Logic Gates, Circuits, Processors, Compilers and Computers

Jan Friso Groote · Rolf Morel ·
Julien Schmaltz · Adam Watkins

Logic Gates, Circuits, Processors, Compilers and Computers

 Springer

Jan Friso Groote (iD)
Department of Mathematics
and Computer Science
Eindhoven University of Technology
Eindhoven, Noord-Brabant, The Netherlands

Rolf Morel
Department of Computer Science
University of Oxford
Oxford, UK

Julien Schmaltz
Department of Mathematics
and Computer Science
Eindhoven University of Technology
Eindhoven, Noord-Brabant, The Netherlands

Adam Watkins
Department of Mathematics
and Computer Science
Eindhoven University of Technology
Eindhoven, Noord-Brabant, The Netherlands

ISBN 978-3-030-68552-2   ISBN 978-3-030-68553-9   (eBook)
https://doi.org/10.1007/978-3-030-68553-9

This Springer imprint is published by the registered company Springer Nature Switzerland AG
The registered company address is: Gewerbestrasse 11, 6330 Cham, Switzerland

This book is for everyone who wants to understand how a computer can do such marvellous calculations, when it is essentially only constructed of simple logic gates.

Preface

Computers have revolutionised the world in well within a century. Dozens of computer processors have been built for every inhabitant of this earth, and this number is rapidly increasing. Most people have little idea of how a computer goes about doing its job. And there is a reason for it. Computers have been designed such that the internal complexity is hidden, not only for those that use computers but even for those who design computer controlled systems, such as hardware engineers, programmers and maintenance staff.

Are computers complex? The answer is both yes and no. Let us first look into the reasons why the answer is yes. Computers are constructed with integrated circuits such as micro-processors. These processors can contain well over a billion components, such as transistors and resistors, all connected with each other in an intricate pattern. And against all odds, this number of components is still growing very rapidly, quickly increasing the complexity of these integrated circuits.

All these systems are man made. This also adds to the complexity as many independent development teams made their own designs. In the history of computer design virtually any conceivable idea has been implemented, and traces of many of these ideas can still be found almost anywhere in computers. The need for backward compatibility makes it hard to remove such ideas. On top of all this hardware many layers of software have been implemented. This makes computer systems very complex objects indeed.

But from a different perspective computers are not at all complex. Many of the essential ideas behind the construction of computers are actually quite straightforward. The purpose of this book is to give a concise, but precise, description of the essence of a computer. After finishing this book the reader should in principle be able to build a computer system from elementary logic components with most of the features that modern computers have, including an elementary operating system and a compiler.

The book starts out with the logic components, *and-*, *not-*, *or-*, and *nand*-gates, that are constructed from transistors. It is explained how such gates can be used to implement any logic function over the boolean values *true* and *false* given by truth tables. These are called combinatorial circuits.

Numbers can be represented by sequences of these boolean values. Not only positive numbers but also negative numbers using the so-called *two's complement* encoding. Using logic gates we can build circuitries that calculate addition, subtraction, multiplication and division on these numbers. Actually, we can implement logic circuits to implement any function on numbers.

An important property of computer systems is that they can store and recall data. We provide the notion of a finite state machine as an abstraction of a system that can interact with its environment and store information about such interactions. Such finite state machines can be implemented using flip-flops and combinatorial circuits.

Using flip-flops it is also possible to build registers, where computer words, representing numbers, instructions and addresses, can be stored. Using registers and a finite state machine it is not particularly difficult to construct a computer that can execute machine instructions or, slightly more abstractly, assembly instructions that form the heart of the execution of a computer program. We show how programs can be written in assembly code, and we even show how a high-level programming language can be compiled into assembly code. This should give the reader a deep understanding about how their Java or C++ programs are executed.

As so many digital components can be packed inside a computer, advanced mechanisms have been added to increase speed and usability. Where initially memories were relatively slow to access, they have been sped up by adding caches. Using interrupts it became possible to let a single processor execute multiple programs simultaneously, serving multiple users at the same time, avoiding that the computer would run idle between tasks. And the single processor machine has been replaced by multiple core computers allowing us to run multiple programs simultaneously.

This increased complexity is nicely shielded from the users by the operating system, together with some hardware support. By using memory protection multiple programs can run simultaneously on a computer in such a way that they cannot access each other's data. Using virtual memory, programs can be written without having to be concerned about the actual memory layout, where it is even possible to use more memory than is physically available. By providing shielding layers around the hardware it is not possible that ordinary programs damage or abuse the hardware infrastructure. This makes modern computers pleasant and secure environments to work in. We will explain the major ideas underlying these concepts.

The Raspberry Pi is very suitable as an experimental platform that stimulates to understand how modern computers work internally. It can be used both as a high-level computer and as a platform for low-level programming. It uses the elegant ARM processor which is an extension of the simple processor that we explain in detail in Chapter 4. We give an overview of the structure of the 32-bit ARM processor and its core instruction set to ease experimentation.

Intended audience. This book is written as an undergraduate level course to help students to understand what a computer is essentially doing. For this reason there are many exercises that all have an answer at the end of this book. It is assumed that the reader has a rudimentary understanding of electronics (resistor, capacitor, transistor). Some experience in common programming languages such as Java or

C++ is needed. Furthermore, the reader is assumed to have elementary mathematical insight to understand basic theorems and proofs, for instance with induction.

Interdependency of the chapters. Chapters 1 to 6 all depend on each other, and should be worked through sequentially. Chapter 7 does not require Chapter 6. The final chapter, Chapter 8, depends on Chapter 7.

Further reading. There are many books written about the structure of computer systems [24, 25, 30, 29, 32, 22, 13, 21], which generally cover the structure of computer systems more extensively, or focus on certain aspects, such as circuits, or assembly programming. This book provides a minimal but complete exposition of all aspects of a computer system such that the essence of how a computer works can be understood completely.

Acknowledgements. This book has been written to support the course Computer Systems (2IC30) at Eindhoven University of Technology, The Netherlands. The course was previously given by Michael Franssen and Rob Hoogerwoord, and the book is based on the structure of the course as developed by them.

Thanks go to the following people for assisting us in writing this book. Special thanks go to Bram Bosch who formally verified many of the circuits, leading to numerous improvements [8], and Alan Mycroft for his many useful comments coming from proof reading large parts of this book. We are also grateful for the helpful remarks by Max Crone, Nikola Djurendic, Bas van Geffen, Bas van Hoeflaken, Quinten van Eijsden, Mohamed Hemza, Anneke Huijsmans, Christine Jacob, Erik Luit, Sebastiaan Peters, Jeroen van Riel, Anson van Rooij, Richard Verhoeven, Sten Wessel and Hans Zantema on drafts of this book.

Nederwetten, Oxford, Vught, Eindhoven,   *Jan Friso Groote*
June 2021   *Rolf Morel*
                                                                  Julien Schmaltz
                                                                   Adam Watkins

Contents

Chapter 1
Basic components and combinatorial circuits

In this chapter we introduce logic gates because they are very useful to describe digital hardware such as computer processors. This was observed by Claude Shannon[1] in his master thesis in 1937 [28]. We show how such gates are constructed using electronic components, such as transistors, and illustrate how circuits with more complex functionality can be constructed efficiently from such elementary gates.

1.1 The three basic logic gates

In Figure 1.1 we find the symbols for three basic logic gates from which digital circuits are built. Each logic gate, or gate for short, is a small hardware component that implements a simple logic function from its inputs to its output. The *and* and *or* gates have two inputs and one output. The *not* gate has one input and one output. A truth table defines the relationship between the input and the output of that gate. A 0 generally means a voltage of 0 V and a 1 represents a higher voltage, for instance 5 V, although today lower voltages, such as 3.3 V, are typical. We discuss the practical realisation of logic gates and their voltages and current flows later in this chapter.

From the truth table it is obvious that the *and* gate has an output of 1 exactly if both inputs are 1. For the *or* gate, the output is 1 if at least one of the inputs is 1. For the *not* gate the output is 1 exactly when the input is 0. Because the *not* gate is a simple gate occurring often it is also written as a single small circle, in particular when joined to another gate.

Using these three basic gates more complex circuits can be made, for instance circuits that add or multiply numbers. When gates are connected such that an output of one gate is never connected to one of its inputs, not even via other gates, the circuit is called *combinatorial*. In this chapter we restrict ourselves to combinatorial

---

[1] Claude Elwood Shannon (1916-2001) was a mathematician and an electrical engineer. He founded the field of information theory, and worked as a cryptanalyst on code breaking and secure communication.

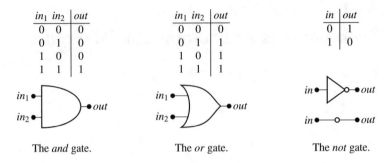

in_1	in_2	out
0	0	0
0	1	0
1	0	0
1	1	1

in_1	in_2	out
0	0	0
0	1	1
1	0	1
1	1	1

in	out
0	1
1	0

The *and* gate.   The *or* gate.   The *not* gate.

Fig. 1.1 Three basic logic gates

circuits. Chapter 3 deals with sequential circuits where outputs are connected to inputs.

A simple but important component is a two-way multiplexer. It has three inputs in_1, in_2 and *sel* and one output *out*. If the selector *sel* is 0, the output *out* equals in_1 and if *sel* is 1, the output is equal to in_2. The truth table that reflects this is depicted in Figure 1.2 on the left. The circuit representing this function is given on the right. Note that there is a *not* gate just before the lower input of the upper *and* gate, drawn as a small circle. Note also that input *sel* is connected to two input wires. It is common to connect wires to the inputs of several gates, but there is a physical limit to the number of gates that a single wire can drive.

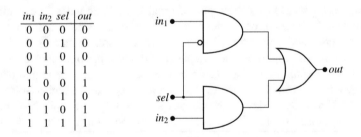

in_1	in_2	sel	out
0	0	0	0
0	0	1	0
0	1	0	0
0	1	1	1
1	0	0	1
1	0	1	0
1	1	0	1
1	1	1	1

Fig. 1.2 The truth table and the combinatorial circuit for a two-input multiplexer

These graphical representations of gates are useful when the circuits are small. When the circuits become more complex a description in textual form tends to work better. Therefore, in text we write $in_1 \wedge in_2$ to represent the output of an *and* gate. Alternative notations that one can encounter are $in_1 \cdot in_2$, $in_1 * in_2$ and $in_1 \& in_2$. The *or* gate is denoted as $in_1 \vee in_2$, and also by $in_1 + in_2$ and $in_1 | in_2$. The *not* gate is denoted as $\neg in$, but also as $\overline{in}$, and !in. The notations with $\wedge$, $\vee$ and $\neg$ are more common in text about logics and are referred to as the *conjunction, disjunction*, and *negation* operators, respectively. The other symbols are more common in the electronics literature.

Exercise 1.1.1. Using logic notation, give the textual representation of the two-input multiplexer depicted in Figure 1.2.

Exercise 1.1.2. Consider a circuit with three inputs in_1, in_2 and in_3 and one output. Make a truth table in which the output is 1 only if exactly one input is equal to 0. E.g., input 011 gives output 1, and input 111 produces 0 as output. Draw a circuit realising this function.

Exercise 1.1.3. Implement an *and* gate with three inputs and a three-input *or* gate using only the basic *and*, *or* and *not* gates. Generalise to an n input *and* gate and n input *or* gate. How many basic gates are necessary? Can you give a proof?

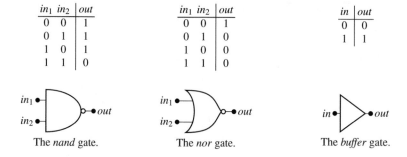

in_1	in_2	out
0	0	1
0	1	1
1	0	1
1	1	0

The *nand* gate.

in_1	in_2	out
0	0	1
0	1	0
1	0	0
1	1	0

The *nor* gate.

in	out
0	0
1	1

The *buffer* gate.

Fig. 1.3 The *nand*, *nor*, and *buffer* basic logic gates

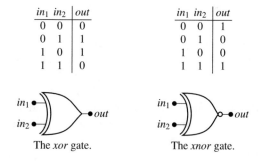

in_1	in_2	out
0	0	0
0	1	1
1	0	1
1	1	0

The *xor* gate.

in_1	in_2	out
0	0	1
0	1	0
1	0	0
1	1	1

The *xnor* gate.

Fig. 1.4 The *xor* and *xnor* logic gates

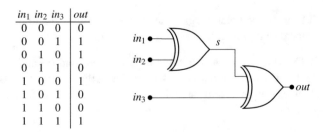

in_1	in_2	in_3	out
0	0	0	0
0	0	1	1
0	1	0	1
0	1	1	0
1	0	0	1
1	0	1	0
1	1	0	0
1	1	1	1

Fig. 1.5 A truth table and a circuit representing the parity function

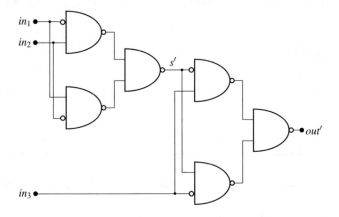

Fig. 1.6 A circuit using only *nand* gates for the parity function

1.2 Other logic gates

There are many other elementary logic gates. All have their own symbol. In Figures 1.3 and 1.4 some are provided, together with their names and truth tables. The *nand* gate is an *and* gate followed by a *not* gate, expressible as $\neg(in_1 \wedge in_2)$. The *nor* is an *or* gate followed by a *not* gate, for which the expression is $\neg(in_1 \vee in_2)$. The buffer just passes its input to the output. Buffers are often used to enhance the input signal. If the buffer is sufficiently strong, in which case it is called an amplifier, it can even be used to drive a light or a motor.

In Figure 1.4 there are two other gates, namely the *xor* and the *xnor*. The first gate outputs a 1 iff (if and only if) the inputs are different and the second outputs 1 iff the inputs are equal. We denote the *xor* gate by $in_1 \oplus in_2$ or $in_1 \not\leftrightarrow in_2$. The *xnor* gate is denoted by $in_1 \leftrightarrow in_2$ and is often referred to as bi-implication in logic.

The parity function is 1 if the number of inputs equal to 1 is odd. For three inputs the parity function is depicted in Figure 1.5. This function can straightforwardly be constructed using two *xor* gates, which is also depicted in this figure. In Figure 1.6 a circuit is drawn using only *nand* gates with exactly the same functionality.

Exercise 1.2.1. Construct the *not* gate only using a *nand* gate or a *nor* gate.

Exercise 1.2.2. Construct a *xor* gate and a *xnor* gate using *and*-, *or*- and *not* gates.

1.3 Physical realisation of gates

Basic gates were initially constructed mechanically using levers, often operated by cog wheels. Later they were made from electronic relays followed by vacuum tubes. Logic gates can even be constructed using hydraulics [27].

These days basic gates are fabricated using transistors, as these are reliable, very small and cheap to produce. Transistors were first demonstrated by Bardeen[2], Brattain[3], and Shockley[4] in 1947, although the concept was patented two decades earlier. In essence transistors are constructed by covering specific parts of pure *semiconductor* wafers, made of e.g. silicon or germanium, with *dopants*, such as boron and phosphorus. Doping changes the available charge carriers of a semiconductor, thereby affecting its conductivity in very precise ways and places.

1.3.1 MOSFET transistors

There are two main types of transistors, the bipolar transistor and the FET (Field Effect Transistor). Although the bipolar transistor was once widely used, it has almost completely been replaced by FETs as FETs are more energy efficient and faster than bipolar transistors. The energy reduction is obtained because switching is done based on voltage levels and not by currents.

A FET has three connections, a gate G, a source S and a drain D. By putting a positive voltage on the gate relative to the source, electrons can be pushed away or be attracted to form or break an electrical connection between the source and the drain, see Figure 1.7. The FET that is most commonly used to make logic gates is the MOSFET (Metal Oxide Semiconductor FET). The name stems from the fact that the gate is made of metal which is isolated using an oxide layer from the connection between the source and the drain. These days the metal gate is often built from alternative materials, such as polycrystalline silicon.

In Figure 1.7 on the left an nMOSFET is sketched. If the voltage at the gate is sufficiently higher than the voltage at the source, electrons are pulled to the gate.

---

[2] John Bardeen (1908-1991) was an American physicist who won the Nobel Prize twice, once for inventing the transistor, and once for the theory of superconductivity.

[3] Walter Brattain (1902-1987) was also an American physicist, born in China. He was known for his knowledge of material science and experimental skills.

[4] William Shockley (1910-1989), an American physicist, was a controversial personality who was on the one hand inventor of the transistor, one of the founders of Silicon Valley and writer of the first textbook on semiconductors, and on the other hand a racist and a defender of eugenics, at his death alienated from most people around him.

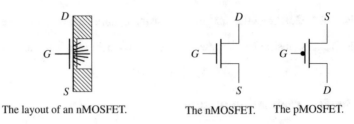

The layout of an nMOSFET.   The nMOSFET.   The pMOSFET.

Fig. 1.7 The layout of an nMOSFET, and the symbols for the nMOSFET and pMOSFET

If there are enough electrons, they can seep away to the drain, and a current can flow from the drain to the source. If the voltage at the gate is equal to the voltage at the source, there are no free electrons to carry the current, and the connection between drain and source acts as an insulator. Only a small current is required to change the voltage at the gate, and a MOSFET only requires energy when actually switching, which explains its energy efficiency. MOSFETs can work at quite low voltages which helps even more.

The pMOSFET is chemically different from an nMOSFET. In a pMOSFET a current can flow if electrons are pushed away from the gate. If the voltage at the gate is sufficiently lower than that of the source, there are free holes for electrons to travel from the drain to the source and current can flow freely. If the voltage at the gate and the source are the same, the connection between the source and the drain behaves as an insulator.

In Figure 1.7 on the right the common symbols for the nMOSFET and the pMOS-FET are provided.

1.3.2 CMOS gates

Early implementations of gates by transistors made use of only nMOSFETs or only pMOSFETs. In case of bipolar transistors, either NPN-, or PNP-transistors were used. When using bipolar transistors this was called TTL logic, and using nMOS-FETs this was often called NMOS. As only one type of transistor was used, such gates were simpler to make. However, such circuits required resistors which dissipate energy even when not switching.

Using both pMOSFETS and nMOSFETS the resistors could be disposed of by giving the transistors complementary roles. This is called CMOS for Complementary MOS. For the voltage at the gate to have the proper effect, every source of an nMOSFET must be connected to the low voltage of the circuit, or to the drain of another nMOSFET. Similarly, the source of a pMOSFET has to be connected to the high voltage, or to the drain of another pMOSFET. In this way a *not* gate, a *nor* gate and a *nand* gate can be constructed in a straightforward manner as shown in Figure 1.8.

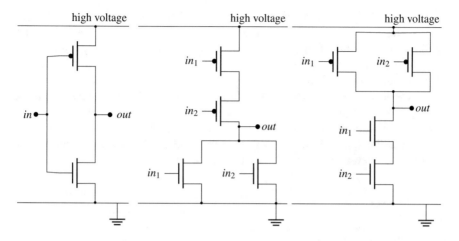

Fig. 1.8 CMOS gates for the *not*, *nor* and *nand*

CMOS is less suitable to directly construct an *and* gate or an *or* gate. The reason is that an input 1 can be used to force to output to 0 using an nMOSFET, and an input 0 can be used to force the output to 1 using a pMOSFET. There is no direct way to force an input 1 to an output 1, or an input 0 to an output 0. These other gates can be constructed, but it is slightly more elaborate.

We explain how the *not* gate works. A high-voltage is a logical 1 and a low voltage is a logical 0. When a high-voltage is put on the input *in*, the nMOSFET is on and the pMOSFET is off. The voltage at the output *out* is pulled down, meaning the logical 1 is inverted to a logical 0. In contrast, when a low voltage is put on the input *in*, the pMOSFET is on and the nMOSFET is off. The output *out* is pulled up. The logical 0 is inverted in a logical 1. The other gates can be understood in a similar way.

Connecting two outputs of gates together should be avoided. This can causes a short circuit as high and low voltage can become directly connected via MOSFETs that are on. Consider connecting the outputs of two CMOS inverters together. If one input is high and the other one is low, there is a massive current flowing through the pFET of one inverter and the nFET of the other inverter. This current can damage the transistors.

1.3.3 Switching delays

Transistors are physical objects. They can switch very quickly from one state to another, but this can still take several picoseconds. These switching times are the reason that digital circuits have a maximum speed at which they can operate. More worrying, they give rise to glitches which are very hard to avoid in designing cir-

cuits. A *glitch* is a temporary change in voltage or logic level before the level settles
at the intended value. Consider Figure 1.9. On the left there is a simple circuit that
will always output 0, independent of whether the input is (in a steady state of) 0 or
1. On the right a timing diagram is drawn. Assume the input is 0 and it switches to
1. In response, but slightly later, the *not* gate switches from 1 to 0, and the *and* gate
also switches from 0 to 1 as temporarily both inputs are 1. After a short while the
and gate responds to the changing output of the *not* gate, and moves back to 0. But
by then the harm has already been done, for a short glitch appeared at the output
out. For a digital circuit, it is important to wait sufficiently long to be sure that all
glitches have levelled out and the circuit has become stable.

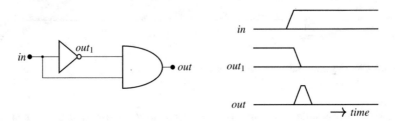

Fig. 1.9 Delay in switching times can give rise to glitches

Most circuits use a *clock* with a typical cycle time of micro- or even (sub-)nano
seconds, corresponding to MHz and GHz frequencies. Each circuit must be stable
within one clock tick. The switching time and the number of sequentially connected
gates determine the maximum clock frequency.

1.3.4 Moore's law

It was quickly recognised that instead of making one transistor on a silicon or germanium wafer, multiple transistors could be constructed by connecting them using
small metal wires on the wafer. In this way not only complete logic gates but even
complete circuits could be fabricated on the wafer with the same ease as making a
single transistor.

In 1965 Moore[5] wrote a short note [20] in which he observed that the number
of transistors that could be put on a wafer was growing exponentially with time. He
predicted that if the growth was sustained, wonders such as a computer in each home
("or at least a terminal to a central computer") would take place. Quite remarkably
Moore's law turned out to be valid for many decades and is still valid today (see Figure 1.10). Due to the growth illustrated by Moore's law, integrated circuits can now

---

[5] Gordon E. Moore (1929-...) obtained a PhD in chemistry. He was co-founder of Intel and
Fairchild Semiconductor.

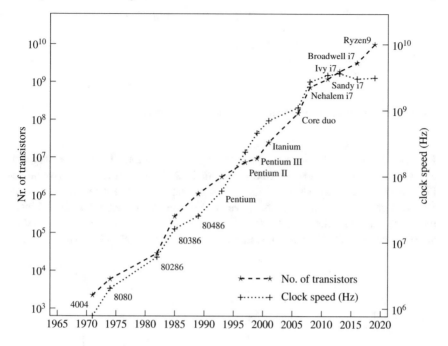

Fig. 1.10 Moore's law

have more than 10 billion (10^{10}) transistors, and this number is still quickly growing. This allows us to construct very complex microprocessors and other circuitry. Until about 2014, an increase in the clock speed followed the increase in transistor counts. Because of physical limitations, this increase in clock speed stopped. Modern architectures obtain more performance by increasing the level of parallelism, for instance, by increasing the number of processor cores.

Exercise 1.3.1. Construct an *and* gate using the CMOS gates from Figure 1.8. Explain why this gate cannot be implemented by just swapping the nFETs and pFETs of the *nor* CMOS gate.

Exercise 1.3.2. Design a CMOS circuit using field effect transistors for a buffer gate, a three-input *or* gate and a two-input *xor* gate.

Exercise 1.3.3. What happens if the output of a gate is connected to the inputs of several other gates? Can it cause damage to connect the output of a gate to one or more of its own inputs?

Exercise 1.3.4. At times it is useful to have an input that can receive the outputs of multiple circuits, though not at the same time. To make this possible, design a CMOS circuit for the *tri-state buffer*, depicted in Figure 1.11. In this figure, *OE* controls whether *in* is forwarded to *out* or if *out* is just disconnected, indicated by Z.

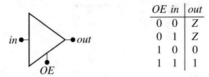

OE	in	out
0	0	Z
0	1	Z
1	0	0
1	1	1

Fig. 1.11 A tri-state buffer either copies over its input or its output is disconnected (Z)

Exercise 1.3.5. The classic transistor is the bipolar transistor. There are two types of bipolar transistors that are depicted in Figure 1.12. At the left the NPN (Negative-Positive-Negative) transistor and the one at the right is a PNP (Positive-Negative-Positive) transistor. Both transistors have three connections, the base, indicated by B, the emitter (E), and the collector (C). Circuits constructed using bipolar transistors are often called TTL (Transistor Transistor Logic) circuits or TTL chips.

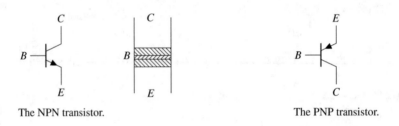

The NPN transistor.   The PNP transistor.

Fig. 1.12 The bipolar NPN and PNP transistors

To understand how an NPN transistor works in a digital circuit, it is sufficient to know that only if there is a small current flowing from the base to the emitter, i.e., through the small arrow, the resistance of the transistor becomes very low and a large current can flow from the collector to the emitter in the same direction. If the base and the emitter have the same voltage, the connection between the emitter and the collector has a very high resistance and it acts as collector and emitter are disconnected.

Which three gates are implemented in Figure 1.13? In this figure the rectangular boxes are fixed resistors. In the diagram on the left when *in* is high, the transistor is conducting and has a low resistance, much lower than the fixed resistor at the top. This means that *out* is pulled down to a low voltage. When *in* is low, there is no current flowing through the arrow, and the resistance of the transistor is much higher than that of the fixed resistor. Hence, *out* is pulled up.

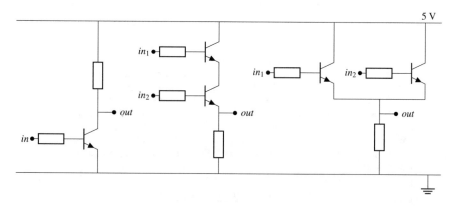

Fig. 1.13 Three gates implemented using bipolar transistors

1.4 Algebraic manipulation and duality

Drawing circuits leads to elegant pictures. But if circuits become larger it is also useful to write circuits as *boolean expressions* using the constants 0 and 1 (sometimes also written as true and false) and the connectives $\vee$, $\wedge$, and $\neg$. The two-input multiplexer from Figure 1.2 is denoted as $(in_1 \wedge \neg sel) \vee (in_2 \wedge sel)$. Note that input *sel* occurs twice in the expression, but this of course represents only one input.

If circuits become even more complex, it is convenient to describe them using a set of equations. The circuit in Figure 1.5 is described by

$$s = in_1 \oplus in_2,$$
$$out = s \oplus in_3.$$

The circuit in Figure 1.6 has the following characterisation:

$$s' = \neg(\neg(\neg in_1 \wedge in_2) \wedge \neg(in_1 \wedge \neg in_2)),$$
$$out' = \neg(\neg(\neg s' \wedge in_3) \wedge \neg(s' \wedge \neg in_3)).$$

Both sets of equations characterise the same function. There are several ways of checking that this is the case. One way is to construct truth tables for both equations, but this is impractical if the number of inputs is large. For n inputs truth tables have 2^n entries. In other words, they grow exponentially with the number of inputs. Therefore, truth tables are useful for small n, but when n is slightly bigger, other techniques are desired to prove that circuits behave the same.

Law	Dual law	Name
$\neg\neg x = x$	$\neg\neg x = x$	Double negation
$\neg 0 = 1$	$\neg 1 = 0$	Constants
$\neg(x \lor y) = \neg x \land \neg y$	$\neg(x \land y) = \neg x \lor \neg y$	De Morgan[6]
$x \lor x = x$	$x \land x = x$	Idempotence
$x \lor 1 = 1$	$x \land 0 = 0$	Zero element
$x \lor 0 = x$	$x \land 1 = x$	Identity element
$x \lor \neg x = 1$	$x \land \neg x = 0$	Excluded middle/Contradiction
$x \lor y = y \lor x$	$x \land y = y \land x$	Commutativity
$x \lor (x \land y) = x$	$x \land (x \lor y) = x$	Absorption
$x \lor (\neg x \land y) = x \lor y$	$x \land (\neg x \lor y) = x \land y$	Complement absorption
$x \land (y \lor z) =$	$x \lor (y \land z) =$	Distributivity
$\quad (x \land y) \lor (x \land z)$	$\quad (x \lor y) \land (x \lor z)$	
$x \lor (y \lor z) = (x \lor y) \lor z$	$x \land (y \land z) = (x \land y) \land z$	Associativity
$x \oplus y = (\neg x \land y) \lor (x \land \neg y)$		Definition of xor
$x \leftrightarrow y = (x \land y) \lor (\neg x \land \neg y)$		Definition of $xnor$
$(x \oplus y) \oplus z = x \oplus (y \oplus z)$		Associativity of xor
$(x \leftrightarrow y) \leftrightarrow z = x \leftrightarrow (y \leftrightarrow z)$		Associativity of $xnor$

Table 1.1 Boolean identities

Another advantage of writing circuits as expressions is that they can be manipulated using algebraic laws. Table 1.1 contains the laws of *boolean*[7] *algebra*. These laws correspond to the valid transformations one can perform on a logic expression. For each equality of the form $t = u$ in this table, the expression t is always equal to the expression u where x, y and z can be any arbitrary boolean expression. This allows for replacing t by u, or u by t in any larger expression without changing the boolean function it represents.

As an example we show that *out* is equal to *out'*. We do that by first showing that s is equal to s'.

$$
\begin{aligned}
s &\overset{\text{Equation for } s}{=} in_1 \oplus in_2 \\
&\overset{\text{Def. of } xor}{=} (\neg in_1 \land in_2) \lor (in_1 \land \neg in_2) \\
&\overset{\text{Double negation}}{=} \neg\neg((\neg in_1 \land in_2) \lor (in_1 \land \neg in_2)) \\
&\overset{\text{De Morgan}}{=} \neg(\neg(\neg in_1 \land in_2) \land \neg(in_1 \land \neg in_2)) \\
&\overset{\text{Equation for } s'}{=} s'.
\end{aligned}
\tag{1.1}
$$

Using this result we can prove in exactly the same way that $out = out'$.

---

[6] Augustus De Morgan (1806-1871), both a mathematician and a logician, contributed to various fields. In particular he made the notion of mathematical induction precise.

[7] George Boole (1815-1864) was a mathematician and logician who developed an algebra to support logical reasoning.

$$
\begin{aligned}
out &\overset{\text{Equation for } out}{=} s \oplus in_3 \\
&\overset{\text{Def. of } xor}{=} (\neg s \wedge in_3) \vee (s \wedge \neg in_3) \\
&\overset{\text{Double negation}}{=} \neg\neg((\neg s \wedge in_3) \vee (s \wedge \neg in_3)) \\
&\overset{\text{De Morgan}}{=} \neg(\neg(\neg s \wedge in_3) \wedge \neg(s \wedge \neg in_3)) \\
&\overset{(1.1)}{=} \neg(\neg(\neg s' \wedge in_3) \wedge \neg(s' \wedge \neg in_3)) \\
&\overset{\text{Equation for } out'}{=} out'.
\end{aligned}
$$

The laws in Table 1.1 have a strong symmetry due to the *duality* of boolean algebra. The principle of duality states that by simultaneously replacing each symbol in a valid equation with its *dual symbol* we obtain the *dual* of the equation, which is again valid. We write $(\phi)^D$ to denote the formula ϕ where all symbols are replaced by their dual.

The operation $(\phi)^D$ leaves variables unaffected. The constants 0 and 1 are dual to each other, i.e., $(0)^D = 1$ and $(1)^D = 0$. The negation operator is *self-dual*, meaning that $\neg$ just maps to $\neg$ in the dual equation. Hence the double negation law is its own dual law. In the same way $\wedge$ and $\vee$ are duals of each other, e.g. $((x \wedge y) \vee x)^D = (x)^D$ turns into $(x \vee y) \wedge x = x$. The dual for each law is indicated in Table 1.1. Observe that not only is a dual law the dual of the corresponding law but also that a law is the dual of its dual law. This is more comprehensibly formulated in a formula: $((\phi)^D)^D = \phi$.

Some of the algebraic laws are not strictly necessary, as they can be proven by the other laws. For instance, Idempotence for $\wedge$ can be proven as follows:

$$
\begin{aligned}
x \wedge x &\overset{\text{Double negation}}{=} \neg\neg x \wedge \neg\neg x \\
&\overset{\text{De Morgan}}{=} \neg(\neg x \vee \neg x) \\
&\overset{\text{Idempotence for } \vee}{=} \neg(\neg x) \\
&\overset{\text{Double negation}}{=} x.
\end{aligned}
$$

The proof that the absorption laws are derivable is slightly more complex. First observe that

$$
\begin{aligned}
x &\overset{\text{Identity element}}{=} x \wedge 1 \\
&\overset{\text{Excluded middle}}{=} x \wedge (y \vee \neg y) \\
&\overset{\text{Distributivity}}{=} (x \wedge y) \vee (x \wedge \neg y).
\end{aligned}
\qquad (1.2)
$$

Using this result we derive

$$
\begin{aligned}
x &\overset{(1.2)}{=} (x \wedge y) \vee (x \wedge \neg y) \\
&\overset{\text{Idempotence}}{=} (x \wedge y) \vee (x \wedge y) \vee (x \wedge \neg y) \\
&\overset{(1.2)}{=} (x \wedge y) \vee x \\
&\overset{\text{Commutativity}}{=} x \vee (x \wedge y).
\end{aligned}
$$

$x\ y$	$\neg x$	$\neg x \wedge y$	$x \vee (\neg x \wedge y)$	$x \vee y$
0 0	1	0	0	0
0 1	1	1	1	1
1 0	0	0	1	1
1 1	0	0	1	1

Table 1.2 A truth table showing that complement absorption is valid

Truth tables are effective for showing that an algebraic law is valid. Consider as an example complement absorption. The truth tables for the left and right hand sides of the law are given in Table 1.2. As the last two columns are identical, this law holds.

Proving that two boolean expressions are not equivalent is known to be NP-complete [11]. This very fundamental result says that there are relatively small boolean expressions for which it is hard to prove equivalence. But ever since computers have been available, people have been working on finding algorithms that, in practice, are able to show that boolean expressions are equal. This field is called Automated theorem proving, and it had limited success until approximately 1990. Since then, various remarkably effective methods have been discovered, and, as it turned out, not all boolean expressions are hard to prove equal. The main achievements were the use of BDDs (Binary Decision Diagrams) [9] and, later, resolution based techniques such as SAT (Satisfiability) and SMT (Satisfiability Modulo Theories) [6]. Proof checkers that implement these methods are now regularly used to show the equivalence of digital circuits. Due to their power and versatility they are finding their way into other areas where they are, for instance, used to solve open mathematical problems.

Exercise 1.4.1. A *xor* gate can also be denoted by $\neg(in_1 \wedge in_2) \wedge (in_1 \vee in_2)$. Prove this using the algebraic laws from Table 1.1.

Exercise 1.4.2. Prove that the complement absorption law (and its dual) can be derived using the other laws.

Exercise 1.4.3. The *xor* and *xnor* are also each others duals, i.e. $(x \oplus y)^D = x \leftrightarrow y$. Write down the algebraic laws that make this explicit. Determine another sense in which these operations are complementary (hint: a truth table might help).

Exercise 1.4.4. Show using truth tables that the laws for absorption and distributivity in Table 1.1 are valid.

1.5 Two-layer circuits

Suppose one wants to make a digital circuit that implements a certain function. If the number of inputs is small, it is easy to write down a truth table. In this section we explain how a truth table can systematically be translated into a simple circuit. As all logic functions can be denoted by truth tables, this shows that all functions can be constructed by logic circuits.

We construct circuits that have just two layers, in order to minimise propagation delay. We either use a layer of *or* gates connected to an *and* gate, or dually, a layer of *and* gates connected to an *or* gate.

Consider the truth table in Table 1.3. It represents the parity function. The output is 1 if and only if the number of 1s in the input is odd. We treat this truth table as an arbitrary one, in the sense that what we present below could apply to any truth table.

in_1	in_2	in_3	out
0	0	0	0
0	0	1	1
0	1	0	1
0	1	1	0
1	0	0	1
1	0	1	0
1	1	0	0
1	1	1	1

Table 1.3 A truth table representing the parity function

Every line in the truth table where the result is 1 corresponds to a so-called *minterm*. This minterm is the conjunction of all inputs; the input is negated if the truth table contains 0 at that point. The line 1 0 0 in Table 1.3 has 1 as the output. Its minterm is $in_1 \wedge \neg in_2 \wedge \neg in_3$. Taking the disjunction of all minterms yields an expression that represents the truth table. This expression is called a *disjunctive normal form*. It can be translated directly into a circuit of *and* gates feeding into an *or* gate. For the parity function, the disjunctive normal form and the circuit are given in Figure 1.14. This circuit is optimal in the sense that no smaller two-layer circuit exists for the parity function.

Due to duality, it is also possible to directly construct a circuit consisting of *or* gates feeding into an *and* gate. For this purpose so-called *maxterms* are constructed for each entry in the truth table where the result is 0. A maxterm is the disjunction of all inputs, where each input that is equal to 1 is negated. For the parity function, the input 0 1 1 leads to the maxterm $in_1 \vee \neg in_2 \vee \neg in_3$. The conjunction of all maxterms is called the *conjunctive normal form*. This conjunction can be understood as a check of whether any of its maxterm conjuncts applied. When the input corresponds to a maxterm there is a maxterm which will be false, which would make the entire conjunction false. If the input did not correspond to any maxterm, then every conjunct will be true and hence the output will be 1. The parity function has four maxterms, which can be used directly to draw a circuit. In Figure 1.15 the conjunctive normal form and the circuit representing the parity function are depicted.

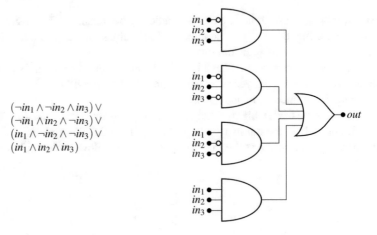

$(\neg in_1 \wedge \neg in_2 \wedge in_3) \vee$
$(\neg in_1 \wedge in_2 \wedge \neg in_3) \vee$
$(in_1 \wedge \neg in_2 \wedge \neg in_3) \vee$
$(in_1 \wedge in_2 \wedge in_3)$

Fig. 1.14 The disjunctive normal form and a circuit for the parity function

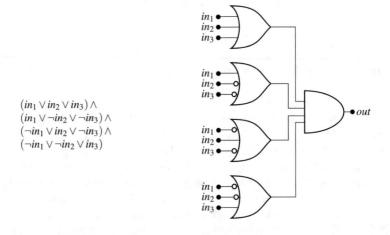

$(in_1 \vee in_2 \vee in_3) \wedge$
$(in_1 \vee \neg in_2 \vee \neg in_3) \wedge$
$(\neg in_1 \vee in_2 \vee \neg in_3) \wedge$
$(\neg in_1 \vee \neg in_2 \vee in_3)$

Fig. 1.15 The conjunctive normal form and the associated circuit for the parity function

Exercise 1.5.1. Systematically derive the disjunctive and conjunctive normal forms for the multiplexer whose truth table is given in Figure 1.2. Draw the circuits. Observe that the obtained circuits contain more gates than necessary.

Exercise 1.5.2. Prove, using the algebraic laws, that the disjunctive normal form in Figure 1.14 is equal to the conjunctive normal form in Figure 1.15.

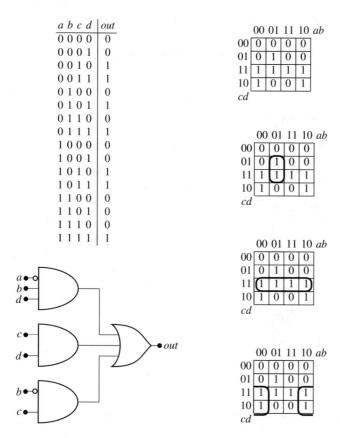

a b c d	out
0 0 0 0	0
0 0 0 1	0
0 0 1 0	1
0 0 1 1	1
0 1 0 0	0
0 1 0 1	1
0 1 1 0	0
0 1 1 1	1
1 0 0 0	0
1 0 0 1	0
1 0 1 0	1
1 0 1 1	1
1 1 0 0	0
1 1 0 1	0
1 1 1 0	0
1 1 1 1	1

Fig. 1.16 A truth table and its Karnaugh map

1.6 Karnaugh maps

For the parity function, the method from the previous section leads to optimal two-layer circuits. But in general this is not the case, and the obtained circuits are too complex and can be simplified. For circuits with relatively few inputs *Karnaugh*[8] *maps* are a useful tool to obtain a minimal two-layer circuit. It only works well for up to five inputs.

The idea is to write a truth table in a matrix of dimension 2×2, 2×4, 4×4 or even 8×4. Each cell in the matrix corresponds to an entry in the truth table. See Figure 1.16. On the left and the top the inputs are explicitly listed. Note that the sequence is different from that commonly used in a truth table. Neighbours differ in only one of the inputs. This means that two cells adjacent to each other

---

[8] Maurice Karnaugh (1924-...) is an American physicist who worked at various research labs, mainly on digital encodings and networks.

in the Karnaugh diagram are neighbours. But a cell in the uppermost row is also a neighbour to the cell in the same column in the lowest row, and two cells in the same row, one in the leftmost column, and one in the rightmost column are also neighbours.

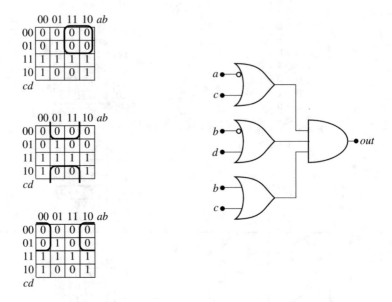

Fig. 1.17 A Karnaugh map covering zeroes

To make a disjunctive circuit, clusters of neighbours of size $2^k \times 2^\ell$ for $k, \ell = 0, 1, 2, \ldots$ must be selected that cover exactly all 1's in the Karnaugh map. These clusters must be as large as possible. They are allowed to overlap. In Figure 1.16 a truth table and its associated Karnaugh map are drawn. There are three clusters. The first drawn cluster, of size two, corresponds to $\neg a \wedge b \wedge d$. The value of input c is not relevant for this output and can be omitted. The cluster drawn in the middle right of the diagram corresponds to $c \wedge d$, and the cluster at the lower right corresponds to $\neg b \wedge c$. By putting disjunctions between the expressions expressing clusters we obtain an expression that is exactly 1 when the truth table is also 1. Moreover, this expression can immediately be transformed into a two-layer circuit, which is minimal.

Dually, by covering the 0's in a Karnaugh map, a conjunctive circuit can be created. The idea is to find maximal clusters of neighbouring nodes that have a value of 0. In Figure 1.17 this is illustrated for the same truth table as in Figure 1.16. For each cluster we write down a maxterm that equals 1 outside the cluster. There are three clusters that correspond to $\neg a \vee c$, $\neg b \vee d$, and $b \vee c$. The minimal conjunctive two-layer expression corresponding to the truth table is $(\neg a \vee c) \wedge (\neg b \vee d) \wedge (b \vee c)$.

It happens that some outputs of a circuit are not relevant, for instance because certain combinations of inputs cannot occur. Such outputs are marked *don't care* using the symbol '*X*'. In a Karnaugh map such outputs can be taken to be a 0, or a 1, depending on which choice makes the clusters as large as possible. In Figure 1.18 a truth table is given with don't cares. The upper Karnaugh map corresponds to the disjunctive circuit at the lower left in this figure. In this diagram all don't cares are taken to be 1. The other Karnaugh diagram corresponds to a conjunctive circuit. This circuit is drawn at the bottom right of the figure.

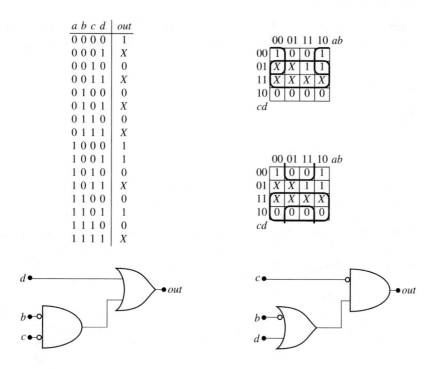

Fig. 1.18 A truth table, Karnaugh maps and circuits with don't cares

Exercise 1.6.1. Prove that the circuits in Figures 1.16 and 1.17 represent the same function by constructing the truth tables for both circuits.

Exercise 1.6.2. Explain why the following cover is not added to the Karnaugh map in Figure 1.17, leading to an extra *or* gate $c \vee d$ in the circuit on the right of Figure 1.17.

	00	01	11	10	*ab*
00	0	0	0	0	
01	0	1	0	0	
11	1	1	1	1	
10	1	0	0	1	
cd					

Exercise 1.6.3. Why are the two circuits in Figure 1.18 not representations of the same boolean function?

Exercise 1.6.4. Draw the 4×2 Karnaugh map for the parity function from Figure 1.5. Explain why the two-layer circuit in Figure 1.14 is optimal and cannot be reduced further.

1.7 Functional completeness of the nand gate

A gate is *functionally complete*, or *universal*, when any boolean function can be computed by a circuit constructed using only this gate. The only commonly used gates that are functionally complete are the *nand* gate and the *nor* gate. This makes it possible to build any circuit using only *nand* gates or only *nor* gates. We show here that the *nand* gate is functionally complete.

From the previous section it follows that any boolean function, represented as a truth table, can be represented as a two-layer circuit using only *and* gates, *or* gates and *not* gates. Using the De Morgan law, we know that an *or* gate can be replaced by an *and* gate and three *not* gates. This shows that any circuit can be constructed using *and* gates and *not* gates only.

A *not* gate can be constructed using a *nand* gate by connecting the input of the *not* gate to both inputs of the *nand* gate. An *and* gate can be constructed from only *nand* gates by replacing the *and* gate by a *nand* gate followed by a *not* gate, which is constructed using a *nand* gate. In Figure 1.19 this is depicted. For each gate on the left, the construction using nand gates is shown on the right.

Exercise 1.7.1. Show that the *nor* gate is functionally complete.

Exercise 1.7.2. Explain why the *not* gate and the *buffer* gate are not functionally complete.

Exercise 1.7.3. For a circuit that consists of only *and* gates, show that if all inputs are 1, the output is 1. This demonstrates that the *and* gate is not functionally complete. In a similar way show that circuits with only *or* gates, circuits with only *xor* gates and even circuits with only *xnor* gates are not functionally complete.

Exercise 1.7.4. *Nand* and *nor* gates are typically implemented with fewer transistors than *and* and *or* gates. Explain why any boolean function can be implemented by a two-layer circuit consisting of only *nand* gates. Dually, show that this is also possible with just *nor* gates.

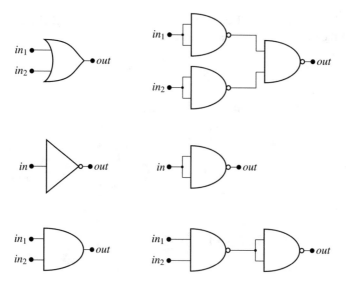

Fig. 1.19 The *nand* gate is functionally complete

1.8 Multiplexers

In this section we have a closer look at multiplexers. A *multiplexer* is primarily used to select a single input out of a number of inputs. A simple two-input multiplexer was shown in Figure 1.2. In Figure 1.20 the standard symbol for a two-input multiplexer is drawn. If *sel* equals 0 the input in_0 is put at the output. If *sel* equals 1 the output *out* is equal to in_1.

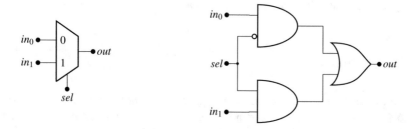

Fig. 1.20 The notation and a realisation of a two-input multiplexer

A general multiplexer has 2^k inputs and a selector consisting of k selector inputs. It can be constructed using $2^k - 1$ two-input multiplexers. This recursive construction is depicted in Figure 1.21. Using a small slash it is indicated that a line can consist of more signal lines. The selectors on the left have a slash labelled with

$k-1$, indicating that the selector consists of $k-1$ boolean signals. Likewise, the inputs of the multiplexers on the left each have 2^{k-1} inputs.

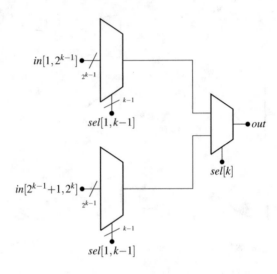

Fig. 1.21 Constructing a multiple-input multiplexer

Exercise 1.8.1. Show how each boolean function with k inputs can be constructed using a 2^k-input multiplexer.

Exercise 1.8.2. A demultiplexer receives one input and k selector signals. Its typical symbol is the mirrored version of the symbol for the multiplexer. It routes the input to one of the 2^k outputs. Construct a four output demultiplexer with two selector signals using standard *and-, or-* and *not* gates.

1.9 Summary

We explained how basic gates, such as *and, or* and *not*, can be realised by transistors. Every boolean function can be implemented as a combinatorial circuit using these gates. Combinatorial circuits are those circuits where the output of a gate is never connected to any of its inputs, either directly or via other gates. Truth tables, Karnaugh diagrams and boolean algebra are useful means to obtain an optimal combinatorial circuit. We also saw that every circuit can be implemented using just *nand* or just *nor* gates, and therefore these gates are called functionally complete.

Chapter 2
Numbers, basic circuits, and the ALU

In this chapter, we discuss the representation of numbers and their manipulation by the central component of a processor, namely, the ALU (Arithmetic Logic Unit). We end with a small section on the representation of alphanumeric characters.

2.1 Representation of unsigned numbers

All data processed by a machine are sequences of bits where a *bit* is a logic unit whose value can be either 1 or 0, or equivalently, true or false. Bits are grouped in fixed length sequences called *words*. A popular length is 8 bits, in which case the sequence is called a *byte*. Nowadays, machine words have lengths that are a multiple of 8, namely 16, 32 or 64, but in the past various other word lengths have been used. For instance the Electrologica X8 had a word length of 27. Below, we use the arbitrary length n for our bit sequences.

We first consider the common representation of natural numbers, i.e. non-negative numbers, those that cannot be preceded by a minus sign. Therefore, such numbers are also called *unsigned numbers*. A bit sequence $\alpha = a_{n-1} \ldots a_0$ of length n is used to represent a natural number, from 0 up to and including $2^n - 1$. The empty sequence of bits is written as ε and it represents 0.

The coding is the usual *positional notation* with base 2. The base-2 interpretation of α as an unsigned number is denoted as $\langle \alpha \rangle_2$ and defined by

$$\langle \alpha \rangle_2 = \sum_{i=0}^{n-1} a_i \cdot 2^i.$$

Initial 0's on the left in a number representation do not change the value. They can be omitted, but sometimes they are written because number representations generally have a fixed length.

Example 2.1.1. In 8 bits the number 255 is represented by $\langle 1111\,1111 \rangle_2$, 32 can be represented by $\langle 100000 \rangle_2$ and by $\langle 0010\,0000 \rangle_2$, and 5 can be represented by $\langle 101 \rangle_2$

© The Author(s), under exclusive license to Springer Nature Switzerland AG 2021
J. F. Groote et al., *Logic Gates, Circuits, Processors, Compilers and Computers*,
https://doi.org/10.1007/978-3-030-68553-9_2

and $\langle 00000101 \rangle_2$. Observe that the empty sequence represents 0, i.e., $\langle \varepsilon \rangle_2 = 0$. As the empty sequence is easily overlooked, it is more customary to represent the number 0 with one or more 0 digits.

The *least significant bit* is a_0, while the *most significant bit* is a_{n-1}. We use the convention that the least significant bit is the last bit of a sequence, but it could as easily be the other way around. Often a word is grouped in bytes. If the most significant byte comes first, this is called *big-endian*[1], otherwise it is called *little-endian*. Even *mixed-endian* formats exist where 16-bit words are big-endian and the bytes in these 16-bit words are little-endian.

By choosing another base b, one obtains another representation. If b is smaller than or equal to 10 it is common to use the digits up to b as the digits of these b-ary numbers. If b is larger than 9 the characters $A, B, \ldots$ are often used for the missing numbers. In this case A stands for 10, B stands for 11, etc.

If $\alpha = a_{n-1} \ldots a_0$ is a sequence of b-ary digits, the base-b interpretation of α is denoted as $\langle \alpha \rangle_b$ and defined by

$$\langle \alpha \rangle_b = \sum_{i=0}^{n-1} a_i \cdot b^i.$$

Example 2.1.2. In base 10, 255 is represented as $2 \cdot 10^2 + 5 \cdot 10^1 + 5 \cdot 10^0$. In base 16 – the *hexadecimal* notation – digits range from 0 to F and 255 is represented as FF, that is, $15 \cdot 16^1 + 15 \cdot 16^0$. In the *octal* representation, which uses base 8, digits range from 0 to 7 and 255 is represented as 377, that is, $3 \cdot 8^2 + 7 \cdot 8^1 + 7 \cdot 8^0$. Table 2.1 gives an overview of the digits of each base.

The following identity is an instance of Horner's[2] rule which allows us to calculate the value of a digit sequence efficiently.

Lemma 2.1.3. Let $b > 1$ be some base, α a digit sequence and a_0 a digit, both over base b.
$$\langle \alpha a_0 \rangle_b = b \langle \alpha \rangle_b + a_0.$$

Proof. We assume $\alpha = a_{n-1} \ldots a_1$. Using this we calculate

$$\langle \alpha a_0 \rangle_b = \sum_{i=0}^{n-1} a_i \cdot b^i = b \cdot \left(\sum_{i=0}^{n-2} a_{i+1} \cdot b^i \right) + a_0 = b \cdot \langle \alpha \rangle_b + a_0.$$

$\square$

Horner's rule allows us to calculate a number with a minimum number of multiplications. Calculating the value of the binary number 111 using Horner's rule goes as follows

---

[1] The terms big-endian and little-endian stem from Jonathan Twist's "Gulliver's Travels" (1726) where a civil war broke out over the question of whether an egg must be opened at the bigger or the smaller end.

[2] William George Horner (1786-1837) was a British mathematician working on number theory, equation solving and optics.

$b_3\,b_2\,b_1\,b_0$	decimal	hexadecimal	octal
0000	0	0	00
0001	1	1	01
0010	2	2	02
0011	3	3	03
0100	4	4	04
0101	5	5	05
0110	6	6	06
0111	7	7	07
1000	8	8	10
1001	9	9	11
1010	10	A	12
1011	11	B	13
1100	12	C	14
1101	13	D	15
1110	14	E	16
1111	15	F	17

Table 2.1 Number representations

$$\langle 111 \rangle_2 = 2\langle 11 \rangle_2 + 1 = 2(2\langle 1 \rangle_2 + 1) + 1 = (2(2 \cdot 1 + 1) + 1) = 7.$$

There is a simple function that can translate a number d into a digit-sequence over base b.

$$T_b(d) = \begin{cases} \varepsilon & \text{if } d = 0, \\ T_b(d \operatorname{div} b)\,a & \text{otherwise, where } a = d \bmod b. \end{cases}$$

Example 2.1.4. Suppose we want to know the base-5 representation of the number 196. The following table indicates the iterative results of the div (quotient) and mod (remainder) calculations, feeding the result of the div back into the function.

	$n \operatorname{div} b$	$n \bmod b$
$T_5(196)$:	39	1
$T_5(39)$:	7	4
$T_5(7)$:	1	2
$T_5(1)$:	0	1

The remainders in reverse order form the sequence 1241 which is the required number in base 5.

If a number representation a in base b must be transformed to a number representation a' in base b', a general method is to translate a to its decimal value d first, and then use the function $T_{b'}(d)$ to calculate a'.

Example 2.1.5. The following pairs of digit sequences all represent the same number. The subscript at each sequence indicates its base.

$$\begin{array}{cc} 21021_3 & 1241_5 \\ 4AB2_{15} & 64256_7 \\ 8888_{14} & A9B6_{13} \end{array}$$

The following lemma, although of little practical use, gives us confidence that our definitions are correct. Encoding and decoding a number yields the same number.

Lemma 2.1.6. Let d be a number and $b > 1$ be some base.

$$\langle T_b(d) \rangle_b = d.$$

Proof. We prove this lemma by induction on d. For the base case, where $d = 0$, we find $\langle T_b(0) \rangle_b = \langle \varepsilon \rangle_b = \sum_{i=0}^{-1} a_i \cdot b^i = 0$.

For the induction step, where $d > 0$, we assume that the lemma holds for all $d' < d$, i.e., $\langle T_b(d') \rangle_b = d'$, which we call the induction hypothesis, and show that the lemma holds for d using the induction hypothesis. We derive

$$\langle T_b(d) \rangle_b \quad = \quad \langle (T_b(d \operatorname{div} b)) (d \operatorname{mod} b) \rangle_b$$
$$\overset{\text{Horner's rule}}{=} b \langle T_b(d \operatorname{div} b) \rangle_b + d \operatorname{mod} b.$$

As $d \operatorname{div} b$ is smaller than d (here $b > 1$ is used), the induction hypothesis yields $\langle T_b(d \operatorname{div} b) \rangle_b = d \operatorname{div} b$. Using this the last result can be rewritten as

$$b (d \operatorname{div} b) + d \operatorname{mod} b.$$

Using modulo calculation this is equal to d.

As we have shown that the lemma holds for $d = 0$, and for any d assuming that it holds for smaller d', the principle of induction says that the lemma holds for all d.
$\square$

Interpreting a bit sequence in base 4, 8, or 16, is simply a matter of choosing how to group bits. In base 4, bits are grouped in pairs, in base 8 one needs 3 bits to represent any digit, and in base 16 four bits represent a digit. The bits can be grouped by putting brackets around the relevant number of bits. If there are not enough bits, 0's can be added to the front. In Table 2.1 the representation of the bit sequence for hexadecimal can be found. The representation for bases 4 and 8 can also be read from the hexadecimal representation by adding 0's in front of the bits.

Example 2.1.7. The following are all equivalent encodings of 185:

$$\langle 1011\,1001 \rangle_2 =$$
$$\langle (10)(11)(10)(01) \rangle_4 = \langle 2321 \rangle_4 =$$
$$\langle (010)(111)(001) \rangle_8 = \langle 271 \rangle_8 \quad =$$
$$\langle (1011)(1001) \rangle_{16} = \langle B9 \rangle_{16}$$

If a number is given in base 4, 8 or 16 and it must be translated to bits, this can be done by replacing each digit by its appropriate bit representation. Translating numbers between any of the bases 2, 4, 8 and 16 is always most conveniently done by going through the binary representation. Actually, as binary notation quickly becomes unreadable, and translation from and to octal or hexadecimal is easy, it is common to represent bit sequences in these number systems.

From now on, we will only use the base-2 representation. We shall therefore write $\langle a \rangle$ instead of $\langle a \rangle_2$.

Exercise 2.1.8. Convert the decimal representation of the decimal number 42 to binary, octal, and hexadecimal representations.

Exercise 2.1.9. Convert the number denoted by 31 in octal representation to binary, hexadecimal, and decimal representations.

Exercise 2.1.10. Convert the base-11 number $A8374$ to base 9, base 12 and base 15.

Exercise 2.1.11. Convert the ternary sequences 22 0220, 1 1111 1112 and 22 1212 0101 0101 to their representations in base 9 without converting them to decimal numbers.

2.2 Two's complement representation of integers

Integers, i.e. numbers that can also be negative, can be represented in different ways as bit sequences. For all common representations the basic idea is to use one bit – generally the leading bit – as a *sign bit* that indicates whether the number is positive or negative. Such number representations are referred to as *signed numbers*.

In this section we explain the prevailing way to represent integers, which is the *two's complement representation*. All major computer processor families – x86, ARM, Power, MIPS, SPARC, ... – implement the two's complement representation. The value of a bit sequence $\alpha = a_{n-1} \ldots a_0$ when interpreted as a two's complement number is denoted by $[\alpha]$ and defined as

$$[\alpha] = -a_{n-1} \cdot 2^{n-1} + \sum_{i=0}^{n-2} a_i \cdot 2^i.$$

Observe that this value is positive or zero if the first bit is 0, and negative if it is 1. For non-negative numbers, the value is determined by the base-2 interpretation of the remaining bits. For negative numbers, the value is determined by taking the base-2 interpretation of the remaining bits and subtracting 2^{n-1} where n is the length of the bit sequence.

Example 2.2.1. Assume 4-bit numbers. The range of the two's complement representation runs from -8 to 7. The range is illustrated in Figure 2.1. We have $[0000] = 0$, $[0111] = 7$, $[1000] = -8$, and $[1001] = -7$.

Note that the smallest number that can be represented with an n-bit representation is -2^{n-1} and the largest is $2^{n-1} - 1$. This implies that this representation is not closed under unary negation: negating the number -2^{n-1}, which is representable as a two's complement bit sequence of length n, yields 2^{n-1}, which cannot be represented as a two's complement bit sequence of length n.

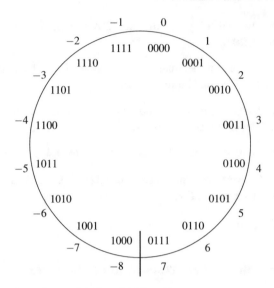

Fig. 2.1 Two's complement representation of 4-bit numbers

The two's complement representation has several properties. The relation between the interpretation as unsigned numbers, using the interpretation $\langle \alpha \rangle$, and two's complement numbers, using the interpretation $[\alpha]$, is given as follows.

Theorem 2.2.2. Let a be either a 0 or a 1 and let α be a bit sequence of length n. It holds that

$$[a\alpha] = -a \cdot 2^n + \langle \alpha \rangle.$$

An interesting property is *sign extension*. It says that initial 0's or 1's can be added or removed from a two's complement number without changing the value it represents, as long as the first bit of the number remains a 0 or a 1, respectively. We state and prove this property.

Theorem 2.2.3 (Sign Extension). Let a be either 0 or 1 and let α be a bit sequence. We find that

$$[a\alpha] = [aa\alpha].$$

Proof.

$$\begin{aligned}
[a\alpha] &= -a \cdot 2^n + \langle \alpha \rangle \\
&= -a \cdot 2^{n+1} + a \cdot 2^n + \langle \alpha \rangle \\
&= -a \cdot 2^{n+1} + \langle a\alpha \rangle \\
&= [aa\alpha].
\end{aligned}$$

$\square$

Example 2.2.4. The 4-bit representation of -4 is 1100. The 8-bit representation of -4 is obtained by adding 1's to the front, which by the previous theorem can be done without changing the value. It is $1111\,1100$. It is also easy to see what the shortest representation of -4 is. We can truncate bits from 1100 as long as the sign bit is unchanged. The shortest representation of -4 in two's complement is 100, which represents $-4+0$. Truncating an additional bit produces 00 which represents a different value.

Another important property is that inverting all bits almost negates the number. We write $\overline{\alpha}$, called α's *inversion*, to indicate that all bits in α have been inverted. In particular for a single bit a this means $\overline{a} = 1 - a$ (or $\neg a$). The property is expressed as follows:

Theorem 2.2.5. Let $\alpha = a_{n-1}\ldots a_0$ be a bit sequence. $[\overline{\alpha}] = -[\alpha] - 1$

Proof. The proof consists of the following calculation, following the definitions.

$$
\begin{aligned}
[\overline{\alpha}] &= -\overline{a_{n-1}} \cdot 2^{n-1} + \sum_{i=0}^{n-2} \overline{a_i} \cdot 2^i \\
&= -(1 - a_{n-1}) \cdot 2^{n-1} + \sum_{i=0}^{n-2} (1 - a_i) \cdot 2^i \\
&= -2^{n-1} + a_{n-1} \cdot 2^{n-1} + \sum_{i=0}^{n-2} \cdot 2^i - \sum_{i=0}^{n-2} a_i \cdot 2^i \\
&= -2^{n-1} + a_{n-1} \cdot 2^{n-1} + 2^{n-1} - 1 - \sum_{i=0}^{n-2} a_i \cdot 2^i \\
&= -(-a_{n-1} \cdot 2^{n-1} + \sum_{i=0}^{n-2} a_i \cdot 2^i) - 1 \\
&= -[\alpha] - 1.
\end{aligned}
$$

$\square$

Example 2.2.6. If we want to represent -8 in two's complement as a 4-bit number, then we derive $-8 = -7 - 1 = -[0111] - 1 = [\overline{0111}] = [1000]$ by Theorem 2.2.5. Similarly, if we want to represent -42 in 8 bits, we write $-42 = -41 - 1$. The representation of 41 is $0010\,1001$. By Theorem 2.2.5 the two's complement representation of -42 is $1101\,0110$.

Example 2.2.7. If we have a number m then we know that $-(-m) = m$. If m is represented in two's complement encoding by α, we can verify that applying negation twice to $[\alpha]$ yields $[\alpha]$. By Theorem 2.2.5 we find $-[\alpha] = [\overline{\alpha}] + 1$. If we negate this result we obtain $-([\overline{\alpha}] + 1)$. By the same theorem we find that this is again equal to $[\alpha]$ as expected.

Exercise 2.2.8. What is the two's complement representation in 8 bits for the numbers -27, -115 and -200? How many leading 1's could be truncated in each case?

Exercise 2.2.9. If unary negation is applied to a two's complement number of a fixed length n representing a number m, the result does not always represent $-m$. For which number is this the case? And why does this not invalidate the observation in Example 2.2.7.

Exercise 2.2.10. Prove that if the most significant bit of a two's complement representation is 0, its interpretation is the same as its interpretation as an unsigned number. That is show that $[0\alpha] = \langle 0\alpha \rangle$.

Exercise 2.2.11. The sign bit of a two's complement number determines the sign: $[a\alpha] < 0$ if and only if $a = 1$. Prove this.

Exercise 2.2.12. Let α be a bit sequence of length n. Prove that $\langle \alpha \rangle - [\alpha]$ is a multiple of 2^n.

Exercise 2.2.13. Give a proof that the sum of a single bit c_0 with bit sequences α and β, each of n bits, always fits in $n + 1$ bits. That is, show that $[\alpha] + [\beta] + c_0 \in \{-2^n, \ldots, 2^n - 1\}$

2.3 Adding unsigned numbers

Addition and subtraction of numbers are important operations. We first concentrate on how we can add two unsigned numbers represented as binary sequences. This can be done in the same way as adding numbers in decimal notation. As an illustration the numbers 142 and 214 are added below:

```
      1 0 0 1 1 1 1 0 (0)  carry bits
      1 0 0 0 1 1 1 0     (142)
      1 1 0 1 0 1 1 0     (214)   +
   ─────────────────────────────────
   (1) 0 1 1 0 0 1 0 0    (356) result
```

We start adding the digits on the right, at the side of the least significant digit. Adding the rightmost digits 0 and 0 yields 0 as a result which is denoted below the bar. For the moment we can ignore the 0 within brackets. Adding the two 1's in the column second from the right yields 10 in binary notation. The 0 is written below the line, and the 1, which is called a *carry*, is denoted on top to be taken into account when adding the third pair of digits from the right. Continuing the addition shows that the carries, denoted on top, are sometimes 0 and sometimes 1.

Note that the result of the addition does not fit into 8 bits. The left-most carry leads to an extra ninth bit in front. If the result is truncated to fit in 8 bits, the result of the addition is incorrect, as in 8 bits it is equal to 100 (decimal notation).

The leftmost carry is called the *carry-out*. The zero within brackets, i.e., the rightmost carry, is called the *carry-in*.

The addition above makes it clear that for adding two binary digits a and b, an additional carry c is also involved. Table 2.2 shows the results of adding these 3 bits together. Bit s is the *sum* bit and bit c' is the *carry* bit. From the table, we can

a b c	c′ s
0 0 0	0 0
0 0 1	0 1
0 1 0	0 1
0 1 1	1 0
1 0 0	0 1
1 0 1	1 0
1 1 0	1 0
1 1 1	1 1

Table 2.2 Binary representation of adding 3 bits

observe that the sum bit is the XOR between the input bits, i.e., $s = a \oplus b \oplus c$. The carry bit c' is 1 if the sum of the three bits is at least 2, which is characterised by $c' = (a \wedge b) \vee (a \wedge c) \vee (b \wedge c)$. One can check that $\langle c's \rangle$ always equals the sum of the three input bits.

When applying this general scheme to the addition of bit sequences α and β it is systematic to add one extra input carry c_0. This is the 0 within brackets in the addition above. We denote this as $\alpha +_{c_0} \beta$, which represents $\langle \alpha \rangle + \langle \beta \rangle + c_0$. If $c_0 = 0$ we often omit c_0, writing $\alpha + \beta$ as the bit sequence representing the sum of α and β.

As addition is an important operation, we define the representation of the sum of two bit sequences α and β, and a single input carry bit c_0 below.

Definition 2.3.1. Let $\alpha = a_{n-1} \ldots a_0$ and $\beta = b_{n-1} \ldots b_0$ be two bit sequences of length n and c_0 an input carry bit. We define the sum $\alpha +_{c_0} \beta$ as a sequence of $n+1$ bits inductively as follows:

1. If $n = 0$, we consider the empty bit sequences α and β, and the bit c_0. The addition $\alpha +_{c_0} \beta$ is defined to be $c_0 \varepsilon$ where ε is the empty sequence.
2. Consider bit sequences $a_n \alpha$ and $b_n \beta$ of length $n+1$ for $n \geq 0$. For α and β having length n, we know that $\alpha +_{c_0} \beta = c_n \gamma$ where c_n is the carry bit and γ is a bit sequence of length n. We define $a_n \alpha +_{c_0} b_n \beta$ as the sequence of $n+2$ bits

$$((a_n \wedge b_n) \vee (a_n \wedge c_n) \vee (b_n \wedge c_n)) \quad (a_n \oplus b_n \oplus c_n) \quad \gamma.$$

The bit sequence $\alpha +_{c_0} \beta$ represents the addition of the sequences of α and β, and the bit c_0. This is confirmed in the following theorem.

Theorem 2.3.2. Let α and β be bit sequences of length n and c_0 a single bit. It holds that

$$\langle \alpha +_{c_0} \beta \rangle = \langle \alpha \rangle + \langle \beta \rangle + c_0.$$

Proof. We prove this theorem by induction on n. The base case is $n = 0$. This means that $\alpha = \varepsilon$ and $\beta = \varepsilon$. The theorem follows by observing that

$$\langle \varepsilon +_{c_0} \varepsilon \rangle \stackrel{\text{def}}{=} c_0 = \langle \varepsilon \rangle + \langle \varepsilon \rangle + c_0.$$

We now discuss the induction step. Assuming that the theorem holds for sequences of length n, we prove that it holds for bit sequences of length $n+1$. Let α and β have length n, the induction hypothesis (I.H.) is $\langle \alpha +_{c_0} \beta \rangle = \langle \alpha \rangle + \langle \beta \rangle + c_0$. Furthermore, by the definition of addition we know that $\alpha +_{c_0} \beta$ equals $c_n \gamma$.

We need to prove

$$\langle a_n \alpha +_{c_0} b_n \beta \rangle = \langle a_n \alpha \rangle + \langle b_n \beta \rangle + c_0.$$

This can be done as follows:

$$
\begin{aligned}
\langle a_n \alpha +_{c_0} b_n \beta \rangle &\overset{\text{Definition 2.3.1}}{=} \langle ((a_n \wedge b_n) \vee (a_n \wedge c_n) \vee (b_n \wedge c_n)) \quad (a_n \oplus b_n \oplus c_n) \quad \gamma \rangle \\
&\overset{(2.1)}{=} (a_n + b_n + c_n)2^n + \langle \gamma \rangle \\
&= (a_n + b_n)2^n + c_n 2^n + \langle \gamma \rangle \\
&= (a_n + b_n)2^n + \langle c_n \gamma \rangle \\
&= (a_n + b_n)2^n + \langle \alpha +_{c_0} \beta \rangle \\
&\overset{\text{(I.H.)}}{=} (a_n + b_n)2^n + \langle \alpha \rangle + \langle \beta \rangle + c_0 \\
&= a_n 2^n + \langle \alpha \rangle + b_n 2^n + \langle \beta \rangle + c_0 \\
&= \langle a_n \alpha \rangle + \langle b_n \beta \rangle + c_0.
\end{aligned}
$$

For the second equality, marked (2.1), we must verify for all values of a_n, b_n and c_n that the identity

$$\langle ((a_n \wedge b_n) \vee (a_n \wedge c_n) \vee (b_n \wedge c_n)) \ (a_n \oplus b_n \oplus c_n) \rangle = a_n + b_n + c_n \qquad (2.1)$$

holds. This corresponds to checking that Table 2.2 is indeed correct. For instance if $a_n = 0$, $b_n = 0$ and $c_n = 0$, we find this holds as $\langle 00 \rangle = 0 = 0 + 0 + 0$. $\square$

In general addition is done with bit sequences of a fixed length n. If the carry c_n is 1, the result of the addition cannot be stored in n bits. It is common that only the n least significant bits of the result are stored, and a special indicator, namely the *carry flag*, is set to the value of c_n such that this problem can be dealt with separately. A capital letter C stands for the carry flag.

Exercise 2.3.3. Calculate the binary result of the addition of 23 and 18 by first converting these numbers from decimal to binary representation and then applying the binary addition scheme. Check the result by converting it back to decimal.

Exercise 2.3.4. Add the two binary numbers $\langle 11011 \rangle_2$ and $\langle 01011 \rangle_2$ according to Definition 2.3.1. Does a carry-out occur?

Exercise 2.3.5. Add the ternary numbers 12212 and 00021 directly. Check the result by a conversion to decimal numbers.

2.4 Adding two's complement numbers

An important reason for using two's complement numbers is that they use the same algorithm for addition as for unsigned numbers. There is one important difference. Whereas a carry bit signifies that the addition of two unsigned numbers has become too large, an *overflow* indicates that the result of adding two's complement numbers does not fit in the allotted number of bits.

We first introduce syntax for *truncation*, i.e. restricting the lengths of bit sequences by discarding leading bits.

Definition 2.4.1. Let $\alpha = a_{n-1} \ldots a_{m-1} \ldots a_0$ be a bit sequence of length n, with $0 \leq m \leq n$. The overbrace operator is defined to restrict the bit sequence to m bits.

$$\overbrace{a_{n-1} \ldots a_{m-1} \ldots a_0}^{\text{length } m} = a_{m-1} \ldots a_0.$$

The following theorem says that if we add two two's complement numbers of length n as if they were unsigned numbers, and restrict the result to length n, the result is correct except for a difference of $(c_n - c_{n-1})2^n$ where c_n and c_{n-1} are carries.

Theorem 2.4.2. Let $\alpha = a_{n-1} \ldots a_0$ and $\beta = b_{n-1} \ldots b_0$ be two bit sequences of length $n > 0$ and let c_0 be a single bit.

$$\overbrace{[\alpha +_{c_0} \beta]}^{\text{length } n} = (c_n - c_{n-1})2^n + [\alpha] + [\beta] + c_0$$

where c_{n-1} and c_n are the two most significant carry bits for the unrestricted addition of α, β and c_0.

Proof. We write $\alpha = a_{n-1}\alpha'$ and $\beta = b_{n-1}\beta'$. Below we use that $\alpha' +_{c_0} \beta' = c_{n-1}\gamma$, following Definition 2.3.1.

$$
\begin{aligned}
\overbrace{[a_{n-1}\alpha' +_{c_0} b_{n-1}\beta']}^{\text{length } n} &\overset{(*)}{=} [a_{n-1} \oplus b_{n-1} \oplus c_{n-1} \quad \gamma] \\
&= -(a_{n-1} \oplus b_{n-1} \oplus c_{n-1})2^{n-1} + \langle \gamma \rangle \\
&= -c_n 2^n - (a_{n-1} \oplus b_{n-1} \oplus c_{n-1})2^{n-1} + c_n 2^n + \langle \gamma \rangle \\
&= -\langle c_n (a_{n-1} \oplus b_{n-1} \oplus c_{n-1}) \rangle 2^{n-1} + c_n 2^n + \langle \gamma \rangle \\
&\overset{(2.1)}{=} -(a_{n-1} + b_{n-1} + c_{n-1})2^{n-1} + c_n 2^n + \langle \gamma \rangle \\
&= -(a_{n-1} + b_{n-1} + c_{n-1})2^{n-1} + c_n 2^n - c_{n-1}2^{n-1} + \langle c_{n-1}\gamma \rangle \\
&= -(a_{n-1} + b_{n-1})2^{n-1} + c_n 2^n - c_{n-1}2^n + \langle \alpha' +_{c_0} \beta' \rangle \\
&\overset{(**)}{=} -(a_{n-1} + b_{n-1})2^{n-1} + c_n 2^n - c_{n-1}2^n + \langle \alpha' \rangle + \langle \beta' \rangle + c_0 \\
&= (c_n - c_{n-1})2^n + [a_{n-1}\alpha'] + [b_{n-1}\beta'] + c_0.
\end{aligned}
$$

At $(*)$ we used Definition 2.3.1 and at $(**)$ Theorem 2.3.2 was used.   □

If $c_n = c_{n-1}$ this theorem shows that 'normal' addition of two's complement numbers yields the desired result. If $c_n - c_{n-1} \neq 0$, it must either be equal to -1 or to 1. In the first case we find (rewriting Theorem 2.4.2)

$$[\alpha] + [\beta] + c_0 = \overbrace{[\alpha +_{c_0} \beta]}^{\text{length } n} + 2^n \geq -2^{n-1} + 2^n = 2^{n-1}.$$

In the second case the difference between the carries is 1 and we observe

$$[\alpha] + [\beta] + c_0 = \overbrace{[\alpha +_{c_0} \beta]}^{\text{length } n} - 2^n < 2^{n-1} - 2^n = -2^{n-1}.$$

In both cases the result of the addition falls outside the range of numbers representable by an n-bit two's complement number. So, exactly if $c_{n-1} \neq c_n$, the addition results in an overflow. An overflow is generally explicitly indicated by setting an *overflow flag* V which is defined to be equal to $c_{n-1} \neq c_n$.

If the addition of α and β above yields a negative number, the $n-1$-th bit of the result is set to 1. As it is very useful to determine that a result is negative, this bit is called the *negative flag*, and it is commonly denoted as N.

Example 2.4.3. If we add $5 + 3$ as 4-bit two's complement numbers, we compute $0101 + 0011 = 1000$ with carries $c_4 = 0$ and $c_3 = 1$. This indicates an overflow. And indeed the result 1000 represents -8, which is incorrect. This is of course due to $5 + 3 = 8$ not being representable as a 4-bit two's complement number. Note that Theorem 2.4.2 says in this case $[1000] = -2^4 + [0101] + [0011] + 0$.

An alternative way of understanding when an overflow occurs is by checking Figure 2.1. Moving three positions in the clockwise direction from 5 crosses the border between the largest positive and the smallest negative number, leading to -8. Crossing this border in additions indicates an overflow.

Exercise 2.4.4. Compute $-4 - 3$ with 4-bit number representations. Do the same for $1 - 7$. Argue whether the results can be represented by 4 bits.

Exercise 2.4.5. Compute $-5 - 5$ with 4-bit number representations. Do the same for $3 + 7$. Argue whether the results can be represented by 4 bits.

Exercise 2.4.6. Compute $-27 - 5$ with 8-bit number representations. Do the same for $-10 + 36$. Argue how many leading 1's and 0's could be dropped.

Exercise 2.4.7. In Theorem 2.4.2 the result of the addition is restricted to n bits. If the result is allowed to grow to $n + 1$ bits we obtain the following identity:

$$\overbrace{[\alpha +_{c_0} \beta]}^{\text{length } n+1} = (a_{n-1} \oplus b_{n-1} \oplus c_{n-1} - c_{n-1})2^n + [\alpha] + [\beta] + c_0$$

where $\alpha = a_{n-1}\alpha'$, $\beta = b_{n-1}\beta'$ and $\alpha' +_{c_0} \beta' = c_{n-1}\gamma$. Prove this. Observe that also in this case an overflow is not solely determined by the most significant carry bit.

2.5 Subtraction

Subtraction for both unsigned and two's complement numbers can be performed using addition and inversion for two's complement numbers (Theorem 2.2.5). Let us first concentrate on unsigned numbers. We calculate the result of subtracting n-bit sequence β from n-bit sequence α, both interpreted as unsigned numbers, as follows:

$$\langle \alpha \rangle - \langle \beta \rangle \stackrel{\text{Theorem 2.2.5}}{=} \langle \alpha \rangle + [\overline{0\beta}] + 1 = \langle \alpha \rangle + [1\overline{\beta}] + 1 =$$
$$\langle \alpha \rangle + \langle \overline{\beta} \rangle - 2^n + 1 \stackrel{\text{Theorem 2.3.2}}{=} \langle \alpha +_1 \overline{\beta} \rangle - 2^n. \tag{2.2}$$

This means that one can subtract β from α by adding α and inverted β with a carry-in set to 1. The additional term 2^n falls outside the n bits that contain the result. However, it indicates that $\langle \alpha +_1 \overline{\beta} \rangle$ must have a carry-out to guarantee that the result is properly representable as an n-bit unsigned number. If there is *no* carry-out, the difference between the numbers is negative and cannot be represented as an unsigned number.

It is confusing that a carry means that the result is not representable in a fixed number of bits for addition and *no* carry means that it is not representable for subtraction. It adds to the confusion that the way people commonly subtract does lead to a carry if the result is *not* representable. Consider the following subtraction of $4 - 7$ in a 4-bit representation. On the left it is given using inversion and addition, on the right using the common subtraction method with borrows.

0 0 0 0 1 carry bits	1 1 1 1 0 borrow bits
0 1 0 0	0 1 0 0
1 0 0 0	0 1 1 1
1 1 0 1	1 1 0 1

As before the carries are in the upmost row. Clearly, carry c_4 is 0 on the left (showing that the result is negative), whereas this carry is 1 on the right (showing that a borrow was required, indicating that the number is negative).

This confusion is so deep that major chip manufacturers have different solutions. The ARM processor uses *no* carry when the result is not representable. The x86 family of Intel does the reverse. We choose to let the carry represent non-representability. As we will later on implement subtraction by addition and inversion, we set the carry flag $C = \neg c_n$ when subtracting.

For two's complement numbers subtraction does not have such confusions. We calculate

$$[\alpha] - [\beta] \stackrel{\text{Theorem 2.2.5}}{=} [\alpha] + [\overline{\beta}] + 1 \stackrel{\text{Theorem 2.4.2}}{=} \overbrace{[\alpha +_1 \overline{\beta}]}^{\text{length } n} - (c_n - c_{n-1})2^n. \tag{2.3}$$

If the resulting addition generates an overflow, the result of the subtraction is not representable. So, for checking the validity of subtraction of two's complement numbers it suffices to inspect the overflow bit in the same way as for addition of two's complement numbers.

Example 2.5.1. To compute as unsigned numbers $6 - 7$, we compute $6 + (-7)$, that is, $0110 + \overline{0111} + 1 = 0110 + 1000 + 1 = 1110 + 1 = 1111$, which is -1. There is no carry out and that means the result is not valid as an unsigned number.

   When computing $6 - 7$ as 4-bit two's complement numbers we obtain $0110 + \overline{0111} + 1 = 1111$ in a similar manner. Both carries c_3 and c_4 are equal to 0. So, there is no overflow and indeed the obtained answer represents -1 as desired.

Example 2.5.2. To compute $-3 - 5$, we compute $-3 + (-5)$, that is, $1101 + \overline{0101} + 1 = 1101 + 1010 + 1 = 10111 + 1 = 11000$. We drop the leading bit and get $[1000] = -8$. The most significant carries were both 1, so the result is valid.

Example 2.5.3. We want to subtract the two's complement numbers -7 and 3. We compute $1001 + \overline{0011} + 1 = 1001 + 1100 + 1 = 10110$. We drop the leading bit and get 0110, which is 6. We observe that $c_4 = 1$ and $c_3 = 0$. The carries are not equal so there is an overflow. And indeed 6 is not the desired result.

Exercise 2.5.4. Compute $116 - 123$ and $123 - 116$ both as unsigned numbers and as two's complement representation, where the numbers consist of 8 bits. Also determine the carry and overflow flags, such that validity of the resulting values can be checked.

Exercise 2.5.5. Calculate using 8-bit two's complement representation: $-120 - 92$. Is the result valid?

2.6 Comparing unsigned and two's complement numbers

Comparing numbers is a common operation. In order to determine that two numbers are equal, it suffices to subtract one from the other to determine whether the result consists of only 0's. This works both for unsigned and two's complement numbers. In order to use such a result, a *zero flag* Z is set when the result of an operation is equal to zero. For two bit sequences α and β, Table 2.3 shows which flags must be inspected to figure out how they are related after subtracting β from α (i.e., $\alpha - \beta$). In order to see that two numbers are not equal, it suffices to check that $Z = 0$ after subtraction, as shown in the row labelled $\alpha \neq \beta$ in the table.

   When inspecting the ordering between two numbers the situation is slightly different. If two unsigned numbers are subtracted a carry flag $C = 1$ (or $c_n = 0$) indicates that the result of the subtraction is negative. In order to determine $\alpha < \beta$, $\alpha +_1 \overline{\beta}$ is calculated following derivation (2.2) from the previous section. The result is $\langle \alpha +_1 \overline{\beta} \rangle - 2^n$. If $C = 0$, the result is positive. If $C = 1$, $\langle \alpha +_1 \overline{\beta} \rangle < 2^n$ and hence the result is negative. By also using the zero flag Z, it can be determined whether $\alpha \leq \beta$. To check that α is larger than (or larger and equal to) β the simple identities $\alpha > \beta = \neg(\alpha \leq \beta)$ and $\alpha \geq \beta = \neg(\alpha > \beta)$ have been used.

	unsigned	two's complement
$\alpha \leq \beta$	$C = 1 \vee Z = 1$	$N \neq V \vee Z = 1$
$\alpha < \beta$	$C = 1$	$N \neq V$
$\alpha = \beta$	$Z = 1$	$Z = 1$
$\alpha \neq \beta$	$Z = 0$	$Z = 0$
$\alpha > \beta$	$C = 0 \wedge Z = 0$	$N = V \wedge Z = 0$
$\alpha \geq \beta$	$C = 0$	$N = V$

Table 2.3 Interpretation of comparison results after subtracting β from α

c_{n-1}	c_n	N	$\alpha < \beta$	$N \neq V$
0	0	0	0	0
0	0	1	1	1
0	1	0	1	1
0	1	1	X	0
1	0	0	X	1
1	0	1	0	0
1	1	0	0	0
1	1	1	1	1

Table 2.4 Resulting flags when subtracting bit sequences $\alpha - \beta$

If α and β represent two's complement numbers, then according to (2.3) subtracting α and β yields the value

$$\overbrace{[\alpha +_1 \overline{\beta}]}^{\text{length } n} - (c_n - c_{n-1})2^n.$$

If $\alpha < \beta$, this result is negative, which means that either $c_{n-1} < c_n$ or $c_n = c_{n-1}$, and the addition of α and $\overline{\beta}$ above yields a negative number. This is indicated by the negative flag N, the $n-1$-th bit of the result.

In Table 2.4 the situation when $\alpha < \beta$ is made explicit in terms of c_{n-1}, c_n and N. There are two entries with don't cares. These denote impossible combinations of c_{n-1}, c_n and N. From the table it can be read that $N \neq V$ is a good indicator for $\alpha < \beta$. This can be straightforwardly extended to the other ordering operators. The result is listed in Table 2.3.

Exercise 2.6.1. Determine whether $0101 = 0111$, $1011 < 1100$, $1011 < 0011$, $0111 < 1000$ and $0111 \geq 0101$ where the bit sequences are interpreted as both unsigned and two's complement numbers. Do so by calculating a subtraction and by interpreting the resulting flags according to Table 2.3.

Exercise 2.6.2. In order to determine that $\alpha < \beta$ it is possible to calculate $\alpha - \beta$, but it is also possible to calculate $\beta - \alpha$. This leads to a different table than Table 2.3. Provide this table.

a b	c s
0 0	0 0
0 1	0 1
1 0	0 1
1 1	1 0

Table 2.5 Rules for adding two bits

2.7 Arithmetic circuits: addition and subtraction

In this section we show how to build logic circuits to compute addition and subtraction. After introducing the half- and the full adder, we present a circuit computing both addition and subtraction for unsigned and two's complement numbers.

2.7.1 Addition: the half- and full adder

We describe a circuit that computes addition in accordance with Definition 2.3.1. Table 2.5 defines the rules for adding two bits. From the table, we can deduce that the sum bit is the exclusive or between the two input bits and that the carry bit is the logic conjunction of the two input bits. That is, we have $s = a \oplus b$ and $c = a \wedge b$. This leads to a circuit composed of an *and* gate and an *xor* gate to compute the addition between two bits. Figure 2.2 shows such a circuit, which is called a *half adder*. This circuit is characterised by the following equations, where we give the outputs s and c the names $HA_s(a,b)$ and $HA_c(a,b)$ for later use.

$$HA_s(a,b) = a \oplus b$$
$$HA_c(a,b) = a \wedge b$$

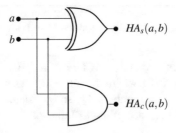

Fig. 2.2 Circuit for a half adder

With two half adders we can compute the addition of three bits as defined in Table 2.2. As observed earlier the sum bit is characterised by $s = a \oplus b \oplus c$ and the new carry has the typical formula $c' = (a \wedge c) \vee (b \wedge c) \vee (a \wedge b)$. This is computed by cascading two half adders as shown in Figure 2.3. This circuit is known as a *full adder*. The following derivation shows that the outputs of the full adder behave as expected.

$$FA_s(a,b,c) = HA_s(c,HA_s(a,b)) = c \oplus HA_s(a,b) = c \oplus a \oplus b = a \oplus b \oplus c$$
$$FA_{c'}(a,b,c) = HA_c(c,HA_s(a,b)) \vee HA_c(a,b) = (c \wedge HA_s(a,b)) \vee (a \wedge b)$$
$$= (c \wedge (a \oplus b)) \vee (a \wedge b) \stackrel{\text{Complement absorption}}{=} (a \wedge b) \vee (a \wedge c) \vee (b \wedge c).$$

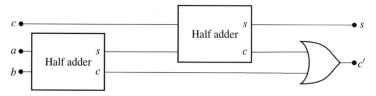

Fig. 2.3 Circuit for a full adder

Addition of two bit vectors of n bits can be computed by cascading several full adders. Figure 2.4 shows an adder for 4-bit numbers. Because the carry is repeatedly passed to the next computation, such a circuit is called a *ripple carry adder* or *carry chain adder*. As signals must pass through a large number of gates, a ripple carry adder can be slow. In the upcoming Section 2.7.3 the faster carry look-ahead adder is explained. Note that all such circuits can be used for both unsigned and two's complement addition.

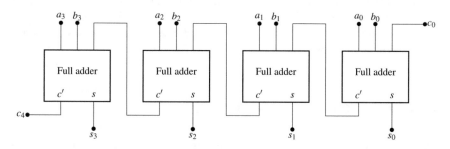

Fig. 2.4 Circuit for a 4-bit ripple carry adder

2.7.2 Subtraction

As explained in Section 2.5 we can use the adder to subtract numbers by inverting the second argument and setting the carry-in to 1. Figure 2.5 shows a circuit using full adders to compute both addition and subtraction. Moreover, it computes the carry flag C, the overflow flag V and the negative flag N. Let $\alpha = a_{n-1} \ldots a_0$ and $\beta = b_{n-1} \ldots b_0$. If input bit op is low, then the first carry is low and every b_i is not inverted. The circuit computes the addition $\alpha + \beta$. If op is high, the initial carry-in is high and every b_i is inverted. The circuit then computes the subtraction $\alpha - \beta$. The carry flag is equal to the carry c_n for addition, and equal to the inverted c_n for subtraction. The overflow flag is calculated by taking the *xor* of c_n and c_{n-1}. The negative flag is equal to s_{n-1}.

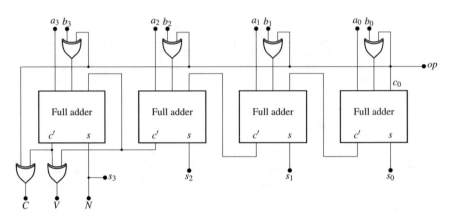

Fig. 2.5 Circuit for a 4-bit signed adder

The essential design idea of an ALU (Arithmetic Logic Unit) is to use one circuit to compute several functions and to use a selection signal, such as op, to determine which function is applied. In Section 2.8 we extend the circuitry to calculate functions such as the bitwise *and* and *or*. The ALU is the workhorse of any processor that can perform all necessary operations on the data floating around in that processor.

2.7.3 The carry look-ahead adder

Ripple carry adders are simple but they are slow. The major issue is that the carry signal propagates sequentially through all full adders. The propagation time is linear in the size of the inputs. Adders are used in many other arithmetic operations. In particular, multiplication consists of repeatedly applying additions. Computations can be sped up considerably if the delay of carry propagation can be reduced.

This is exactly what the *carry look-ahead adder* does. The idea is to calculate the carry signals in advance. Looking at addition, a carry is generated in one of the following two cases:

- both a_i and b_i are 1, or

- when a_i or b_i is 1 and the carry is 1.

Consider the design of a full adder (see Figure 2.3), and define p to be the first partial sum and g the first carry. By definition of the half adder, we have the following:

$$p = a \oplus b \text{ and } g = a \wedge b.$$

We can express the final sum and carry bits as functions of p and g as follows:

$$s = p \oplus c \text{ and } c' = g \vee (p \wedge c).$$

We can observe that if $g = 1$ a carry is generated and whenever $p = 1$ "the previous carry" is propagated. Bits g and p are therefore called *carry generate* and *carry propagate*. The key observation is that the value of p and g only depends on the input bits, and not on the previous carry.

To help understand this computation, the boolean expressions of the four carries generated by our 4-bit adder (Figure 2.4) can be expressed as follows:

$c_1 = g_0 \vee (p_0 \wedge c_0)$

$c_2 = g_1 \vee (p_1 \wedge c_1) = g_1 \vee (p_1 \wedge (g_0 \vee p_0 \wedge c_0)) = g_1 \vee (p_1 \wedge g_0) \vee (p_1 \wedge p_0 \wedge c_0)$

$c_3 = g_2 \vee (p_2 \wedge c_2) = g_2 \vee (p_2 \wedge g_1) \vee (p_2 \wedge p_1 \wedge g_0) \vee (p_2 \wedge p_1 \wedge p_0 \wedge c_0)$

$c_4 = g_3 \vee (p_3 \wedge c_3)$

$\quad = g_3 \vee (p_3 \wedge g_2) \vee (p_3 \wedge p_2 \wedge g_1) \vee (p_3 \wedge p_2 \wedge p_1 \wedge g_0) \vee (p_3 \wedge p_2 \wedge p_1 \wedge p_0 \wedge c_0)$

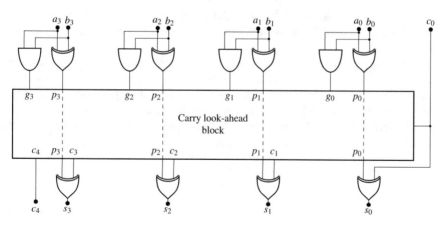

Fig. 2.6 Block diagram for a 4-bit carry look-ahead adder

It is clear from these equations that all carry bits are functions of initial carry bit c_0 and inputs bits in α and β. They can therefore be computed as soon as all these inputs are available. Thus, calculations of all c_i can be done in a two-layer circuit, so in constant time, albeit with a quadratic number of components. The construction of the carry look-ahead adder consists of computing each p_i and g_i using a half adder, then inserting a carry look-ahead block computing all carries following the above equations, and finally computing the results using *xor* gates. This structure is illustrated in Figure 2.6.

The carry look-ahead adder is only one of the adders that have been designed to speed up addition. An alternative is the *conditional sum adder*. In this adder all additions are done with the carry input set to both 0 and 1. Using a multiplexer the results of the right calculations are selected.

Exercise 2.7.1. In Figure 2.5 the zero flag Z is missing. Design a circuit to calculate it.

Exercise 2.7.2. In number of gates, what is the difference in propagation delay for the final carry out for a 4-bit ripple carry adder and a 4-bit carry look-ahead adder. What is the difference in delay for 32-bit adders (the *xor* gate counts for two gate delays)?

Exercise 2.7.3. Construct a 2-bit conditional sum adder.

2.8 The arithmetic logic unit (ALU)

An ALU (*Arithmetic Logic Unit*) is a circuit taking two bit sequences as inputs and computing different arithmetic and logic functions. The ALU forms the heart of a computer processor. An ALU is typically able to compute addition and subtraction. It is generally also able to apply logic operations in a pairwise way on all the bits of both inputs. E.g., if bit sequences have length four, then $0011 \wedge 0101$ results in 0001.

Each ALU has different functions depending on what the processor requires. We desire an ALU that computes addition, subtraction, conjunction, disjunction, and exclusive or. Besides that it must be able to select one of the inputs and forward it to the output, sometimes being incremented or decremented by one. In summary, we wish to design an ALU that with input bit sequences α and β can put the result of one of the following operations on its output:

A: α	$A+B$: $\alpha+\beta$	$A \wedge B$: $\alpha \wedge \beta$
B: β	$A-B$: $\alpha-\beta$	$A \vee B$: $\alpha \vee \beta$
	$A+1$: $\alpha+1$	$A \oplus B$: $\alpha \oplus \beta$
	$A-1$: $\alpha-1$	

We start out with a 1-bit ALU based on a ripple carry adder and later we concatenate n copies tó obtain an n-bit ALU. Figure 2.7 shows our 1-bit ALU. Inputs a_i and b_i are the i-th bits of the input and c_i represents the carry from its $i-1$-th neighbour. Bits op_0, op_1 and op_2 are used to select the required operation that the ALU must perform. If $op_0 = 0$, the ALU computes the output r_i selected by bits op_1 and op_2 as explained in the following table:

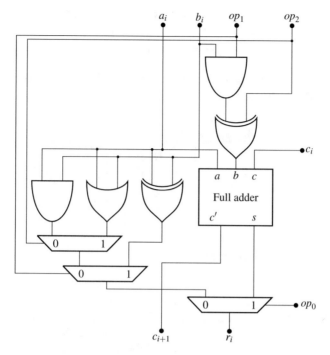

Fig. 2.7 A 1-bit arithmetic logic unit (ALU)

op_1	op_2	r_i	c_{i+1}
0	0	$a_i \wedge b_i$	X
0	1	$a_i \vee b_i$	X
1	0	$a_i \oplus b_i$	X

The carry output c_{i+1} gets various values depending on the input. However, with input $op_0 = 0$, this output is meaningless, and we stress this by setting X's in its output column.

Note that when the input is set to $op_1 = 1$ and $op_2 = 1$ no operation is defined. As it stands this ALU calculates the exclusive or, but by leaving this input undefined, it is possible to add another operation to the ALU and still keep the current ALU backwards compatible.

If $op_0 = 1$, the ALU computes the arithmetic operation specified by op_1 and op_2. To understand the different functions, let us compute the input b of the full adder.

op_1	op_2	b
0	0	0
0	1	1
1	0	b_i
1	1	$\neg b_i$

Bits op_1 and op_2 provide the full adder with inputs 0, 1, b_i or its inverse. In the first four rows of Table 2.6 the effect on the outputs c_{i+1} and r_i is shown. The result of the addition of three values is output c_{i+1} r_i and therefore it stretches over the two columns on the right.

The three last rows contain the output of the 1-bit ALU when op_0 is set to 0, as already mentioned earlier.

$ALU.op = op_0$	op_1	op_2	c_{i+1}	r_i
1	0	0	$a_i + 0 + c_i$	
1	0	1	$a_i + 1 + c_i$	
1	1	0	$a_i + b_i + c_i$	
1	1	1	$a_i + \neg b_i + c_i$	
0	0	0	X	$a_i \wedge b_i$
0	0	1	X	$a_i \vee b_i$
0	1	0	X	$a_i \oplus b_i$

Table 2.6 Encoding of ALU operations

We can combine several 1-bit ALUs from Figure 2.7 to build a full ALU. Figure 2.8 shows a 4-bit ALU with the carry flag (C), the negative flag (N), and the overflow flag (V) in exactly the same way as Figure 2.5. Note that these flags only have a useful meaning when the ALU is used for addition or subtraction.

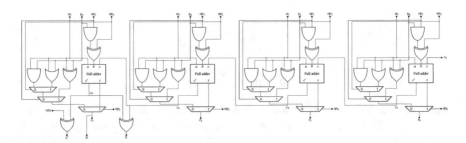

Fig. 2.8 A 4-bit arithmetic logic unit

Exercise 2.8.1. Extend the circuit of the 1-bit ALU of Figure 2.7 such that it can also output b. Indicate how the ALU must be configured to perform this operation.

Exercise 2.8.2. Our final design still computes the overflow flag using the last two carries. Propose a solution to compute the overflow flag without using internal signals.

2.9 Multiplication

Arithmetic logic units can be extended with all kinds of other functions. As an illustration we show how the product of two bit sequences α and β can be computed. We do this in a way very similar to the common method for the multiplication of ordinary digital numbers. Consider the multiplication of two 4-bit numbers. The computation is as follows:

$$
\begin{array}{ccccccccc}
 & & & & a_3 & a_2 & a_1 & a_0 \\
 & & & & b_3 & b_2 & b_1 & b_0 \\
\hline
 & & & & a_3\wedge b_0 & a_2\wedge b_0 & a_1\wedge b_0 & a_0\wedge b_0 \\
 & & & a_3\wedge b_1 & a_2\wedge b_1 & a_1\wedge b_1 & a_0\wedge b_1 & & + \\
\hline
 & r_{51} & r_{41} & r_{31} & r_{21} & r_{11} & r_{01} \\
 & & a_3\wedge b_2 & a_2\wedge b_2 & a_1\wedge b_2 & a_0\wedge b_2 & & & + \\
\hline
 & r_{62} & r_{52} & r_{42} & r_{32} & r_{22} & r_{12} & r_{02} \\
 & a_3\wedge b_3 & a_2\wedge b_3 & a_1\wedge b_3 & a_0\wedge b_3 & & & & + \\
\hline
r_{73} & r_{63} & r_{53} & r_{43} & r_{33} & r_{23} & r_{13} & r_{03}
\end{array}
$$

This diagram does not depict the carries that are used in the additions.

In general, the computation can be expressed by the following formula:

$$
\langle \alpha \rangle \cdot \langle b_{n-1}\ldots b_0 \rangle = \sum_{i=0}^{n-1} \langle \alpha \rangle \cdot b_i \cdot 2^i.
$$

Note that the multiplication with 2^i can easily be achieved by putting bit 0 i times at the end of the result.

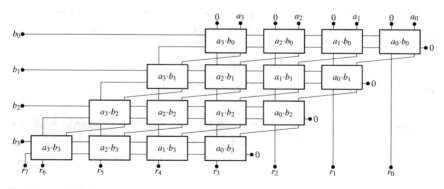

Fig. 2.9 4x4 multiplier array

A combinatorial implementation of a multiplier is shown in Figure 2.9. This figure shows a multiplier array for the multiplication of two 4-bit numbers. Each individual block has the structure given in Figure 2.10.

A disadvantage of this multiplier is that the signal path from a_0 to r_7 is quite long. There are many proposed optimisations for this problem. Options are to use

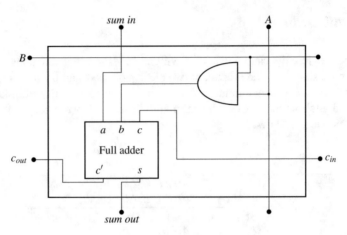

Fig. 2.10 Basic building block for the multiplier array

faster adders like the carry look-ahead adder, or more advanced forms like the *carry save adder*, where carries are stored and only incorporated in the multiplication at the very end. Another option is to use higher-radix multiplication (say, compute in base 4 instead of base 2). In Booth-encoding[3] the second number β is interpreted as a sequence of 2-bit numbers each representing a two's complement number.

A commonly used alternative is to calculate multiplication iteratively, i.e., multiplying α with one bit of β at a time. This substantially reduces the number of gates that are needed, but it requires special circuitry to store intermediate results and control the multiplication in time. Sequential circuits can do this, see Chapter 3.

Exercise 2.9.1. Division can be implemented using combinatorial circuits by performing sequences of subtraction. Design a circuit for a 3-bit division.

2.10 Alternative representations for numbers

We detailed the two's complement representation for integers. This representation is dominant today; however there are other representations that have their own specific purposes.

---

[3] Andrew Donald Booth (1918-2009) was a British engineer working on crystallography, who took part in the design of the first computers in the United Kingdom, including the first magnetic drum memory. Later he worked on the automatic translation of natural languages.

2.10.1 Sign and magnitude

A straightforward representation for integers is the *sign and magnitude* representation. Similar to the two's complement representation, the idea is to use the leading bit as a sign bit, which is 0 to indicate positive numbers and 1 to indicate negative ones. The remaining bits determine the absolute value using the unsigned representation. The range of a n-bit sequence is then $\{-(2^{n-1}), \ldots, 2^{n-1}\}$. This representation has the pleasant property that it is symmetric around 0, but it has the following drawbacks:

- There are two representations for 0. For example, for 4 bits we have $+0 = 0000$ and $-0 = 1000$;
- Addition and subtraction are more complicated than for two's complement numbers.

Adding numbers with different sign bits requires subtraction *and* comparison. The basic idea is to subtract the smallest number from the biggest one and use the sign of the latter. To know which one is the biggest, a comparison is needed. This complication in addition induces a higher cost in hardware. The sign and magnitude representation is primarily used in the floating-point number representation for real numbers.

2.10.2 One's complement

One's complement is another representation for integers. Whereas n-bit negative numbers in two's complement are obtained by subtracting a positive number from 2^{n-1}, one's complement numbers are obtained by complementing each individual digit.

The leading bit is the sign bit. For positive numbers with a sign bit 0, the value is determined by the unsigned representation of the remaining bits. For negative numbers with a sign bit 1, the remaining bits are interpreted as the positive number from which $2^{n-1} - 1$ is subtracted. This leads to the definition of $[\alpha]_{\bar{1}}$ being the value of a bit sequence $a_{n-1}\alpha$ of length n in one's complement representation by

$$[a_{n-1}\alpha]_{\bar{1}} = \langle \alpha \rangle - a_{n-1} \cdot (2^{n-1} - 1).$$

A pleasant property of this representation is that to invert the sign, one simply needs to invert all bits. Besides that, it has the same disadvantages as the sign and magnitude representation. There is a double representation of 0. In four bits 0000 and 1111 both represent 0. Moreover, addition and subtraction are less straightforward than in two's complement representation.

2.10.3 Floating-point numbers

The use of real numbers is commonplace. Within computers real numbers are represented as *floating-point numbers*. Floating-point numbers have the shape $\pm n \times b^m$ where n and m are arbitrary numbers and b is a fixed base, generally 2 or 10. The numbers n and m have a fixed number of bits. In the IEEE 754-2008 standard the 64-bit representation of a floating-point number uses $b = 2$ and assigns 52 bits to n, 11 bits to m and 1 bit is reserved for the sign. The 52 bits of n are implicitly assumed to be preceded by a 1, yielding a precision of 53 bits. The smallest positive number that can be represented is 2^{-1022} whereas the largest representable number is 2^{1023}. There are special representations for $-\infty$, $+\infty$ if the result of a calculation cannot be represented. There is even a representation *NaN* standing for 'not a number', which is used if the sign of the result cannot be determined.

2.10.4 Parity bits and Hamming codes.

Bit sequences that are stored or transferred may get garbled. One way to detect this is to add extra redundant bits. The simplest scheme is adding a *parity bit*, which is a bit that encodes whether the total number of ones in the bit sequence is odd or even. If one bit is unintentionally flipped, this can be detected by a simple piece of circuitry. Of course, if two bits are flipped this will not be detected by a parity bit.

By adding more redundant bits error detection becomes more reliable. Examples are encodings such as two-out-of-five, repetition or adding a checksum. The first uses 5 bits with three 0's and two 1's, where each decimal is represented by three 0's and two 1s. Repetition is simply the idea that instead of sending each bit once, each bit is sent several times. With a checksum a particular value is calculated over the whole bit sequence, which is then attached to it.

These schemes are more precise than adding a single parity bit but still do not offer the possibility of correcting data. Hamming[4] codes add more bits to a sequence and support the possibility of correcting some bits in case of errors.

2.10.5 Gray code

A huge disadvantage of the unsigned number encoding system is that numbers that are close can have totally different representations. For instance, 0111 and 1000 represent the consecutive numbers 7 and 8, yet have *no* bit in common.

---

[4] Richard Wesley Hamming (1915-1998) was an American mathematician who developed Hamming codes, Hamming numbers, the Hamming distance, and many other concepts important for computer science.

The basic idea of the *reflected binary code*, also known as the Gray code[5], is to represent unsigned numbers in such a way that when a number is incremented by 1, exactly one bit is modified. Table 2.7 shows the Gray code representation of 4-bit unsigned numbers in comparison with the decimal, hexadecimal and octal encodings.

b_3 b_2 b_1 b_0	decimal	hexadecimal	octal
0 0 0 0	0	0	00
0 0 0 1	1	1	01
0 0 1 1	2	2	02
0 0 1 0	3	3	03
0 1 1 0	4	4	04
0 1 1 1	5	5	05
0 1 0 1	6	6	06
0 1 0 0	7	7	07
1 1 0 0	8	8	10
1 1 0 1	9	9	11
1 1 1 1	10	A	12
1 1 1 0	11	B	13
1 0 1 0	12	C	14
1 0 1 1	13	D	15
1 0 0 1	14	E	16
1 0 0 0	15	F	17

Table 2.7 Gray code encoding of 4-bit unsigned numbers

Classically, Gray codes are used in position detectors. If two codes are under the detector and the detector cannot clearly determine which one, the error that the detector makes is at most one off. They are also used to transfer information where the value should be approximately correct. If one component communicates its clock value to another component when the clock value can be increased at any moment, the use of Gray codes ensures that the receiver will always receive (almost) the correct clock value.

Exercise 2.10.1. Prove the property that $[\overline{\alpha}]_{\overline{1}} = -[\alpha]_{\overline{1}}$ with α a bit sequence of at least length 1.

Exercise 2.10.2. Which values do the bit sequences 1010 and 0101 represent in the unsigned, two's complement, sign and magnitude, and one's complement representations?

Exercise 2.10.3. Convert the numbers -6 and 3 to 4-bit sign and magnitude representation. Give a procedure to perform the comparison needed to find the operand with the largest magnitude. Calculate the addition of -6 and 3 using the procedure for sign and magnitude representation.

---

[5] Frank Gray (1887–1969) was a researcher at Bell labs working especially on the development of television, for which he developed what is now known as the Gray code.

dec	hex	char		dec	hex	char	dec	hex	char	dec	hex	char
0	00	NUL	null	32	20	space	64	40	@	96	60	`
1	01	SOH	start of heading	33	21	!	65	41	A	97	61	a
2	02	STX	start of text	34	22	"	66	42	B	98	62	b
3	03	ETX	end of text	35	23	#	67	43	C	99	63	c
4	04	EOT	end of transmission	36	24	$	68	44	D	100	64	d
5	05	ENQ	enquiry	32	25	%	69	45	E	101	65	e
6	06	ACK	acknowledge	33	26	&	70	46	F	102	66	f
7	07	BEL	bell	34	27	'	71	47	G	103	67	g
8	08	BS	backspace	35	28	(	72	48	H	104	68	h
9	09	TAB	horizontal tab	36	29	)	73	49	I	105	69	i
10	0A	LF	line feed, new line	32	2A	*	74	4A	J	106	6A	j
11	0B	VT	vertical tab	33	2B	+	75	4B	K	107	6B	k
12	0C	FF	form feed, new page	34	2C	,	76	4C	L	108	6C	l
13	0D	CR	carriage return	35	2D	−	77	4D	M	109	6D	m
14	0E	SO	shift out	36	2E	.	78	4E	N	110	6E	n
15	0F	SI	shift in	32	2F	/	79	4F	O	111	6F	o
16	10	DLE	data link escape	33	30	0	80	50	P	112	70	p
17	11	DC1	device control 1	34	31	1	81	51	Q	113	71	q
18	12	DC2	device control 2	35	32	2	82	52	R	114	72	r
19	13	DC3	device control 3	36	33	3	83	53	S	115	73	s
20	14	DC4	device control 4	32	34	4	84	54	T	116	74	t
21	15	NAK	negative acknowledge	33	35	5	85	55	U	117	75	u
22	16	SYN	synchronous idle	34	36	6	86	56	V	118	76	v
23	17	ETB	end of trans. block	35	37	7	87	57	W	119	77	w
24	18	CAN	cancel	36	38	8	88	58	X	120	78	x
25	19	EM	end of medium	32	39	9	89	59	Y	121	79	y
26	1A	SUB	substitute	33	3A	:	90	5A	Z	122	7A	z
27	1B	ESC	escape	34	3B	;	91	5B	[	123	7B	{
28	1C	FS	file separator	35	3C	<	92	5C	\	124	7C		
29	1D	GS	group separator	36	3D	=	93	5D	]	125	7D	}
30	1E	RS	record separator	32	3E	>	94	5E	^	126	7E	~
31	1F	US	unit separator	33	3F	?	95	5F	_	127	7F	del

Table 2.8 The ASCII character encoding table

Exercise 2.10.4. Convert the numbers 3 and 5 to 4-bit one's complement representation. Calculate $3 - 5$ using a procedure similar to the one used for two's complement representation.

2.11 Representation of character sets

There are several formats that encode text in bits. The desire for such codes predates the use of computers. In order to replace costly operators transmitting messages in Morse[6] code, methods were devised to operate a mechanical printer over a telegraph line. Baudot[7] invented a reliable system where characters were represented in 5 bits.

---

[6] Samuel F.B. Morse (1791-1872) was an American painter. He became interested in rapid long-distance communication after the news of his wife dying reached him too late.

[7] Jean-Maurice-Emile Baudot (1845-1903) was a French telegraph engineer. His only education consisted of a local primary school. The unit *baud* standing for the number of bits that can be transferred per second is named after Baudot.

Since that time various other encodings have been proposed, but by far the most important is the *American Standard Code for Information Interchange* or *ASCII* encoding standardised in 1963. It was primarily meant to send data to a teleprinter and consisted of 7 bits. The ASCII character encoding can be found in Table 2.8.

The first 32 entries in the table are control signals for the printer, among which the line feed (LF), meant to scroll the paper one line up, and the carriage return (CR), intended to move the print head back to the left so that printing could start on a new line. To begin printing on an empty line both a carriage return and a line feed had to be sent to the printer.

The ASCII text format became the prevalent representation for simple text files. It was considered unnecessarily wasteful to store both a line feed and a carriage return. Unfortunately, some operating systems have retained a line feed (LF) as the end of line (especially Unix) while older Apple operating systems used a carriage return (CR). Windows systems use both a carriage return followed by a line feed to indicate the end of a line (CR-LF). This hampers the compatibility of ASCII text files between computers with different operating systems.

Because computers increasingly used the 8-bit byte, it was natural to extend the ASCII code to 256 symbols. This has been done in many different ways. Ultimately, this encoding was standardised in ISO/IEC 8859, which defined 16 different extensions of the 7-bit ASCII encoding for different parts of the world. This was not a very practical solution as texts using the extended character set were only legible in the regions where they were written.

The expansion of computing into parts of the world that did not use the Latin alphabet, and communication between them, drove the foundation of *The Unicode Consortium* in 1991. The initial 16-bit Unicode encoding system has now expanded to encompass seven encoding schemes using either 8, 16 or 32 bits. Together these currently represent 154 different writing systems using 143,859 characters including various graphical symbols and emojis [10]. The need for backward compatibility with systems such as ASCII, and the use of code 'planes', gives Unicode a maximum capacity of 1,111,998 characters.

2.12 Summary

We explained the unsigned and two's complement representations to encode numbers into machine words. Logic circuits were provided to add and subtract such numbers and calculate the carry, overflow, zero and negative flags based on the outcome of such an operation. It was shown how to extend such a circuit to a basic but fully fledged ALU that can be used as the heart of a simple microprocessor. Finally, a short overview was given of other encodings of numbers, as well as encodings of other data types, such as character sets.

Chapter 3
Sequential circuits

In this chapter we show that it is possible and useful to connect the outputs of gates to their inputs. Such circuits are called *sequential circuits*. By connecting outputs to the inputs, gates can store data. This allows us to design circuits that 'remember' past inputs, such as registers and random access memory.

3.1 A one-time latch

Consider the diagram in Figure 3.1 which consists of a single *or* gate. Assume that input *in* is set to 0 and *out* is also 0. This is a stable situation. Now suppose *in* becomes 1. Signal *out* would also become 1. This situation is not stable. Input *y* follows *out* and becomes 1, too. If *in* switches back to 0, output *out* will remain 1. Whatever happens to input *in* the output will remain 1. Output *out* is 1 if input *in* has been 1 once. Clearly, this circuit has a memory function although in this simple form it finds little use.

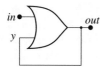

in y	out
0 0	0
0 1	1
1 0	1 (unstable)
1 1	1

Fig. 3.1 A simple one-time latch

Exercise 3.1.1. What happens if the *or* gate in Figure 3.1 is replaced by an *and* gate?

Exercise 3.1.2. Depending on the type of physical gates used, the initial value of the output of a gate may be undefined. A one-time latch constructed from a single gate of this type could be triggered during initialisation, rendering the circuit altogether

© The Author(s), under exclusive license to Springer Nature Switzerland AG 2021
J. F. Groote et al., *Logic Gates, Circuits, Processors, Compilers and Computers*,
https://doi.org/10.1007/978-3-030-68553-9_3

useless. Suppose that an external signal *init* is provided that is 1 during initialisation and 0 afterwards. Modify the one-time latch of Figure 3.1 such that after the *init* signal goes to 0 the *out* signal is (initially) 0.

3.2 The set-reset flip-flop/set-reset latch

Using two gates, we can make an element that will retain its value until it is set, or reset, explicitly. This element is called a *set-reset flip-flop*, and it is one of the most basic sequential logic circuits. It is depicted in Figure 3.2 using *nor* gates. The circuit has two inputs *reset* and *set* that are used to set output *out* to 0 (reset) or to 1 (set).

If both *reset* and *set* are equal to 0, the flip-flop keeps the value *out*. Using the truth table this can be verified. If *reset* is equal to 1 and *set* is equal to 0, then *out* becomes 0, and consequently *y* becomes 0 locking *out* to 0. Similarly, if *set* is 1, and *reset* is 0, the flip-flop is locked to contain 1.

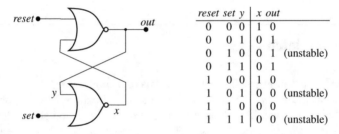

reset	set	y	x	out	
0	0	0	1	0	
0	0	1	0	1	
0	1	0	0	1	(unstable)
0	1	1	0	1	
1	0	0	1	0	
1	0	1	0	0	(unstable)
1	1	0	0	0	
1	1	1	0	0	(unstable)

Fig. 3.2 A set-reset flip-flop with *nor* gates

The set-reset flip-flop has two important disadvantages. The first one is that it is very sensitive to glitches. A single glitch on one of the inputs is enough to change the value of a flip-flop. Another disadvantage is that if both inputs are equal to 1, it is unclear which value the flip-flop will get when both inputs go to 0. If *reset* goes to 0 first, the output will become 1. If *set* goes to 0 first, the output becomes 0. If both inputs change at (almost) the same time and it is not clear which one goes first, the outcome is unknown. It is called *metastability* when it is possible that inputs can change in such a way that outputs cannot be predicted. Such behaviour is undesired and therefore it should be prevented.

A solution is to add a gate signal *G* that indicates when the input is stable. Only when *G* equals 1 can the set and reset signals change the value of the flip-flop. If *G* is 0 the flip-flop remains unchanged. In Figure 3.3 a *gated* set-reset flip-flop is depicted. A gated flip-flop is generally called a latch. Therefore a gated set-reset flip-flop is also called a *set-reset latch*.

Exercise 3.2.1. In Figure 3.4 a flip-flop with *nand* gates is depicted. Explain how this flip-flop is reset and set. Which inputs make this flip-flop become metastable?

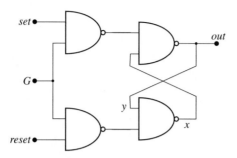

Fig. 3.3 A gated set-reset flip-flop/set-reset latch

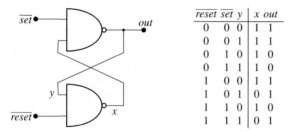

reset	set	y	x	out
0	0	0	1	1
0	0	1	1	1
0	1	0	1	0
0	1	1	1	0
1	0	0	1	1
1	0	1	0	1
1	1	0	1	0
1	1	1	0	1

Fig. 3.4 A set-reset flip-flop with *nand* gates

Exercise 3.2.2. We would like to construct a gated flip-flop that toggles its output whenever the input G is 1. We take the circuit from Figure 3.3 and connect *out* to both *reset* and *set*. We use a *not* gate between *out* and *set*. What problem does this circuit have?

3.3 The D-latch/D-flip-flop

If we have a gate signal available we do not need separate set and reset signals. We can replace them with a single input. A *data*- or *D-latch* (or *gated D-flip-flop*) acquires the input on data signal D when the gate signal G is 1. If G is 0 it remains stable. Its circuit is depicted in Figure 3.5. On the right the common diagram for the gated D-latch is given.

A disadvantage of the gated D-flip-flop is that while G is 1, the input D and output Q are directly connected. Every change in D is directly reflected in Q. It is better to have a circuit that reads the input at a single instant in time for instance when G goes from 0 to 1. This is called *edge-triggered*. Edge-triggered flip-flops are generally referred to as 'flip-flops', as opposed to latches which are gated. An edge-triggered D-flip-flop has a control signal C and reads its input D while C *moves* from 0 to 1.

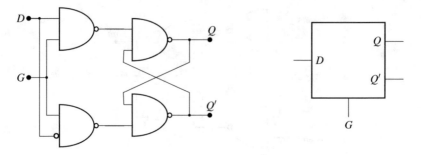

Fig. 3.5 A D-latch/gated D-flip-flop

Typically, C is a clock input. A *clock* is a signal that repeatedly goes from 1 to 0 and back to 1 again typically with a MHz or GHz frequency. Whenever the clock becomes 1, the flip-flop reads a new value. Most circuits are controlled by a clock and as such they are called *synchronous logic*. They consist of D-flip-flops interconnected with some combinatorial circuitry where the D-flip-flops are connected to the clock. When the clock ticks (i.e. goes up) the D-flip-flops change their content simultaneously, after which the combinatorial logic calculates new input for the flip-flops to read at the next clock tick.

We can use the circuit from Figure 1.9 to construct an edge-triggered D-flip-flop. This circuit generates a glitch whenever C goes up. We connect this circuit to the gate input G of the D-latch, see Figure 3.6. Whenever C goes up, the D-latch reads its input.

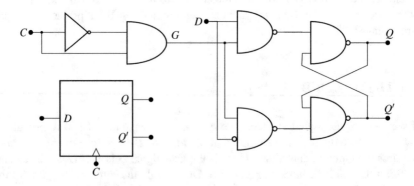

Fig. 3.6 An simple edge-triggered D-flip-flop

This edge-triggered D-flip-flop is not very reliable. The glitch activating the D-flip-flop must be one sufficiently long such that the flip-flop can store the value of D into Q, and sufficiently short such that when D becomes unstable Q cannot

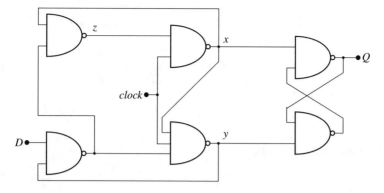

Fig. 3.7 A stable edge-triggered D-flip-flop

be affected anymore. A change in temperature influences the length of the glitch making the D-flip-flop possibly unstable.

A stable edge-triggered D-flip-flop is provided in Figure 3.7. While the clock is low, x and y are 1, and the set-reset flip-flop on the right maintains the output Q. As x and y are 1, signal z follows the value of input D. When the clock goes to 1, the signal z becomes fixed to the value of D at that moment, and x and y become equal to respectively $\neg z$ and z. This sets the output of Q to the value that D had when the clock rose. This value is kept unchanged not only while the clock is 1, but also when the clock goes back to 0. The output Q only changes when the clock rises again.

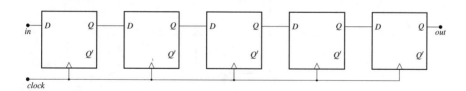

Fig. 3.8 A shift register constructed using D-flip-flops

Using edge-triggered D-flip-flops it is possible to make a shift register as shown in Figure 3.8. The input *in* is read by the leftmost D-flip-flop at the first upgoing flank of the clock. At the second upgoing flank this value is forwarded to the second flip-flop, and during subsequent clock ticks this signal ripples from left to right.

This only works if the output Q of each flip-flop remains stable for a while after the clock goes up. This time is called the *output hold time*. The output hold time must be larger than the *hold time*, which is the time after the upgoing clock flank during which the input D is read. Because the use of D-flip-flops as in the shift register is very important, many D-flip-flops are especially constructed with the output hold time being larger than the hold time.

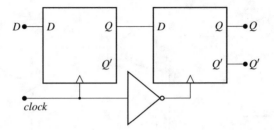

Fig. 3.9 A master-slave D-flip-flop

Alternatively, when it cannot be guaranteed that the output hold time is larger than the hold time, a *master-slave D-flip-flop* can be used, see Figure 3.9. A master-slave D-flip-flop is constructed from two edge-triggered D-flip-flops. The first one reads the input at the upgoing flank of the clock. During this time the second flip-flop keeps the output stable. Only at the downgoing flank of the clock is input D forwarded to the second flip-flop and the output Q becomes D.

Exercise 3.3.1. Design an edge-triggered D-flip-flop that reads its data on each down going flank of the signal C.

Exercise 3.3.2. In Figure 3.9 a master-slave D-flip-flop is constructed using two D-flip-flops. Is it possible to construct it using two D-latches instead?

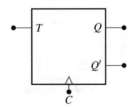

Fig. 3.10 The commonly used diagram for a T-flip-flop

Exercise 3.3.3. Figure 3.10 depicts the diagram for the T-flip-flop which is used to toggle the stored bit. The T-flip-flop is edge-triggered and has a single input T which when high negates the current outputs. Design a circuit that implements the T-flip-flop.

Exercise 3.3.4. The J-K flip-flop is a mixture of a clocked set-reset flip-flop and the T-flip-flop from the previous question. It is edge-triggered like the D-flip-flop. When the input J is 1 and K is 0 at the clock pulse, the flip-flop is set to 1. If J is 0 and K is 1, the flip-flop is set to 0. When both J and K are 0 the flip-flop retains its value. When both J and K are 1, the flip-flop negates its current value, like the T-flip-flop. Design a J-K flip-flop.

3.4 Registers

One flip-flop can store only a single bit. By putting n flip-flops side by side one can store n bits simultaneously. This is called an n-bit *register*. Such registers can be built using gated D-latches or edge-triggered D-flip-flops. To control the register efficiently, the signals G or C of each latch/flip-flop are combined and all the flip-flops in the register read their input simultaneously.

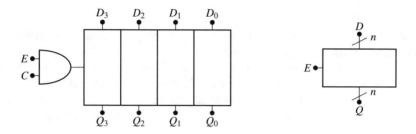

Fig. 3.11 A 4-bit register and an n-bit register

Often the input signal is combined with an extra explicit *enable* signal E. This enable signal provides an extra means to control whether the register will read its input when the signals G or C allows it. On the left of Figure 3.11 a 4-bit register is depicted, constructed using four edge-triggered D-flip-flops. Whenever C becomes 1, while E is 1, the register reads the input value. When E is 0 the input of the register is not enabled, and the register remains unchanged when the clock goes up.

On the right an n-bit register is drawn. The small slashes at the input D and the output Q indicate that the signals are n bits wide. The clock input is not explicitly indicated to simplify the picture. In synchronous logic all registers are connected to the clock and drawing all clock inputs unnecessarily clutters the picture.

If there are multiple registers and their outputs are used as inputs for other registers, a large number of connections and multiplexers are required. There is an alternative, namely the use of a *databus* or *bus* for short. Essentially, an n-bit bus is nothing more than a set of n connecting wires. The register whose output is required puts its content on the bus. The circuits needing this output can then read it from the bus.

There is a problem in connecting multiple registers to a single bus. The outputs of two gates cannot be connected as this leads to a short-circuit. To avoid this problem the *tri-state buffer* has been developed. It is depicted in Figure 3.12 on the left and its truth table can be found in the middle. When the output enable signal OE is 1 the buffer puts its input *in* to the output *out*. If OE is 0 the output is disconnected from the input. It has a so-called high-impedance signal which is denoted using the letter Z. This means that the output is neither connected to 1 nor to 0. In the answer of Exercise 1.3.4 an implementation using MOSFETs is provided. It is safe to connect

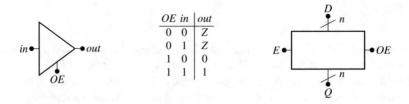

Fig. 3.12 A tri-state buffer with outputs 0, 1 and Z, and a tri-state output register

multiple outputs of tri-state buffers as long as the output of at most one is enabled and the others are set to high impedance.

A tri-state output register is a register for which the outputs run through tri-state output buffers. Such a register has an extra input signal *OE* (Output Enable) that is used to either set the output to to the content of the register or to the high-impedance value Z. The symbol for the register is depicted in Figure 3.12 on the right.

3.5 Finite state machines

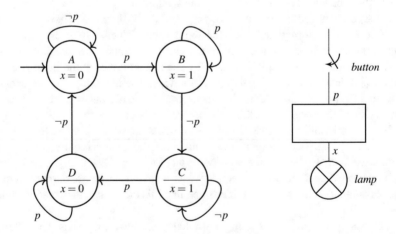

Fig. 3.13 A finite state machine for a one-button switch

Deterministic finite state machines are an alternative way of looking at digital circuits. They are often used to model sequential behaviour where the output changes according to both the inputs and the values stored within the circuit. Finite state machine models can systematically be translated into digital circuits.

3.5.1 An example state machine with four states

A finite state machine consists of a number of states and transitions between these states. We write each state as a circle and each transition as an arrow from state to state. In Figure 3.13 an example of a simple finite state machine is drawn for a one-button switch. The idea is that the system moves from state to state via the transitions.

The initial state is the state where the process starts when the system is started up. It is drawn with an incoming arrow not originating from another state. Each state has a name, denoted above the line in a state. Furthermore, in each state some outputs are set and these are denoted below this line. For the switch in Figure 3.13, the output is the single signal x. In the initial state A it is set to 0. Each transition is labelled with a condition expressed as a logic formula over the input signals. The input signal of the switch is p. In each state the transition is taken that corresponds with the current input. So, in state A, the process stays in state A as long as p is low. If p becomes 1, then the system goes to state B where it will stay until p becomes low again. Note that when traversing from state A to state B, the output x changes from 0 to 1. To simplify drawing state machines, transitions that remain in a state are generally never drawn. All inputs that change the state are drawn on outgoing transitions of that state. All remaining inputs leave the state machine in that particular state.

The system in Figure 3.13 is a state machine to control a light bulb using a single button switch. When the button is released the input p of the state machine is 0. When the button is pressed, signal p is 1. Pressing and releasing the button once toggles the state of the light, which can be off ($x = 0$) or on ($x = 1$).

In the initial state A, the light is off. As long as the button is not pressed, the state machine remains in state A. When the button is pressed, p becomes 1, the transition to state B is taken and the state machine will stay in this state as long as the button remains pressed (which means as long as $p = 1$). The output x changes from 0 to 1, so the light turns on. When the button is released, p becomes 0. So, the transition to state C labelled with $\neg p$ is taken and the light stays on. When the button is pressed again the state machine goes to state D, switching the light off, and when the button is again released, the state machine is again in its initial state and the light is off.

3.5.2 Encoding the state machine

We want to build state machines using logic gates. We start out by making both an output- and a state-transition table. In the output table it is denoted for each state how the output signals must be set. For the state-transition table it is indicated for

state (old)	p	state (new)
A	0	A
A	1	B
B	1	B
B	0	C
C	0	C
C	1	D
D	1	D
D	0	A

state	x
A	0
B	1
C	1
D	0

Fig. 3.14 The output table and the state-transition table for the one-button switch

each state and each input what the next state will be. The output- and state-transition tables for the one-button switch are depicted in Figure 3.14.

state	s t
A	0 0
B	0 1
C	1 0
D	1 1

state	s t
A	0 0
B	1 0
C	1 1
D	0 1

state	s_A s_B s_C s_D
A	1 0 0 0
B	0 1 0 0
C	0 0 1 0
D	0 0 0 1

Fig. 3.15 Three possible state encodings for the one-button switch

If there are n states, we need at least $\lceil \log_2(n) \rceil$ *boolean state variables* or *boolean variables* to represent the state. A boolean variable is a signal that holds a value of 0 or 1 until it is explicitly changed. Typically, a flip-flop is used to represent a boolean variable.

For our one-button switch with four states, we require at least two boolean variables. In Figure 3.15 we provide three possible state encodings. In the leftmost table the states A to D are simply encoded by the binary numbers 0 to 3. We call the two boolean variables that are used s and t. In the table in the middle the states are encoded using Gray codes. In the rightmost table *one-hot* encoding is used. In this encoding there are as many boolean variables as there are states, and at most one variable is set at any time. This may be more costly in the number of flip-flops but it can still be attractive because less complex combinatorial circuitry is often required.

In this case we choose the Gray encoding from the table in the middle in Figure 3.15, as the signal s exactly matches the desired output x. Using this encoding we can rewrite the output- and state-transition tables from Figure 3.14 by replacing the state names by their explicit encoding. The result can be found in Figure 3.16. The state-transition table describes how the new values for s and t need to be constructed using the old values of s and t, and the input p. We construct the combinatorial circuit for doing so using two Karnaugh diagrams in Figure 3.17, one for setting the new value of s and one for the new value of t.

s t (old)	p	s t (new)
0 0	0	0 0
0 0	1	1 0
1 0	1	1 0
1 0	0	1 1
1 1	0	1 1
1 1	1	0 1
0 1	1	0 1
0 1	0	0 0

s t	x
0 0	0
1 0	1
1 1	1
0 1	0

Fig. 3.16 The output and the state-transition tables with explicit state encoding

	00	01	11	10	st
0	0	0	1	1	
1	1	0	0	1	
p					

	00	01	11	10	st
0	0	0	1	1	
1	0	1	1	0	
p					

Fig. 3.17 Two Karnaugh diagrams for s (left) and t (right)

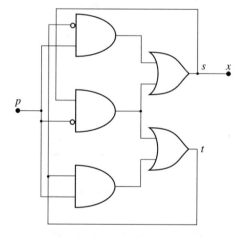

Fig. 3.18 A state machine for the one-button switch in asynchronous logic

3.5.3 Realising the state machine using logic gates and flip-flops

In Figure 3.18 the state machine is constructed using *and* and *or* gates. The boolean state variables are two signals s and t. The output x is directly connected to the state s; as designed, no gates are required to construct x from the state. Following the Karnaugh diagram, $s := (s \wedge \neg p) \vee (\neg t \wedge p)$ and $t := (s \wedge \neg p) \vee (t \wedge p)$. As the expression $s \wedge \neg p$ can be shared, only three *and*s are required.

   This circuit is very simple, fast and if constructed with field effect transistors, very energy efficient. Such circuits are studied widely under the name of *asyn-*

chronous logic or *delay insensitive circuits*. Unfortunately, these circuits are very hard to design correctly as they are very sensitive to glitches.

The solution for the glitch problem lies in the use of a clocked n-bit register built from D-flip-flops. The required circuit is depicted in Figure 3.19. The slashes on the signal lines indicate that these consist of n signals. Using the current value Q of the register, the combinatorial circuit calculates the output and a new value for D. This new input for D is read when the clock goes up. The output hold time of the D-flip-flops must be longer than the hold time, as for the shift register, guaranteeing that Q remains stable until the new value for D is read. This takes care that the new value for the register is calculated based solely on its previous content. If Q would take over the value of D too soon, and the combinatorial circuit is sufficiently fast, the value of D could become unstable before D is read, leading to metastability, making the register useless.

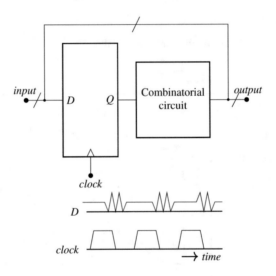

Fig. 3.19 An edge-triggered D-flip-flop controlled by a single clock

We construct the state machine for the one-button switch using a single clock and two edge-triggered D-flip-flops, one for variable s and one for t. It is depicted in Figure 3.20. The combinatorial circuit required is exactly the same as that in Figure 3.18.

Although much easier to construct because the problem of glitches can be ignored, a clocked state machine has the disadvantage that the state changes only occur with the rising edge of the clock. This not only limits the speed of a state machine, it also can cause inputs to be overlooked. The input p could be a very short pulse, shorter than a clock pulse, and may go unnoticed. In practice this is rarely a problem, as clocks are very fast. And if it is a problem, an extra flip-flop can be used which has the purpose of reading input p and preserving it until the next clock tick.

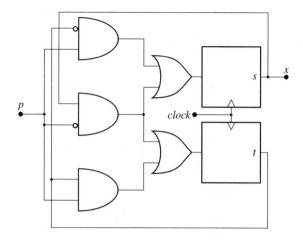

Fig. 3.20 A clocked state machine for the one-button switch

The clocked circuit that we constructed is called a *Moore*[1] *machine*. The output depends only on the state variables. This means that a change in the input only shows up in the output one clock tick later. In a *Mealy*[2] *machine* the output can depend directly on the input and the state. A Mealy machine generally requires fewer flip-flops to represent the state than a Moore machine because input that can be forwarded directly to the output does not need to be recalled. Connecting various Mealy machines together can lead to large combinatorial circuitry depth, reducing the overall clock frequency. In Figure 3.21 a schematic sketch of both a Moore and a Mealy system is given. Because Mealy machines change the outputs when the inputs change, it is common to write both inputs and outputs on the transition, in the form *input/output*. The behaviour of the one-button switch has been depicted in Figure 3.21 at the bottom as a Mealy state machine where the output x is put behind the slash in each transition.

Exercise 3.5.1. Construct the unclocked and clocked circuits for the state machine in Figure 3.13. Use the binary state encoding for the state variables, see the leftmost table of Figure 3.15. Why is it not possible to construct a correct unclocked circuit for the state machine with this encoding? (Hint: What would the effect of propagation delay be for this circuit?)

Exercise 3.5.2. Change the state machine in Figure 3.13 such that the light will change state when the button switch is released, instead of changing state when it is pressed. Design a clocked circuit for this state machine.

---

[1] Edward F. Moore (1925–2003) was a mathematician and computer scientist working on digital circuits and cellular automata, the latter being an inspiration for Conway's Game of Life.

[2] George H. Mealy (1927–2010) was a mathematician and professor at Harvard University. In 1955 he presented a paper called "A method for synthesising sequential circuits".

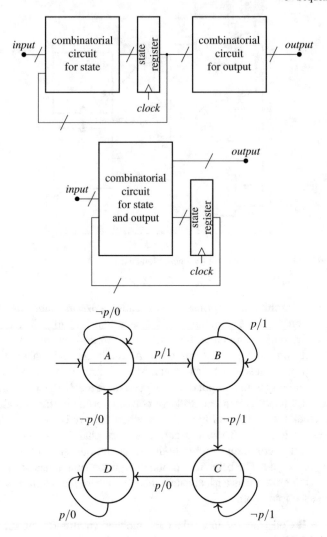

Fig. 3.21 A Moore machine (top), a Mealy machine (middle) and a Mealy state machine (bottom)

Exercise 3.5.3. It is not guaranteed that the flip-flop will start in its initial state, unless special flip-flops are used. So, an explicit reset signal r is needed which is equal to 1 for a short time when the system starts. Extend the state machine for the one button switch with this explicit reset signal and implement it using edge-triggered D-flip-flops.

Exercise 3.5.4. Build a clocked circuit that has one input and one output. The output becomes 1 after the input has been 1 for at least two clock cycles. Design this circuit

both as a Moore and a Mealy machine. Note that the Mealy machine only requires
one flip-flop, whereas the Moore machine requires two.

Exercise 3.5.5. An alarm system needs to be constructed. The system is based
around a motion detector input m, a disable button d, an output b connected to an
alarm bell, and an indicator light l. The alarm bell and the light have to be activated
as soon as the motion detector is triggered. The alarm bell can only be turned off by
the disable button. When the alarm bell has been silenced it will not ring again for
the current disturbance. The indicator light stays on after the alarm bell to indicate
an ongoing disturbance. Permanently pressing the disable button means the system
completely ignores detected motion. Design a state transition diagram for the alarm
system and implement it using edge-triggered D-flip-flops and a single clock.

Exercise 3.5.6. A set-reset flip-flop can be described as an automaton with two
states. See Figure 3.22. Design a clocked circuit for this flip-flop and compare the
result with the set-reset flip-flop.

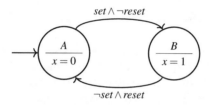

Fig. 3.22 An automaton for a set-reset flip-flop

Exercise 3.5.7. The unclocked state machine for the one-button switch in Figure 3.18 is not stable if no assumptions can be made about the relative speeds at
which the logic gates change outputs, based on their inputs. Give a sequence where
the output x can change arbitrarily often where s, t and x are *false* and p switches
from *false* to *true*.

3.6 Random access memory

Memory can be constructed using an array of registers. Each register consists of m
D-flip-flops where m is called the *word size*. Such memory is called *SRAM* (*static
random access memory*). Generally, for some number n there are 2^n registers in such
an array. Using multiplexers we can use n signal lines to select a particular register.
These signal lines are called the *address* of the memory.

An array of RAM consisting of m-bit wide registers is depicted in Figure 3.23.
The input is an m-bit wide signal called *in*. This input signal is connected to all the
registers. The *write* signal is connected via a demultiplexer to the registers. When

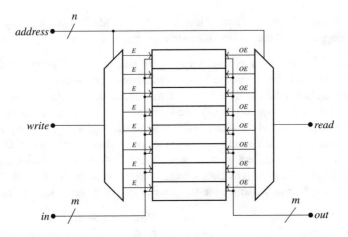

Fig. 3.23 Memory as a readable/writeable set of registers

write is set to 1 the register indicated by the *n*-bit wide *address* signal adopts the value available at *in*.

When the *read* signal is set to 1, the content of the *m*-bit wide register indicated by *address* is put at the output *out*. The address is decoded using a demultiplexer. If the signal *read* is 0, all of the registers will have their outputs set to the high-impedance value Z, not setting signal *out* to any value. It is common that the input *in* and the output *out* are connected to the same data bus. In this case the signals *read* and *write* should not be set to high simultaneously.

Besides static RAM there is dynamic read only memory or DRAM. It uses small capacitors to store bits which require less space than flip-flops. As these capacitors leak, they must be refreshed regularly, for which DRAM components require special hardware. When requiring memory at a given address, it may take a number of cycles for the DRAM to acquire the data, as the clock of the DRAM has a much lower frequency than the clock of a processor using it. Due to its internal structure, it is often cheaper to obtain the data from consecutive addresses sequentially from DRAM. This data is then stored in cache memory built of static RAM which can be accessed with the clock speed of the processor.

3.7 Finite state machines to control registers

The combination of finite state machines and registers is particularly powerful. In the next chapter we show how a simple but full-fledged computer processor can be constructed. Here, as an illustration, a first-in, first-out queue of registers is constructed. The purpose of this queue is to temporarily store a number of values. Such

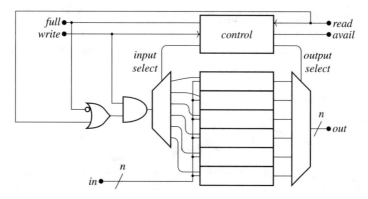

Fig. 3.24 An efficient queue of registers

a circuit can, for instance, be used when a source provides data in bursts that cannot be processed sufficiently quickly.

Our register queue is drawn in Figure 3.24. It has m plain registers each containing n bits. In this design we use registers that do not have a tri-state output. A register value that must be stored is offered at *in*, together with a *write* signal. Writing takes place when there is an empty register, or when a value is being read from the queue simultaneously, which frees up a register.

Reading a register value is done by setting *read* to 1. The value of the first register in the queue will be available immediately at *out*.

There is a finite state machine, called *control*, that ensures that the values in the registers are properly stored and delivered. The finite state machine *control* has two outputs, namely *full* and *avail*. Signal *full* equals 1 when the queue is full. Signal *avail* equals 1 if the queue contains at least one element.

When the *write* signal is true, and the queue is not full or a value is being read, the input of the demultiplexer on the left in Figure 3.24 is set to 1 to indicate that the value at *in* can be read.

As an output, the signal *avail* indicates that data is available. The register to be read is chosen using a demultiplexer and the internal signal *output select*.

The signals *input select* and *output select* consist of $\lceil \log_2(m) \rceil$ bits selecting the register to be written to and the register to be read, respectively. Reading and writing to the registers can happen simultaneously. To determine these signals, *control* recalls the number i of values in the registers as well as the index j of the register that is next to be read. The value of *output select* equals j. The value of *input select* is equal to $(i + j) \bmod m$. Observe that both when the queue is empty ($i=0$) and when the queue is full ($i=m$) the value being written into the queue is stored in register j. In particular when the queue is full and values are both read and written, the written value replaces the one being read.

We provide a finite state automaton to control a register queue with two registers, to keep the automaton simple. It is depicted in Figure 3.25. The states are labelled $S_{i,j}$. On the transitions the inputs *write* and *read* are shown. Recall that self-loops on states are not drawn. If a transition is only labelled with a *write* signal, this means that this transition is taken for any value of *read*. Note that it is possible to read and write the register queue simultaneously, if there is at least one element in the queue.

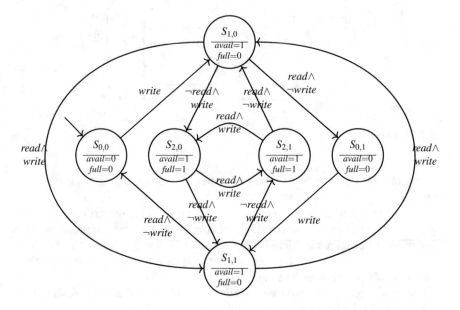

Fig. 3.25 A finite state machine to control a two-register queue

The outputs *avail* and *full* are depicted in each state. They are immediately derivable from the name $S_{i,j}$ of a state. If $i = 0$ then there are no filled registers and *avail* is 0. If $i = 2$ both registers are filled, and *full* is equal to 1.

Due to lack of space, the signals *input select* and *output select* are not drawn explicitly. But as indicated above they are derivable from the name of each state. State $S_{i,j}$ has as *output select* the value of j. The value of *input select* is $(i+j) \bmod 2$. Using the technique outlined in Section 3.5 a Moore machine can be constructed using three D-flip-flops controlling this register queue.

Exercise 3.7.1. Design a Moore machine implementing the state machine of Figure 3.25 using three D-flip-flops controlling the outputs *avail*, *full*, *input select* and *output select*.

3.8 Hardware description languages

Designing digital circuits by hand using truth tables or Karnaugh maps only works if the circuits are small. But in reality circuits are very large with up to billions of components. In order to design such circuits special hardware design languages have been developed. These languages can describe individual gates, but they can also use typical programming constructs like for loops to describe many signals at once, and instantiate building blocks from libraries. Designing a modern circuit often consists of combining circuits from various libraries and connecting them together. These designs look more like a program written in a higher-level programming language than a description of hardware.

There are two major hardware description languages, namely Verilog [31] and VHDL, which stands for VHSIC-HDL or Very High-Speed Integrated Circuit Hardware Description language [1]. A typical description of a D-flip-flop Q with an input D and an enable signal *enable* in VHDL is

> **process**
> > **begin**
> > > **if** rising_edge(*clock*) **and** *enable* = '1'
> > > **then** $Q \Leftarrow D$;
> > > **end if**;
> > **end process**;

Note that the value of Q remains unchanged when there is no rising clock, or when the flip-flop is not enabled.

Components can be declared using the keyword **entity**. A register of D-flip-flops looks like

> **entity** REGISTER **is**
> > **generic**
> > > (WIDTH : **in** *natural* := 16);
> > **port**
> > > (*enable* : **in** *std_logic*;
> > > *clock* : **in** *std_logic*;
> > > D : **in** *std_logic_vector*(WIDTH−1 **downto** 0);
> > > Q : **out** *std_logic_vector*(WIDTH−1 **downto** 0));
> > **end entity** REGISTER;

The physical implementation of these components and their inter-connection is known as a *microarchitecture* in hardware. Registers such as that defined above can be used wherever an arbitrary number of D-flip-flops is required. The number of flip-flops is often a power of 2. Typically, these registers will be used to store binary numerical values.

3.9 Summary

In this chapter we explained how sequential circuits can be constructed by connecting the output of gates to their inputs, which makes it possible for circuits to have memory. This started out with the construction of gated latches and edge-triggered flip-flops, of which the D-flip-flop is the most important. Using multiple D-flip-flops, registers were constructed to store machine words, and with some multiplexers/demultiplexers static random access memory was designed.

Using Moore or Mealy deterministic finite state machines digital controllers can be designed. We showed how to systematically implement these controllers in asynchronous logic, which does not use a clock, or synchronous, clocked sequential logic. By combining registers and finite state machines, elaborate digital hardware can be designed, such as a queue of registers for autonomous buffering of data.

Chapter 4
An elementary processor

In the previous chapter we have seen how we can construct registers, finite state machines and memory. Here we combine these ingredients to form a computer that can execute a program.

A *program* is a sequence of instructions allowing some apparatus to perform various tasks. Before systems became programmable, they were only able to repeatedly do a fixed sequence of tasks, or they required tight human control. One of the first successful programmable devices was the Jacquard loom[1], a French machine which could weave textiles with different patterns depending on a set of punched cards forming its program. These machines were highly successful but only after the mechanism had been improved by De Vaucanson[2]. Sir Charles Babbage[3] designed the Analytical Engine, a mechanical computer with many components still found in modern computers, which was also programmable by punch cards.

In contemporary computers the instructions are stored in RAM instead of on punched cards. For the early computers, such as the Mark I, the program would be loaded from punched cards into the memory for programs and the data would go via the same route to separate memory for the data [23]. John von Neumann[4] observed that there is no reason to treat programs and data separately. They can both be stored in RAM and be treated in exactly the same way [34]. His proposal that data and instructions be stored and accessed together led to the development of the *von Neumann architecture* which has become predominant in computer processor design.

---

[1] Joseph Marie Charles, nicknamed Jacquard, (1752-1834) was a merchant, building a programmable loom in 1804.

[2] Jacques de Vaucanson (1709-1782) was a French inventor known for his mechanical machines such as an automatic flute player and the digesting duck.

[3] Charles Babbage (1791-1871) was a philosopher, mathematician and electrical engineer who designed the mechanical Difference Engine for printing calculation tables for logarithms and trigonometric functions. Subsequently, he developed the Analytical Engine. He also contributed to cryptography, theology and the science of factory production.

[4] John (János Lajos) von Neumann (1903-1957), born in Hungary, was an American/Hungarian mathematician with contributions in virtually all areas of mathematics and computer science.

© The Author(s), under exclusive license to Springer Nature Switzerland AG 2021   73
J. F. Groote et al., *Logic Gates, Circuits, Processors, Compilers and Computers*,
https://doi.org/10.1007/978-3-030-68553-9_4

In this chapter we present a simple computer processor architecture in full detail along with its corresponding instruction set in which programs can be written. We also show how the instructions are executed on the architecture. All commonly existing computer processors have the same fundamental structure as the one presented here, although they are generally far more complex.

4.1 The general structure of the processor

The processor defined in this chapter implements a pure von Neumann architecture. It has a number of registers to store data values and instructions, an ALU (*arithmetic logic unit*) to perform calculations on the contents of registers and some memory (RAM) to store data values between calculations. The values in the registers and in RAM consist of 16-bit words, except for the *CC* register. The ALU is also suitable for 16-bit operations.

The processor executes programs written as a sequence of machine code instructions. A machine code instruction typically expresses that some ALU operation such as addition or subtraction must be carried out on values in the registers and the result must be returned to a register. Another typical use is that register values must be transferred to or from RAM. There are also control instructions that allow for blocks of code to be conditionally executed or looped over repeatedly.

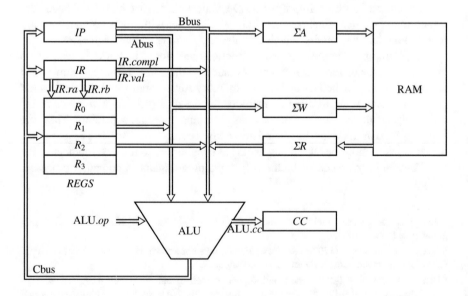

Fig. 4.1 The basic data path for our simple processor

The structure of the processor is depicted in Figure 4.1 which is called the *basic data path*. It has a number of specific registers and a number of general registers, all connected by three 16-bit buses: the Abus, the Bbus and the Cbus. The processor is clocked, and during each clock tick data is moved from and to the registers via these buses. During each clock tick and for each bus, one component can write to that bus and multiple components can read. As there are multiple buses, multiple data transfers are possible on each clock tick.

The specific registers are the instruction pointer (*IP*) pointing to the next instruction to be executed, the instruction register (*IR*) containing the current machine code instruction, the address register for memory (ΣA), the read and write registers for memory (ΣR and ΣW), and the 4-bit flags register (*CC*). The flags register is used to store the flags C, N, V and Z resulting from calculations in the ALU. The general registers (*REGS*) consist of R_0, R_1, R_2 and R_3 which store values used for calculations in the program.

Each specific register has its own select signal *sel* that, if set to 1, causes the register to read the value available on the bus that is connected to its input. As an example, if $\Sigma A.sel$ is set to one, then, when the clock signal rises, the value which is on the Bbus at that moment is read into register ΣA. These select signals are not shown explicitly in Figure 4.1.

For each register connected to a bus, there is also an output enable (*oe*) signal. If this is set, the output of the register is made available on the bus. Only one register at a time can be enabled to set its output onto the bus, as otherwise a short-circuit can occur and the processor may be damaged. If a register is connected to multiple buses, an extra letter is added to the output enable signal to indicate the bus. For the register *IP* there are two output signals, namely *IP.oea* and *IP.oeb*. The same holds for the general registers which have *REGS.oea* and *REGS.oeb*.

Instructions in the *IR* register can contain 9 bits of data which can be passed to the Bbus. Because the Bbus is 16 bits wide the data must be extended. The output signal *IR.val* extends the 9 bits with 0's. The output signal *IR.compl* takes the 9 bits as a two's complement value and extends the sign bit to the full 16-bit width as shown in Section 2.2. The register *IR* can output either *val* or *compl*, using the signals *IR.oev* or *IR.oec*, respectively.

For the general registers there is one select signal for input into the registers *REGS.sel*, and three signals *REGS.oea*, *REGS.oeab* and *REGS.oeb* for output. The selection of which particular registers are input and output is determined by two 2-bit signals *IR.ra* and *IR.rb* that are extracted from the instruction in the *IR* register. These signals correspond to specific bit positions in the instruction in *IR*. This is discussed later when we deal with the shape of instructions in machine code.

When *REGS.sel* equals 1 it reads the value on the Cbus into the register indicated by *IR.ra*. When *REGS.oea* is 1, the register value indicated by *IR.ra* is put on the Abus. When *REGS.oeab* is 1, the register value indicated by *IR.ra* is put on the Bbus. Likewise, when *REGS.oeb* is 1, the value of *IR.rb* is put on the Bbus. Note that the contents of two registers can be put on the buses, provided the buses are different. It is also possible to put the contents of one register onto both the Abus and the Bbus simultaneously.

The ALU can be instructed to perform a certain operation via its input ALU.*op*. It is the same ALU as defined in Section 2.8, although it also outputs the zero flag Z. Concretely, the ALU outputs the four flags C, N, V and Z from *ALU.cc*, and these can be read into the 4-bit flag register *CC* by setting *CC.sel* to 1. We show later how the *CC* flags are used in the execution of instructions.

The RAM is addressed using the value in the address register ΣA. When RAM.*sel* equals 1, then the content of the write register ΣW is read into the address indicated by ΣA. If the output enable signal of the RAM equals 1, the content of the RAM indicated by the address register is available to be read into the ΣR register.

By setting the select and output enable signals of the registers, data can be transferred throughout the processor. By instructing the ALU to perform the appropriate instruction, values can be added, subtracted or compared. For instance, if an address is already available in ΣA, and the content w of the RAM at this address must be moved to register *IR*, this can be done by setting $\Sigma A.oe$ and $\Sigma R.sel$ at the first clock tick. At the end of this clock tick the value w is read in ΣR. At the next clock tick $\Sigma R.oe$ is set. The ALU is set to pass the content of the Bbus directly to the Cbus (see Exercise 2.8.1) and *IR.sel* is set to read this value directly into the register *IR*. After this second clock tick, *IR* contains w.

Using multiple buses, it is possible to move the contents of several registers in one clock tick. For instance while the content of ΣR is moved via the Bbus and the Cbus to *IR*, the content of *IP* can be moved simultaneously via the Abus to ΣW. And if need be, we could change the layout of the simple processor, for instance by adding an extra Dbus, or extra registers, to give it more functionality or to move data around in fewer clock cycles.

Exercise 4.1.1. The instruction register *IR* is loaded with an instruction to add the contents of the registers R_0 and R_1 and place the result into R_0. The ALU's flags also need to be saved. How should the relevant select and output enable signals be set to execute this instruction? What should the additional signals (*IR.ra*, etc.) correspond to?

Exercise 4.1.2. We want to calculate the disjunction of three different values, two of which are already in *REGS*, namely in R_0 and R_1. The data in *IR* contains the address of the third value. The result should be stored in the register R_0 and the flags should be saved in *CC*. Show how all the relevant signals should be set indicating in which clock cycle they are used. Use no more than three clock cycles.

Exercise 4.1.3. Suppose we wish to copy a value from the register R_0 into the RAM while keeping the values in *REGS* and *IP* available for subsequent operations. The address where this value is to be stored has to be calculated by adding up the value of the R_1 register with a signed value embedded in the current instruction in *IR*. Why is it not possible to execute this instruction on the basic data path? Modify the basic data path in Figure 4.1 such that it is possible to execute this instruction in three clock cycles. Show how all the relevant signals should be set.

4.2 The instruction set

Our processor uses a simple set of machine code instructions that is a good representation of the variety of instructions that are found in most computer processors
[16, 2, 17]. The set is suitable to write any sequential program. For parallel programming we introduce a few more instructions later.

Each machine code instruction is a sequence of 16 bits and therefore not very
readable. This is the reason that machine code instructions are generally presented
as *assembly instructions* or *mnemonics*. An *assembler* is a program that translates
assembly instructions to machine code. We first present our instruction set as assembly instructions. How they are represented as bit sequences is explained later.

Instruction	Mode	Effect	Flags
STOR R_i [$expr$]	(in)direct	RAM[$expr$] $\leftarrow R_i$	N,Z
LOAD R_i $expr$	register/immediate	$R_i \leftarrow expr$	N,Z
LOAD R_i [$expr$]	(in)direct	$R_i \leftarrow$ RAM[$expr$]	N,Z
ADD R_i $expr$	register/immediate	$R_i \leftarrow R_i + expr$	C,N,V,Z
ADD R_i [$expr$]	(in)direct	$R_i \leftarrow R_i +$RAM[$expr$]	C,N,V,Z
SUB R_i $expr$	register/immediate	$R_i \leftarrow R_i - expr$	C,N,V,Z
SUB R_i [$expr$]	(in)direct	$R_i \leftarrow R_i -$RAM[$expr$]	C,N,V,Z
AND R_i $expr$	register/immediate	$R_i \leftarrow R_i \wedge expr$	N,Z
AND R_i [$expr$]	(in)direct	$R_i \leftarrow R_i \wedge$RAM[$expr$]	N,Z
OR R_i $expr$	register/immediate	$R_i \leftarrow R_i \vee expr$	N,Z
OR R_i [$expr$]	(in)direct	$R_i \leftarrow R_i \vee$RAM[$expr$]	N,Z
XOR R_i $expr$	register/immediate	$R_i \leftarrow R_i \oplus expr$	N,Z
XOR R_i [$expr$]	(in)direct	$R_i \leftarrow R_i \oplus$RAM[$expr$]	N,Z
BRA $disp$	immediate	$IP \leftarrow IP + disp$	-
BCC $disp$	immediate	$IP \leftarrow IP + disp$ if $C = 0$	-
BCS $disp$	immediate	$IP \leftarrow IP + disp$ if $C = 1$	-
BPL $disp$	immediate	$IP \leftarrow IP + disp$ if $N = 0$	-
BMI $disp$	immediate	$IP \leftarrow IP + disp$ if $N = 1$	-
BVC $disp$	immediate	$IP \leftarrow IP + disp$ if $V = 0$	-
BVS $disp$	immediate	$IP \leftarrow IP + disp$ if $V = 1$	-
BNE $disp$	immediate	$IP \leftarrow IP + disp$ if $Z = 0$	-
BEQ $disp$	immediate	$IP \leftarrow IP + disp$ if $Z = 1$	-
BRS R_i $disp$	immediate	RAM[$R_i - 1$], IP, $R_i \leftarrow IP$, $IP + disp$, $R_i - 1$	-
RTS R_i	indirect	IP, $R_i \leftarrow$ RAM[R_i], $R_i + 1$	-

Table 4.1 The instruction set of our simple processor

The instructions are listed in Table 4.1. They only refer to the registers $R_0, \ldots, R_3$,
IP and CC, and the RAM. This is the *programmer's model* of the processor. It is not
necessary to know about the other registers when writing programs for this processor.

The instructions can roughly be divided into four categories. In the first category are store and load instructions. Store (STOR) instructions are used to write
data to memory and load (LOAD) instructions are used to read data into registers
$R_0, \ldots, R_3$. The arithmetic instructions ADD, SUB, AND, OR, and XOR are used

for calculations with data. The branch instructions BRA, BCC, etc. are used to jump to other parts of the program, often depending on how the flags in the flag register CC are set. The last two instructions are branch to subroutine (BRS) and return from subroutine (RTS). These are primarily used to implement procedure calls.

Table 4.1 shows the arguments for each instruction. Arguments can be one of the four registers or a 9-bit value. The expression R_i refers to a register, *disp* is a 9-bit value in two's complement notation representing a displacement and *expr* refers to a register or an unsigned 9-bit value. When a 9-bit value is used as an *expr*, it is first transformed into a 16-bit value by adding 0's as the most significant bits. Note that *expr* values are therefore always non-negative.

For each instruction the effect is indicated in the third column in the table. For instance, for LOAD R_i *expr* the effect is that the value represented by *expr* is copied to register i. If *expr* is a register, the content of that register is moved to register i. If *expr* represents a value, that value is moved into R_i. For example, after the execution of LOAD R_3 17 register R_3 contains the value 17. And likewise, after the execution of ADD R_1 R_2 the register R_1 contains the sum of the values that the registers R_1 and R_2 had before executing this instruction.

The load and arithmetic instructions come in several variants, namely with (in)direct and register/immediate addressing modes. In register/immediate mode the argument is used directly in the instruction. An example of *register* mode is the instruction LOAD R_0 R_1, which results in the contents of register R_1 being copied to R_0. In *immediate* mode the argument value is placed in the destination, for example, LOAD R_0 20 which places the decimal value 20 into R_0. With the (in)direct modes, the argument is denoted within square brackets and it represents an address in RAM. For example in the *direct* mode instruction LOAD R_0 [10] the content of the memory at address 10 is copied into R_0. The *indirect* mode instruction LOAD R_1 $[R_2]$ copies the content of the RAM at the address given by the value in register R_2 to register R_1.

Note that the results of the load and the arithmetic operations are always stored in one of the four registers. To store data in memory, the STOR instruction must be used. As the second argument of the STOR instruction always refers to memory, it is only available in the (in)direct modes.

The fourth column of Table 4.1 shows the condition code flags that are set as the result of each operation. Observe that setting the carry and overflow flags only makes sense for addition and subtraction. When the instructions become more complex, there can be reasons to set the flags in a more selective way.

The branch instructions are used to jump to other parts of the program. This is done by changing the value of the register *IP* containing the instruction pointer. After executing a branch instruction, the next instruction that is executed is taken from the new address held within register *IP*.

We use the immediate argument *disp* of a branch instruction as a relative displacement compared to the current instruction pointer which points to the next instruction to be executed. The value *disp* is interpreted as a two's complement number. If the value of *disp* is negative, a jump backward in the program is made. If it is zero or higher, a forward jump is performed. For example, BRA 1 causes the program to jump over the next instruction and BRA -2 causes the program to jump to the instruction just before this branch instruction. The instruction BRA -1 jumps to itself and causes an infinite loop. When this instruction is executed, the instruction pointer is increased by one, which is subsequently decreased by 1 due to the branch instruction. Therefore, the branch instruction BRA -1 is executed continuously.

The advantage of using relative jumps is that the jumps are valid independent of where the program is stored in memory. In such a case the code is called *relocatable*. If the argument *disp* were an absolute address, the program would have to be stored at a fixed place in memory in order to be executed successfully. When a computer is used for several purposes, it is not always possible to store the program at a fixed place in memory as this might have been taken by other programs or data. Relocatable code can be placed anywhere in memory providing that a sufficiently large block of memory is available.

The argument *disp* only consists of 9 bits. This means that only backward jumps of 256 instructions and forward jumps of size 255 are possible relative to the current instruction. For large programs, this is an unpleasant restriction, as jumps exceeding these limits must be constructed from multiple smaller jumps. Fortunately, for the programs in this book we do not require such large jumps to be made.

The BRA instruction always changes the instruction pointer. But often a conditional jump is required. For this purpose, instructions set the Z, N, V, C condition code flags and a conditional jump only takes place when its corresponding flag has the right value. If not, the jump is ignored and the next instruction is executed. There are eight conditional jump instructions, one for each value the four condition code flags can take. As an example, the instruction BCC *disp* changes the instruction pointer with *disp* only if the carry flag is clear, i.e., equal to 0. The BCS instruction only branches to a new address when the carry flag is set.

This instruction set is sufficient to write programs. As an illustration, we provide a program that loads a number from address 0 in memory and adds it repeatedly to the content of address 1. The number of times addition takes place is given by the number at address 2, which is assumed to be larger than 0 initially. The values in memory are first loaded into registers, where the calculations take place. At the end the sum is stored at address 1 in memory.

```
LOAD R0 [0]   ; Load RAM[0] into register R0.
LOAD R1 [1]   ; Load RAM[1] into register R1.
LOAD R2 [2]   ; Load RAM[2] into register R2.
   ADD R1 R0  ; Add registers R0 and R1; store the result in register R1.
   SUB R2 1   ; Decrement register R2 by 1.
   BNE -3     ; Jump to the add instruction if Z is not set, i.e., if R2 did not
              ; become 0. Otherwise, continue with the store instruction below.
STOR R1 [1]   ; Store the sum into RAM[1].
```

Note that because the instruction pointer always points to the next instruction to be executed, the relative jump is based on the difference between the destination address and the address following the jump instruction.

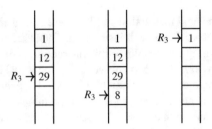

Fig. 4.2 The processor stack

The last category of instructions contain the branch to subroutine (BRS) and the return from subroutine (RTS) instructions. These are used for calling functions. For the execution of functions the notion of a *stack* is essential. A stack is nothing more than a neatly arranged pile of values to which new elements can be added and removed from the top. Our stack grows down, and therefore, the top of the stack is at the bottom. A stack is typically implemented as a block of memory in RAM, see Figure 4.2 where three different stack configurations are drawn.

There is a *stack pointer* that points to the last occupied position at the top of the stack. We systematically use register R_3 to hold the stack pointer. The register holding the stack pointer is often also denoted as *SP*. Some processors have a specially designated register to hold the stack pointer.

Now consider a deliberately simple function f, say, increasing the content of register R_0 by two. This function may be called from anywhere in the program, and when the function is finished, the program must return to the instruction directly after the place where it was called. Therefore, this *return address* must be stored somewhere. This is typically done on the stack.

The instruction BRS R_3 *disp* calls the function f by performing three actions. It first decreases register R_3, i.e., the stack pointer, by one such that it refers to the next empty place beyond the top of the stack. It then puts the instruction pointer, which already refers to the next instruction, on the stack. Finally, it replaces the instruction pointer with the address of the function f such that f is executed next. The argument *disp* has the value $addr_f - addr_{BRS} - 1$ where $addr_{BRS}$ is the address of the branch to subroutine instruction and $addr_f$ is the address where the function f resides in memory.

When the function f is finished with its calculation, it executes a return from subroutine, RTS R_3, instruction. This replaces the content of the instruction pointer with the value on the top of the stack. This is the return address that was stored when the BRS instruction was executed. The RTS R_3 instruction also increments the stack pointer by one, as this return address is of no further use and does not need to be stored on the stack.

Concretely, the program has the following shape:

ADD R_0 2   ; The function f is located here, adding 2 to R_0.
RTS R_3 ; The calculation of f is finished. Return to the
                                    ; instruction directly after the place where f
                                    ; was called.
...   ; There can be other instructions here.
BRS R_3 *relative_address_of_f* ; Call the function f.
...   ; When f is finished, execution proceeds here.

Exercise 4.2.1. Consider the assembly program on page 79. Why is it a bad idea to place this program at address 0 in memory?

Exercise 4.2.2. Instead of using a stack, is it possible to use a dedicated register or memory address to store the return value?

Exercise 4.2.3. Besides having a stack with register R_3 another stack could be constructed with register R_2 as a stack pointer. Is there a fundamental reason why this should be avoided?

4.3 The instruction fetch and the register transfer language

To execute an instruction on our processor, it must first be moved from RAM to the instruction register *IR*. This is called the *instruction fetch*. The instruction is subsequently decoded, any additional data fetched from memory and the instruction executed. After that, if need be, the results are written back to memory.

In this section we focus on implementing the instruction fetch on our simple processor. For the instruction fetch, the instruction at the address indicated by the instruction pointer *IP* must be moved to the instruction register. To facilitate this, the content of the register *IP* must be moved to the address register *ΣA* in the first clock cycle. The instruction pointer must also be increased to prepare it for the next instruction. This is done by sending it through the ALU, adding one and storing the increased value back in *IP*. In the second clock cycle, the instruction at that address is moved to the read register *ΣR*. Finally, in the third cycle, the content of *ΣR* is moved to *IR*.

A convenient and precise way to describe such movements is by using *register transfer language*. For each clock cycle, there is a single line that shows how the content of registers and RAM is copied into each other via various buses and the ALU.

$$R_0, R_1, R_2, \ldots \leftarrow expr_0, expr_1, expr_2, \ldots$$

This is a simultaneous assignment. Each expression $expr_i$ is assigned to a register or a RAM address R_i in the same clock cycle.

The expression is either another register, including the flag outputs of the ALU, an ALU operation applied to two registers, or the output of the RAM. After each register, the bus over which the signals from that register travel can be denoted. Denoting this bus is a good habit, as it makes it clear which buses are used. During one clock cycle, a bus can only be used for one transfer of data. Moreover, there are sometimes situations where signals can travel via different buses. Denoting them explicitly makes it clear which one was intended.

This register transfer language is specific for the data path in Figure 4.1 although it allows for small changes in the data path. In Appendix C, the precise syntax of the register transfer language is defined.

For the general purpose registers, we use the name *RA* to refer to the register selected by *IR.ra* whose value is placed on the Abus due to *REGS.oea* being 1. The register *RB* is similarly defined, namely the register selected by *IR.rb* which is put on the Bbus. We use the register name *RAB* when *REGS.oeab* equals 1, i.e., when the register indicated by *IR.ra* is put on the Bbus.

1. $\Sigma A, IP \leftarrow IP(\text{Bbus}), IP(\text{Abus})+1$.
2. $\Sigma R \leftarrow \text{RAM}[\Sigma A]$.
3. $IR \leftarrow \Sigma R(\text{Bbus})$.

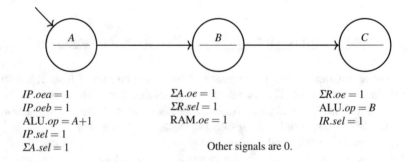

$$IP.oea = 1 \qquad\qquad \Sigma A.oe = 1 \qquad\qquad \Sigma R.oe = 1$$
$$IP.oeb = 1 \qquad\qquad \Sigma R.sel = 1 \qquad\qquad ALU.op = B$$
$$ALU.op = A+1 \qquad\quad RAM.oe = 1 \qquad\qquad IR.sel = 1$$
$$IP.sel = 1$$
$$\Sigma A.sel = 1 \qquad\qquad\qquad \text{Other signals are 0.}$$

Fig. 4.3 A finite state machine orchestrating the instruction fetch

From this description in register transfer language, it is quite straightforward to construct a finite state machine that performs the corresponding register transfers. The finite state machine that orchestrates how machine code instructions are carried out on a machine is often called the *execution unit* and the part that carries out the instruction fetch is depicted in Figure 4.3. Note that there are no signals on the transitions. On consecutive clock ticks the execution unit moves independently of any input signal, first from state *A* to *B* and then to *C*. The outputs of this state machine control the simple processor. Each state of the finite state machine corresponds to a line in the register transfer program in its shorter form and the outputs in each state enable exactly the right data transfers in the processor. There are quite a number of outputs in each state, so they are written below each state. Signals that are not explicitly set to 1, can be assumed to be set to 0. These are omitted to save space. In state B ALU.*op* is not set. This is not problematic because the output of the ALU is not used. The signal ALU.*op* can be set to any value, which could be indicated by setting it to a don't care value *X*.

Note that the third step of the register transfer description is executed when moving from state C to a subsequent state. Here inputs do play a role because the machine code instruction that has been fetched, must be executed. Transitions leaving state C are discussed in Section 4.5 and they are not depicted in Figure 4.3.

Exercise 4.3.1. Give the description in register transfer language for loading the contents of the RAM at the address stored in the register RB and calculating the sum of this value with the value in register RA. Store the result in the register RA and set the CC flags.

Exercise 4.3.2. Suppose the simple processor just finished executing an instruction. The next instruction is to *XOR* the values of the register RA selected by *IR.ra* and the register RB selected by *IR.rb*. Save the result in the first register. Describe in register transfer language how this operation is to be performed. First execute the instruction fetch.

Exercise 4.3.3. It is possible to only use two clock cycles to fetch an instruction by removing the register ΣR and connecting the RAM directly to the Bbus. Write the fetch in register transfer language for this new data path and adapt the finite state machine accordingly.

4.4 The format of machine code instructions

Each instruction of the simple processor is encoded as a 16-bit sequence. This can be done in many ways, and our encoding is rather arbitrary and could easily be done differently. But it is good practice to choose a systematic encoding, because this leads to less complex circuitry and also simpler assemblers that translate the assembly code to machine code.

The STOR, LOAD and arithmetic instructions are translated to 16-bit machine code according to the following scheme.

$$op \; op \; op \; op \; r \; r \; 0 \; v \; v \; v \; v \; v \; v \; v \; v \; v$$
$$op \; op \; op \; op \; r \; r \; 1 \; r \; r \; 0 \; 0 \; 0 \; 0 \; 0 \; 0 \; 0$$

The first encoding refers to the direct and immediate mode variants of the instruction with a register and a 9-bit value, and the second bit sequence is the indirect and register mode encoding of instructions operating on two registers. The first 4 bits indicate to which assembly instruction this machine code word refers. This is often called the *opcode*. It is defined according to the following table.

STOR 0 0 1 1 (in)direct

LOAD 0 1 0 0 register/immediate   AND 1 0 1 0 register/immediate

LOAD 0 1 0 1 (in)direct   AND 1 0 1 1 (in)direct

ADD   0 1 1 0 register/immediate   OR   1 1 0 0 register/immediate

ADD   0 1 1 1 (in)direct   OR   1 1 0 1 (in)direct

SUB   1 0 0 0 register/immediate   XOR 1 1 1 0 register/immediate

SUB   1 0 0 1 (in)direct   XOR 1 1 1 1 (in)direct

The letters $r\,r$ represent the number of the register upon which the machine code instruction must operate. As we only have four registers in our simple processor, 2 bits are sufficient to indicate a register. The first instruction format operates on only one register. The second format refers to two registers.

When an instruction is loaded into the *IR* register, the first pair of bits $r\,r$ indicate a register from the *IR.ra* signal and the second pair of bits $r\,r$ indicate a register from the *IR.rb* (see Figure 4.1). The *IR.ra* signal determines which register is put on the Abus (if *REGS.oea* is 1) and into which register the content of the Cbus is put (if *regs.sel* is high). The 2 bits *IR.rb* determine which register outputs its content on the Bbus (if *REGS.oeb* is 1).

The 9 bits indicated with the letter v in the first instruction refer to the 9-bit value. Note that when this value is put on the Bbus, the 9 bits must be extended to 16 bits by adding seven zeroes at the front. This requires dedicated circuitry, not explicitly indicated in Figure 4.1.

The conditional branch instructions have the following format:

$$0\ 0\ 0\ 1\ c\ c\ c\ d\ d\ d\ d\ d\ d\ d\ d\ d$$

where the 3 bits indicated by c refer to the condition used in the conditional branch, given by the table below.

BNE 0 0 0 $Z = 0$ BVC 1 0 0 $V = 0$

BEQ 0 0 1 $Z = 1$ BVS 1 0 1 $V = 1$

BPL 0 1 0 $N = 0$ BCC 1 1 0 $C = 0$

BMI 0 1 1 $N = 1$ BCS 1 1 1 $C = 1$

The 9 bits indicated by a d refer to the displacement. Note that if the displacement of a conditional branch instruction is put on the Bbus it must be preceded by 0's or 1's to transform it into a proper 16-bit two's complement number.

There are three assembly instructions left, namely BRA, BRS and RTS, and for these we use the following encoding:

BRA: $0\ 0\ 0\ 0\ 0\ 0\ 0\ d\ d\ d\ d\ d\ d\ d\ d\ d$

BRS: $0\ 0\ 0\ 0\ r\ r\ 1\ d\ d\ d\ d\ d\ d\ d\ d\ d$

RTS: $0\ 0\ 1\ 0\ r\ r\ 0\ 0\ 0\ 0\ 0\ 0\ 0\ 0\ 0\ 0$

As explained previously the bit positions indicated by r refer to a register. The d's refer to a displacement.

Exercise 4.4.1. Check that each assembly instruction is encoded in a unique machine code instruction. Also identify which bit sequences are available to encode additional assembly instructions, in case we would like to enlarge our set of machine code instructions.

Exercise 4.4.2. Someone proposes adding an instruction NEG R_i to calculate the additive inverse of a number, with the effect $R_i \leftarrow -R_i$. Give an encoding for the new instruction and implement it on the basic data path (see Theorem 2.2.5 for a hint). Argue why one might prefer adding the new instruction by giving at least two advantages and one disadvantage of doing so.

Exercise 4.4.3. Suppose the simple processor is modified such that there are eight general purpose registers. Show that it is possible to encode the instructions in 16 bits, while retaining 9 bits for data values for all relevant instructions. How much space would be left for additional instructions?

4.5 Implementing instructions on the processor

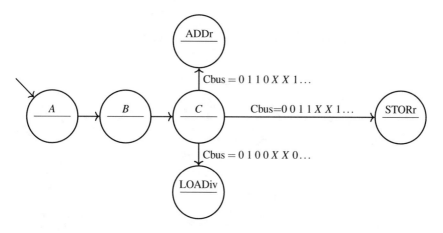

Fig. 4.4 The execution unit selects the execution of the machine code instruction

When the instruction is moved via the Cbus to the instruction register *IR*, the execution unit uses the relevant bits to determine what the instruction is and it moves to a state where this particular instruction is executed. For each load and arithmetic instruction, there are four states, depending on whether the instruction is direct, indirect, immediate or register. For the LOAD instructions these four states have the names LOADr (register), LOADiv (immediate value), LOADi (indirect) and LOADd (direct). For the store instruction, there are two states, namely one for the direct and another for the indirect store. In Figure 4.4 these states are drawn for three store/load/arithmetic instructions. In total there are 29 such states, including those for the BRS, RTS and jumps.

In order to extend the execution unit for each individual instruction, we describe the implementation of each instruction first in register transfer language. We start with describing the STOR R_i $[R_j]$ instruction, i.e., the indirect register-based store instruction. We assume that the instruction fetch has taken place. Essentially, the instruction moves the content of register R_i to RAM[R_j]. Therefore, the content of register R_j must be moved to ΣA and the content of register R_i must be transferred to ΣW. Subsequently, the content of ΣW must be moved into RAM at the address provided by ΣA.

4. ΣA, ΣW, $CC \leftarrow RB(\text{Bbus})$, $RA(\text{Abus})$, ALU.cc.
5. RAM[ΣA] $\leftarrow \Sigma W$.

Note that RA corresponds to R_i and RB corresponds to R_j. When this last register transfer has been carried out the store instruction is completed and the next instruction can take place. Recall that the STOR instruction sets the CC flags. This is achieved by passing the content of the ABus through the ALU and setting CC with this result.

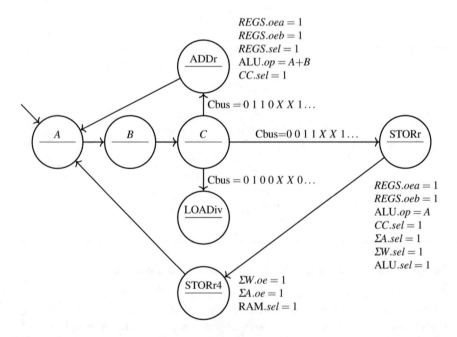

Fig. 4.5 The execution unit selects the execution of the machine code instruction

The translation of this register transfer code leads to additional states in the execution unit. The states for the STORr (register mode) and ADDr (register mode) instructions are depicted in Figure 4.5. Observe that when going from state STORr and STORr4 there are no inputs. Note also that from the state STORr4 there is a transition to state A, which means that a new instruction will be fetched after the execution of STOR R_i $[R_j]$ is finished.

Now assume that the fetched instruction was a direct register addition: ADD R_i R_j. The effect is that the contents of R_i and R_j must be added and stored in R_i. Moreover, the CC flags must be set. This can be achieved in one clock cycle. This can be phrased by extending the register transfer description for the fetch by

4. $RA, CC \leftarrow RA(\text{Abus}) + RB(\text{Bbus}), \text{ALU}.cc$.

In Figure 4.5, the precise signal settings to implement this instruction on the simple processor are also given.

We now show how the branch instructions are implemented. We consider the BEQ $disp$ instruction, namely, branch if the Z flag is equal to 1. The important extension to implementing the store/load and arithmetic instruction is that the execution unit must also inspect the CC flags to determine how the instruction must be executed. If $Z = 1$, the next instruction to be executed is $IP + disp$. If $Z = 0$, essentially nothing needs to be done, as IP already points at the next instruction.

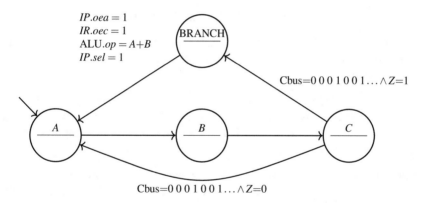

Fig. 4.6 The execution unit finite state machine for the BEQ instruction

We look at the register transfer instruction that in case $Z = 1$ must be executed after the fetch.

4. $IP \leftarrow IP + IR.compl$.

The translation into states of the execution unit is given in Figure 4.6. The state BRANCH is the state where displacement is added to the instruction pointer.

If the BEQ instruction is executed when $Z = 0$, nothing needs to be done. Therefore, there is a transition directly from state C to A. See also Figure 4.6. All nine branch instructions can be mapped onto the simple processor, by either jumping to the state BRANCH if branching is due, or by directly jumping to state A. This means that the condition on the transition from C to BRANCH and for C to A is large. In Figure 4.6 only that part of the condition belonging to the BEQ instruction is depicted.

There are two remaining instructions, namely branch to subroutine (BRS) and return from subroutine (RTS). Implementing these is reasonably straightforward, and we leave this as an exercise. For BRS two extra states are required. RTS can be implemented with four extra states. This means that our execution unit can be built with only 59 states implementing all instructions. This state machine can be constructed as a Mealy machine with a state of 6 bits.

When the processor is reset or powered up, a special address is loaded into the instruction pointer, for instance the address 0. At this address lies the first instruction of a program to be executed. Often the RAM is replaced by a small piece of read only memory (ROM) containing a basic program, or an elementary operating system that allows for the loading of more advanced programs into RAM.

Exercise 4.5.1. Implement the instructions LOAD R_i R_j, SUB R_i [*address*], and BMI *disp* in register transfer language. Use the register names RA and RB for R_i, R_j. For the branch instruction show both cases.

Exercise 4.5.2. Consider the following doubly indirected, indexed load instruction:

$$\text{ADD } R_i + [[R_j]] \qquad\qquad R_i \leftarrow R_i + \text{RAM}[\text{RAM}[R_j]].$$

where the flags must be set for the value loaded into register i. Indicate using register transfer commands how this instruction could be implemented. The instruction fetch can be skipped.

Exercise 4.5.3. Give the register transfer commands to implement XOR R_i [R_j], including the commands to fetch the instruction. Describe the relevant part of the state machine of the execution unit. Indicate which signals of the simple processor must be set to 1.

Exercise 4.5.4. Give the register transfer commands to implement BRS and RTS, including the instruction fetch. Draw the relevant part of the state machine of the execution unit.

4.6 Optimisation of the execution of instructions

A lot of effort is put into optimising the execution of instructions. We show how our simple processor can be made twice as fast by fetching the next instruction, whilst executing the previous one. This is called *prefetching*.

Modern processors may well go beyond this. Most of them operate on a pipeline of instructions that are in transit from memory to guarantee that the processor never has to wait for an instruction to be fetched. The pipeline preprocessor tries to foresee which branches will be selected, such that it only needs to load those instructions that will be executed. This is called *branch prediction*.

By using multiple buses and ALUs, instructions can even be executed simultaneously. But this is tricky, as an instruction that writes to a memory address must be executed before any subsequent instruction that reads the written result. The processor then only executes those instructions that do not depend on instructions that have not been executed yet. But this often leads to instructions being executed in a different order than they occur in the program. This is known as *out-of-order execution*. Most processors only respect the order of instructions operating on the same address, which is adequate for sequential programs but requires care when it comes to parallel programming.

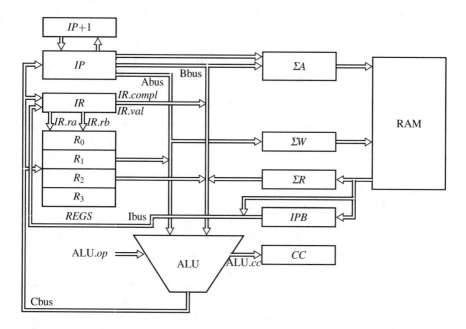

Fig. 4.7 The prefetch data path for our simple processor

We will restrict ourselves to prefetching, and will not reorder the execution of instructions. But in order to make prefetching possible, we need to make a few changes to our basic data path. The extended data path is found in Figure 4.7, which we call the *prefetch data path*. One extra register is added, called the instruction prefetch buffer, or *IPB*. This register is used to temporarily store the next instruction. This register is connected to the instruction register with a separate instruction bus, called the Ibus thus avoiding the need to use the ALU and the Bbus for moving instructions to the instruction register. The register *IPB* is bypassed making it possible to read an instruction from memory into the instruction register within one clock cycle.

Furthermore, we add a separate simple adder to the instruction pointer *IP* such that we can increase the instruction pointer without having to use the ALU.

When executing instructions in the prefetch data path, we ensure that during the last clock cycle of each instruction the next instruction is moved via the Ibus to the instruction register. The execution unit can use this information to jump directly to the state belonging to the execution of this next instruction. This means that with prefetch no extra clock cycles are spent on fetching instructions.

Concretely, we take care that at the end of each instruction the following three properties hold:

1. The next instruction to be executed is present on the Ibus.
2. The register ΣA contains the address of the next instruction to be executed.
3. The instruction pointer IP contains the address of the current instruction plus 2.
   It refers to the next-next instruction.

When the processor starts, two clock cycles are needed to prepare the registers to meet the properties stated above. These are

1. $\Sigma A, IP \leftarrow IP(\text{Bbus}), IP+1$.
2. $IR, \Sigma A, IP \leftarrow \text{RAM}[\Sigma A](\text{Ibus}), IP(\text{Bbus}), IP+1$.

The execution of the direct add with registers ADD R_i R_j can be performed in one clock cycle.

3. $RA, CC, IR, \Sigma A, IP \leftarrow RA(\text{Abus}) + RB(\text{Bbus}), \text{ALU}.cc, \text{RAM}[\Sigma A], IP, IP+1$.

Observe that all three requirements are preserved when executing this instruction.

As another example we show how the instruction XOR RA [*address*] is implemented by providing a description in register transfer language. We will start the numbering at 3 to indicate the assumption that the register transfers mentioned under clock cycles 1 and 2 above have been executed.

3. $\Sigma A, IPB \leftarrow IR.val(\text{Bbus}), \text{RAM}[\Sigma A]$.
4. $\Sigma R \leftarrow \text{RAM}[\Sigma A]$.
5. $RA, CC, IR, \Sigma A, IP \leftarrow RA(\text{Abus}) \oplus \Sigma R(\text{Bbus}), \text{ALU}.cc, IPB(\text{Ibus}), IP, IP+1$.

Note that in clock cycle 3, the next instruction is stored in IPB. This frees the register ΣA for a subsequent transfer from memory.

When prefetching instructions, the processor assumes that the two next instructions to be executed are at addresses IP and $IP+1$. But when a jump occurs, this is not true. Therefore, jumps are particularly tricky with prefetching. First, we look at a branch instruction in case the condition for a jump is not true. The register transfers are pretty straightforward.

3. $IR, \Sigma A, IP \leftarrow \text{RAM}[\Sigma A], IP, IP+1$.

However, if the branch is taken, four clock cycles are required.

3. $IP \leftarrow IP(\text{Abus}) - 1$.
4. $IP \leftarrow IP(\text{Abus}) + IR.compl(\text{Bbus})$.
5. $\Sigma A, IP \leftarrow IP, IP+1$.
6. $IR, \Sigma A, IP \leftarrow \text{RAM}[\Sigma A], IP, IP+1$.

In cycle 3 the instruction pointer is corrected, as it points two addresses beyond the current address. In cycle 4 the address for the next instruction is loaded in IP. Finally, in cycles 5 and 6 prefetching of the next instructions is prepared.

In Table 4.2 we put the number of clock cycles required for each instruction, with and without prefetching. The number of accesses to memory are also listed. This number includes the memory access to obtain the instruction itself. Due to the processor architecture we can only read one word from memory at any time, so the number of memory accesses provides a lower bound on the number of clock cycles

Instruction	Mode	#cycles without prefetch	#cycles with prefetch	#memory accesses
STOR R_i [expr]	indirect	5	2	2
LOAD R_i expr	direct	4	1	1
LOAD R_i [expr]	indirect	6	3	2
ADD R_i expr	direct	4	1	1
ADD R_i [expr]	indirect	6	3	2
SUB R_i expr	direct	4	1	1
SUB R_i [expr]	indirect	6	3	2
AND R_i expr	direct	4	1	1
AND R_i [expr]	indirect	6	3	2
OR R_i expr	direct	4	1	1
OR R_i [expr]	indirect	6	3	2
XOR R_i expr	direct	4	1	1
XOR R_i [expr]	indirect	6	3	2
BRA $disp$	direct	3/4	1/4	1
BCC $disp$	direct	3/4	1/4	1
BCS $disp$	direct	3/4	1/4	1
BPL $disp$	direct	3/4	1/4	1
BMI $disp$	direct	3/4	1/4	1
BVC $disp$	direct	3/4	1/4	1
BVS $disp$	direct	3/4	1/4	1
BNE $disp$	direct	3/4	1/4	1
BEQ $disp$	direct	3/4	1/4	1
BRS R_i $disp$	direct	6	6	2
RTS R_i	direct	6	5	2

Table 4.2 The number of clock cycles per instruction before and after optimisation

required. From this it is obvious that half of the instructions are already optimally implemented.

Exercise 4.6.1. Describe how the instructions LOAD R_i *value* and STOR R_i [R_j] can be implemented in one and three clock cycles, respectively, using prefetching.

Exercise 4.6.2. Give the exact register transfers for implementing both the BRS and RTS instructions using the prefetch data path.

4.7 More advanced instructions

By extending the data path it is possible to implement far more complex processor instructions. In this section we give a few examples of such instructions.

A fundamental discussion is whether a processor should have a simple and straightforward or a complex and versatile set of instructions. The advantage of *RISC (Reduced Instruction Set Computer)* is that the logic of processors is simple, allowing for more registers and logic to speed up the execution of instructions. The advantage of *CISC (Complex Instruction Set Computer)* is that programs require fewer instructions and are therefore smaller, but more complex circuitry is needed to execute these instructions. The Intel x86 processor family has a CISC instruction set, whereas the instruction set of the ARM processor is a RISC.

As the number, and complexity, of instructions increases it is unlikely that they will fit in a single word. If single instructions stretch over multiple words, the instruction fetch becomes more complicated, and the instruction register must be enlarged. However, having instructions of different sizes does have advantages. Frequently used instructions can be short, whereas rarely employed instructions can have a bigger footprint. This allows program size to be minimised.

Many contemporary processors have more advanced arithmetic instructions, not only add and subtract but also multiply and divide (with remainder) instructions. For our simple processor, the natural multiplication instructions are MUL R_i *expr* and MUL R_i *[expr]*. Many processors support floating-point numbers together with all common operations on them, including trigonometric functions (sin, cos, etc.), exponentiation and logarithms.

Another useful extension is relative indirect addressing. Assume a register points to an array (see Section 5.4.1) containing words and the value at array position 2 must be obtained. It is possible to increase the register by 2, obtain the value and decrease the register again. As this is a very common operation, instructions of the shape

$$\text{STOR } R_i \ [R_j + index]$$
$$\text{LOAD } R_i \ [R_j + index]$$
$$\text{ADD } R_i \ [R_j + index]$$

can be used. The effect of the STOR instruction is RAM$[R_j + index] \leftarrow R_i$. If register R_1 contains the address of the array, copying the value at position 2 of the array into register R_2 can be done using the instruction LOAD R_2 $[R_1 + 2]$.

Relative indirect addressing is also very useful to access values stored on the stack. The element at the top of the stack can be loaded in register R_0 by the instruction LOAD R_0 $[SP + 1]$. If the content of register R_2 needs to be stored on the stack, say 3 words above the stack pointer, this can be performed using the instruction STOR R_2 $[SP + 3]$.

Even more complex instructions can be conceived where an address is determined by calculations with multiple registers and constants. A possibility is, for instance, STOR R_i $[R_j + R_k]$ where the address of the data that must be stored is determined by adding the content of two registers. This is useful if R_j points to the base address of a data structure and R_k contains an index into it. When traversing the data structure, the value of R_k must often be increased. For this, instructions of the shape STOR R_i $[R_j + (R_k{+}{+})]$ have been devised with the effect that

$$RAM[R_j + R_k], R_k \leftarrow R_i, R_k + 1$$

where the register R_k is auto-incremented during the assignment.

In the next chapter we show how multiple programs can be run as simultaneous processes on our simple processor. An important observation is that if these programs communicate by only reading and writing from and to memory they cannot accomplish certain simple tasks. In particular, they cannot solve the *consensus problem.* Consider a number of processes numbered from $1, \ldots, n$ each having a set of numbers S_i. The intersection of this set is not empty, i.e., $\bigcap_{i=1}^{n} S_i \neq \varnothing$. In the consensus problem the processes must all select the same number $j \in \bigcap_{i=1}^{n} S_i$.

The consensus problem can be solved when a simple *test and set* instruction TESTSET $[R_i]$ is available. The effect of this instruction is

$$\text{if } RAM[R_i] = 0, \text{ then } RAM[R_i] \leftarrow 1.$$

It is important that this instruction is carried out atomically; between checking the value in memory and writing to it, another process may not write to the same address. The flags must be set in accordance with the value at $RAM[R_i]$. So, in particular the flag Z is 1 iff the assignment is executed. All modern processors support running multiple programs simultaneously, and henceforth they all have instructions such as the test and set instruction.

A more elaborate variant of the test and set instruction is *compare and swap*. The instruction CMPSWP $[R_i]\ R_j\ R_k$ has as effect

$$\text{if } RAM[R_i] = R_j, \text{ then } RAM[R_i] \leftarrow R_k.$$

The content of memory pointed at with R_i is only changed when it is equal to R_j. It is also important that this instruction is executed atomically. Note that in order to implement the compare and swap instruction substantial changes to our instruction format and the data path of our processor are necessary.

Exercise 4.7.1. Implement the test and set instruction TESTSET $[R_i]$ on the processor with the simple data path. Assume that R_i can be put on the Bbus using *RAB*. Also assume that the last 9 bits of the instruction are 0 0 0 0 0 0 0 0 1. Using *IP.val* the value 1 can be obtained. It is not necessary to implement the instruction fetch. Write two implementations in register transfer language, namely one where $RAM[R_i]$ is equal to zero, and one where it is not.

4.8 Input and output

Processors communicate with their surrounding world. In this section we make a minimal extension to the processor such that *I/O* (*input and output*) is possible. We add two registers, one to which the outside world can write, and another in which the processor can put information that can be read by external parties.

In contemporary computers there are many input and output registers connected to the hardware surrounding the processor. This hardware comprises all the devices that the processor can control such as memory controllers, network communication devices, and video controllers. There can be special instructions in the processor to read and write to these registers, or there can be a part of the RAM that is connected to the input and output devices. In the latter case standard STOR and LOAD instructions can be used to communicate with these external devices.

Input and output can be very simple such as reading the last key that was hit on the keyboard, or switching an LED on or off. But it can also be very complex such as instructing the network hardware to send a message from memory through the network, or instructing the disk hardware to read a block of data into memory.

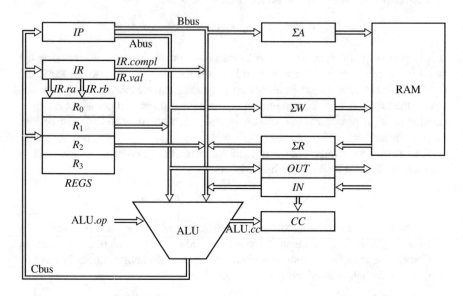

Fig. 4.8 The basic data path extended with an input and an output register

In our simple approach we add two new 16-bit registers *OUT* and *IN*. The register *OUT* is connected to the Abus. The register *IN* is connected to the Bbus and register *CC*. The simple data path with input and output is depicted in Figure 4.8. The outside world consists of circuitry that can always read the *OUT* register and also write to the *IN* register by setting some input data and enabling *IN.sel* when the clock goes high. When *IN.sel* is high during multiple clock ticks, this is seen as multiple writes into the *IN* register.

Instruction	Effect	Flags
IN R_i	$R_i \leftarrow IN$	C,N,V,Z
OUT R_i	$OUT \leftarrow R_i$	-
IN R_i	0 0 1 0 r r 1 0 0 0 0 0 0 0 0 0	
OUT R_i	0 0 1 0 r r 0 1 0 0 0 0 0 0 0 0	

Table 4.3 The effect and machine code representation of the input and output instructions

We define two new instructions, IN R_i and OUT R_j. Their effect and machine code representations are shown in Table 4.3. When the instruction IN R_i is executed, the overflow flag V is set to 1 when register *IN* has been written to more than once whilst its previous content has not been read. When no new data has been written between two contiguous IN instructions, the carry flag will be set. The other flags are all set to zero during this instruction. The flags are not affected when the OUT instruction is executed.

As an illustration we can write a small program that counts the number of keystrokes on a keyboard in register R_1. For this purpose we assume that a keyboard is connected to register IN. Whenever a key is hit, the keyboard enables the input select $IN.sel$ of this register during one up going clock signal, writing a bit representation into it. If the processor is too slow, and misses a keystroke, the program must jump to a separate error handling routine. The assembler program is provided below

```
LOAD R₁ 0   ; Set the number of keystrokes to 0.
    IN R₀     ; This is the beginning of the keyboard polling loop.
              ; R₀ now contains the last key that was hit if Z is 1,
              ; and if V equals 1 a keystroke has been missed.
    BVS 3     ; The flag V is 1. At least one keystroke has been missed. Jump
              ; to the error handling code.
    BCC −3    ; The flag Z is zero. No new key has been read. Jump to the
              ; beginning of the loop.
    ADD R₁ 1  ; Count the keystroke.
    BRA −5    ; Jump back to the beginning of the loop.
    ...       ; This is the place for error handling code when a keystroke
              ; is missed.
```

The technique that the program above uses to continuously read the input to determine whether new data has arrived is called *polling*. This is particularly inefficient as it uses the full capacity of the processor while a keystroke may only come once in a billion clock cycles. The processor could be used for other, more useful calculations while waiting for the next keystroke, or if the hardware would allow it, go into a sleep mode only to become active when a new keystroke arrives. This can save a substantial amount of energy. In the next section interrupts are explained. The interrupt technique makes both approaches technically possible.

Exercise 4.8.1. Note that the program above is not particularly useful as the content of register R_1 is not made available to the outside world. Adapt the program such that whenever a new keystroke is read, the number of keystrokes is written into the register OUT.

Exercise 4.8.2. Implement the IN and OUT instructions using register transfer language on the basic data path with input and output registers, see Figure 4.8. Include the instruction fetch.

4.9 Interrupts

In the previous section we have seen that it is useful when the outside world can give a signal to the processor indicating that some data is available, or that another event of interest has happened. Such a signal is called an *interrupt*. Interrupts are very important as they not only allow the processor to efficiently react to external stimuli but are also essential in allowing the processor to run multiple programs simultaneously.

As with the input and output mechanism, we will provide our processor with the minimal necessary extension to allow interrupts and to explain the essential idea. Standard processors have multiple types of interrupts, some with high and others with low priority, some that can be disabled and others which cannot.

An interrupt is an electrical signal. Whenever the signal goes high it sets an interrupt flag in a register. When the execution unit has finished the current instruction, and is about to execute the instruction fetch, it checks whether the flag is set. If it is set, the execution unit fetches the next instruction from a special address where the interrupt routine can be found and it resets the interrupt flag. This is known as calling an interrupt handler or *ISR* (*interrupt service routine*). If the interrupt bit is not set, the execution unit fetches and executes the next instruction in the normal way.

At the end of the interrupt service routine the processor must continue executing the program from the address where it was interrupted. This address is called the *return address* and it must be stored somewhere. When the address is stored in a designated register, it is not possible for a second interrupt to be handled until the first interrupt service routine has finished. To allow multiple simultaneous interrupts, the stack is the most convenient place for storing return addresses. As in our processor register R_3 points to the stack, the return address is put at RAM$[R_3]$.

When the interrupt subroutine is executed, the flags in the flag register CC are most likely be set to new values. When returning to the interrupted program, the original values of the flags need to be restored as well. For this reason they are also stored on the stack, i.e., when the interrupt routine is called, RAM$[R_3 - 1]$ is set to the value of register CC. Note that the stack pointer R_3 is decremented by 2 when the interrupt routine is called.

Instruction	Effect
RTI	$R_3, IP, CC \leftarrow R_3+2, \text{RAM}[R_3+1], \text{RAM}[R_3]$
OUT R_i	0 0 1 0 0 0 0 1 1 0 0 0 0 0 0 0 0

Table 4.4 The return from interrupt instruction

When returning from the interrupt subroutine both the instruction pointer, the flags and the stack must be restored. There is a special instruction return from interrupt (RTI) for this purpose. Its effect and its machine code are listed in Table 4.4.

The other registers R_0, R_1 and R_2 can also be changed in the interrupt routine. These are not saved and restored automatically. It is left to the programmer of the interrupt routine to ensure that when the RTI is complete, the registers are restored properly. In the next chapter we will look at how to write a proper interrupt routine.

Interrupts can come from outside the processor, but they can also be generated internally. For instance, when an attempt is made to execute a machine word that does not present a proper instruction, the processor can generate an *internal interrupt*, which is also called an *exception*. Similarly, when an attempt is made to read from or write to non-existent memory such an exception can also be generated. The interrupt handler can then decide how to appropriately handle the problem, which might be to terminate the program and bring the processor into a safe state, as returning back to the program may only increase the trouble.

Such internal interrupts are considered so useful that most processors have special *software interrupt* instructions, also called *traps*. These software interrupts generally have a number as an argument, such as

$$\text{TRAP 15} \quad \text{; Generate software interrupt no 15.}$$

Often there are variants that are conditionally executed, based on the values of the flags. Software interrupts are widely used for system calls because they can change the mode of the processor, which is important to implement security and protection mechanisms inside a processor. This is further explained in Section 7.2.1.

Exercise 4.9.1. When a subroutine finishes, the stack pointer is increased. The return address is now just beyond the top of the stack. Can this address safely be read and used?

4.10 Summary

We gave an overview of a simple processor, starting with how registers, the ALU and RAM are connected by buses. We introduced the programmer's model of a processor along with a 16-bit instruction set. There are instructions for calculations on values in registers, moving data to and from memory, and control flow. Instruction execution is governed by a state machine which orchestrates the movement of data within the processor. Of the myriad ways this process can be optimised, we highlighted prefetching. We concluded with how I/O and interrupts allow processors to interact with the outside world and deal with exceptional conditions.

Chapter 5
Assembly programming

In this chapter, we discuss writing programs using the assembly instructions for the simple processor introduced in the previous chapter. The principles common to all programming languages are discussed, such as the structuring of assembly code and how data structures can be manipulated. The focus, however, is on how higher-level features, e.g. data structures, procedure calls and multithreading, can be realised using assembly language.

5.1 Labels and comments, EQU and CONS

An assembly program consists of a list of assembly instructions, such as LOAD, STOR, ADD, etc. We use the assembly instructions of our simple processor (see Table 4.1), with some syntactical extensions that make them easier to read and write.

Even in the early days of assembly programming it was observed that sequences of assembly instructions are hard to comprehend. It is therefore important to annotate assembly programs with comments, aiding the comprehensibility of the programs, not just for the sake of others but also for an author looking back at their own code. We write comments after assembly instructions, and use a semicolon to start a comment.

Using jump instructions, such as BRA, BEQ and BRS, it is possible to implement *if-then-else* conditions and loops. Calculating the relative displacements for jumps is quite error prone. This is the reason to introduce the notion of a *label*. A label is put in front of an instruction followed by a colon, for example while_loop: ADD $R_i value$. The label represents the address where that instruction is stored, assuming that the program is stored at address 0. We call this the *program position* of the labelled instruction. For example, LOAD R_i while_loop loads the address of the above labelled ADD instruction into a register. A program, called an *assembler*, is responsible for converting assembly instructions into machine code and will automatically substitute the right values for the labels.

J. F. Groote et al., *Logic Gates, Circuits, Processors, Compilers and Computers*,
https://doi.org/10.1007/978-3-030-68553-9_5

When a label is used in a jump instruction, the program position is used to determine the relative displacement. Let a_2 be the address of a branching instruction whose jump destination is a_1, e.g., a_2 : BRA a_1. The assembler calculates the argument of the branch instruction to become $a_1 - a_2 - 1$. The -1 is to compensate for the fact that the instruction pointer is pointing at the next instruction. This effect is exactly what we desire. For example the instruction BRA while_loop will jump directly to the labelled ADD instruction.

In order to keep code intelligible it is a good habit to use mnemonic names for not only labels but also, more generally, for other values. The EQU keyword can be used to bind a name to a value. If EQU *name value* is used, then the string *name* can be used in the remainder of an assembly program to represent *value*. A line in the assembly code using EQU only introduces an abbreviation and does not lead to the generation of a machine code instruction. Instructions in assembly code that do not directly translate to processor operations are commonly known as *pseudo instructions*.

A simple loop that counts from 100 to 0 is given by the following assembly program:

```
                EQU initial_value 100   ; Introduce a mnemonic name for 100.
                LOAD R0 initial_value   ; Set register 0 to the value 100.
while_loop: SUB R0 1                    ; Decrement register 0 and set the Z flag.
                BNE while_loop          ; Repeat as long as last result was not zero.
end_while:  ...
```

A common occurrence is code that should only be executed when some condition holds. In high-level programming languages the *if-then-else* construct is used for this purpose. In assembly it typically has the following shape, where, as an example, two unsigned numbers are read from memory, compared, and the larger value is stored at the output address.

```
                EQU input1 100      ; Names for input and output addresses.
                EQU input2 101      ;
                EQU output 102      ;
                LOAD R0 [input1]    ; Load the first input in register 0.
                SUB R0 [input2]     ; Subtract input2 and set the processor flags.
                BCS else_branch     ; If the C flag is set, the second input is larger.
then_branch: LOAD R0 [input1]      ; Load the first input again, as the content of R0
                                    ; has been changed by the subtraction above.
                STOR R0 [output]
                BRA after_else      ; Jump to the instruction after the if-then-else.
else_branch: LOAD R0 [input2]      ; Obtain input2 to store it at the output.
                STOR R0 [output]
after_else:     ...                 ; Code after the if-then-else.
```

Sometimes it is useful to store data directly within the program code. For this purpose the CONS pseudo instruction is introduced. CONS *value* inserts a single word containing *value* at that spot in the machine code program. For instance, it might be useful to store the powers of two instead of calculating them each time they are required. The following code provides a table with the powers of two and introduces a label for it.

```
powers_of_2_table: CONS 1    ; Table with the powers of 2.
                   CONS 2    ;
                   CONS 4    ;
                   CONS 8    ;
                   CONS 16   ;
                   CONS 32   ;
                   CONS 64   ;
                   CONS 128  ;
                   CONS 256  ;
                   CONS 512  ;
                   . . .
```

Note that the label powers_of_2_table contains the address of the beginning of the table provided the program is loaded at address 0. But generally the program is loaded at another address, and therefore additional effort is required to let the program access the table correctly.

The program below, labelled power_of_2, puts 2^n in register R_0. It assumes that n is the value in R_0 at the start of execution of the program. Additionally it is assumed that register R_3 contains the address of the top of the stack. We no longer assume that the program is located at address 0.

First, the BRS instruction stores the address of the next instruction on top of the stack, by using calc_pos as a relative displacement. This address is the actual memory location (during execution) of the instruction labelled calc_pos. The difference between the actual address of calc_pos and the program position of calc_pos is the memory location of the first instruction of the program. By summing this address with the program position of the powers_of_2_table we can access the table to obtain the required value. Note that this is not conventional usage of the BRS instruction, as we do not jump back to the address that was pushed to the stack.

```
power_of_2: BRS R₃ calc_pos           ; Branch to the next instruction to save
                                       ; its actual address.
calc_pos:   LOAD R₁ [R₃]              ; Load this instruction's memory
                                       ; address into a register.
            ADD R₃ 1                   ; Restore the stack pointer.
            SUB R₁ calc_pos            ; Calculate the actual start of the program.
            ADD R₁ powers_of_2_table   ; Add the program position of the table.
            ADD R₁ R₀                  ; Calculate the correct index into the table.
            LOAD R₀ [R₁]              ; Load the nth power of two from the
                                       ; table.
```

Exercise 5.1.1. Write an assembly program that reads three unsigned numbers from memory and stores the largest value of the three as an output at a fixed address. Introduce names for the (arbitrary) memory addresses that are accessed. See Table 2.3 on how to compare numbers.

Exercise 5.1.2. Assume that an address *seq_start* has been defined using EQU, and that it points to the first element of a sequence of numbers. The length of the sequence is *seq_length*. The sequence is contiguous in memory, i.e. can be accessed at subsequent addresses. Write an assembly program that adds up all the numbers and stores the sum in the address indicated by *cumul_sum*.

Exercise 5.1.3. Explain why the following program generally does not load the value 10 into register R_0.

> constant_store: CONS 10   ; Store constant 10.
> program_body: LOAD R_0 [constant_store] ; Load 10 into register R_0.

5.2 Arithmetic calculations

Assembler programs continuously carry out calculations. If these calculations are carried out with unsigned numbers the ALU flags can be used in a straightforward way for conditional jumps. If the numbers represent two's complement numbers, the situation is a little bit more delicate and more care is required. The effects of comparing two's complement numbers on the processor flags are listed in Table 2.3.

As an illustration, we provide a two's complement number in each of the registers R_0 and R_1 and subtract these to determine which of the numbers is smaller. According to Table 2.3, the first one is smaller than the second if $N \neq V$. As we do not have instructions to compare flags directly we check whether N is 1 and subsequently whether V is 1, etc. In code this can be done as follows:

> cmp_two's_compl: SUB R_0 R_1 ; Subtract the registers to set the flags.
>   BMI flag_N_is_one ; Jump if $N = 1$.
>   BVS smaller   ; Here N is 0. If $V = 1$ jump to smaller.
>   BRA larger_or_eq: ; Flags N and V are both 0.
> flag_N_is_one: BVC smaller   ; Flag N is 1. If $V = 0$, jump to smaller.
> larger_or_eq: . . .   ; Here we know that $R_0 \geq R_1$.
>   . . .
> smaller: . . .   ; Here we know that $R_0 < R_1$.

Arithmetic operations may give results that do not correctly fit in the number of bits available. If this is not explicitly checked, programs will perform calculations with these erroneous values, which will propagate to other areas of the program. Such situations lead to erroneous results, the cause of which can be hard to trace back. Therefore, it is always a good habit to check explicitly that the results of a calculation are valid. To determine which flags should be checked it is necessary to know if the numbers that are being compared are unsigned or use two's complement representation.

We provide an example where two unsigned numbers in R_0 and R_1 are added and the result is checked for an overflow.

ADD $R_0 R_1$	; Add the registers and set the flags.
BCS overflow_handler	; If an overflow occurred, jump to the
	; error handler.
...	; Normal continuation of the program.
overflow_handler: ...	; Error handler for an overflow.

Our simple processor only provides basic arithmetic operations, essentially only addition and subtraction. More complex operations can, of course, be calculated. We provide a program that performs the multiplication of two unsigned numbers. We assume that the numbers to be multiplied are located at addresses with labels $operand_1$ and $operand_2$, and the result is stored at the address $result$. The calculation is performed in 16 iterations where the iterations are counted by a variable i that runs from 0 to 16. We describe the program in terms of i, although i is not explicitly part of the program. We write the value at address $operand_1$ as α and the value at address $operand_2$ as $\beta = b_{15} \ldots b_0$.

For correctness of the calculation it is essential that whenever the program is at mult_loop the registers contain the following values:

$$R_0 = \alpha 2^i, \qquad R_1 = 2^i, \qquad R_2 = \alpha \sum_{j=0}^{i-1} 2^j b_j.$$

This is called an *invariant* of the loop. Clearly, when $i = 16$ the register R_2 contains the required value. Note that in the code the 16*th* iteration is detected by overflowing R_1, whereupon the register takes on 0 as value. Also note that in the program we care about whether the (intermediate) results are representable in 16 bits, and hence have branches to an error handler.

multiplication:	LOAD R_0 [$operand_1$]	; $R_0 := \alpha = \alpha 2^i$, as initially $i = 0$.
	LOAD R_1 1	; $R_1 := 2^i$.
	LOAD R_2 0	; $R_2 := \alpha \sum_{j=0}^{i-1} 2^j b_j$.
mult_loop:	AND R_1 [$operand_2$]	; Check whether bit i of β, i.e., bit b_i, is set.
	BEQ prepare_loop	; If $b_i = 0$ go to prepare_loop.
	ADD $R_2 R_0$	; $R_2 := R_2 + R_0$.
	BCS overflow_error	; Check for overflow.
prepare_loop:		; Here it holds that $R_2 = \alpha \sum_{j=0}^{i} 2^j b_j$.
	ADD $R_1 R_1$	; Double R_1. Now $R_1 = 2^{i+1}$, except if i=16.
	BEQ ready	; If i=16, then R_1=0 and multiplication done.
	ADD $R_0 R_0$	; After this instruction $R_0 = \alpha 2^{i+1}$.
	BCS overflow_error	; Check for overflow.
	BRA mult_loop	; Loop back. Here i can be thought to be in-
		; cremented by 1 and the invariant is valid
		; again.

ready: STOR R_2 [*result*] ; Here it holds that $R_2 = \alpha \sum_{j=0}^{15} 2^j b_j = \alpha \beta$.
                        ...   ; Rest of the program.
overflow_error: ...   ; This is the place to handle an overflow.

Exercise 5.2.1. Assume that register R_0 contains a value in two's complement representation. Provide assembly instructions to convert it to an unsigned number in register R_1. If the conversion fails, jump to a piece of code labelled conversion_error.

Exercise 5.2.2. Assume that registers R_0 and R_1 both contain two's complement numbers. Write assembly code to add these into R_0, and if an overflow occurs, jump to a piece of code with the name overflow.

Exercise 5.2.3. Write a program that takes an unsigned number at some memory address *input*, divides it by two and outputs it to the memory at address *output*. Our instruction set is not particularly suited for this operation but it can be done. Most processors have a standard instruction to divide a number by 2^n, which is often called a shift right.

5.3 A timed loop

Sometimes a program needs to be time-sensitive. This usually corresponds to interacting periodically with some other hardware: a display might need to be refreshed at a certain frequency, or some input device needs to have its buffers read every so often.

In the previous chapter the simple processor instructions were implemented by specifying what their behaviour should be for a number of clock cycles. When the frequency of the processor clock is known, it is possible to calculate exactly how much time is needed to execute a program. For this we need to know the number of cycles that it takes to run each instruction that our program uses. This can be found in Table 4.2.

The following example executes a loop 14 times. Each instruction is annotated with the number of clock cycles that it uses, where we assume we do not use prefetching.

```
timed_loop: EQU counter 14      ; EQU does not run during code execution.
            EQU address 100     ;
            LOAD R0 0           ; A direct LOAD requires 4 clock cycles.
            STOR R0 [address] ; A STOR needs 5 clock cycles.
            LOAD R1 counter   ; 4 cycles.
while_loop: ADD R0 1            ; All direct arithmetic instructions require 4
                               ; clock cycles.
            STOR R0 [address] ; 5 cycles.
            SUB R1 1            ; 4 cycles.
            BNE while_loop      ; Uses 4 cycles when the branch is taken,
                               ; and only 3 cycles when it is not.
end_while:  ...
```

In this case the entire fragment needs 250 clock cycles to get to end_while. If the clock speed for the processor is set to 1 MHz then the code executes in exactly a quarter of a millisecond.

On modern processors there is no one-to-one correspondence between an instruction and the time that it requires to execute, and the timed loop technique sketched above cannot be used. These processors will use techniques such as caching, out-of-order execution, branch prediction, and many more to try to optimise execution time on the fly. For example, if an instruction is in the (level one) cache, it can be executed quickly, whereas, if it is in main memory it may take up to hundreds of clock ticks before the instruction is fetched. For modern processors, running several programs simultaneously, it is hard to predict where instructions reside.

As an alternative, most processors provide hardware timers that can be set to provide an interrupt after a certain time interval. Using timers allows a processor to be programmed to act at roughly the intended times. But in these modern environments it is hard to guarantee exact timings.

Exercise 5.3.1. Write an assembly program that loads a positive *timer* value from an address in memory and waits for the *timer*'s value in milliseconds before it can continue on to execute other code. Assume that the processor does not use prefetching and has a clock speed of 1 MHz.

5.4 Basic data structures

It is possible to store data in memory wherever it is convenient. However, it is useful to structure how data is stored. The three data structures discussed below are as elementary as they are fundamental to the efficient implementation of low-level systems.

5.4.1 Arrays

Often multiple data values need to be stored that are closely related. When these values have the same *type* (e.g., unsigned numbers, integers, etc.) and they are stored consecutively in memory, we refer to these values collectively as an *array*. Each value in an array can consist of multiple words, and we call this number the size of an array element.

An important property of arrays is that accessing an element of an array is easy and can be done quickly. To access a value of an array the address of the first element and an index are needed. The first address is often called the *base* address. The index of the first element in an array is 0.

By multiplying the size of an element and the index an *offset* into the array is calculated. The memory address of the required value is obtained by adding the offset to the base address. Typically we introduce mnemonic names for the base address of an array, for the number of elements it contains and for the size of its elements.

As an example we show how to add up all the unsigned numbers in an array of size n. In this case the size of an array element is 1 and therefore no explicit multiplication with the size is needed. The result of the addition is stored at the address *sum*.

```
sum_up_array EQU base_address ...   ; The base address of the array.
             EQU array_size ...     ; The size n of the array.
             EQU sum ...            ; The address where the sum is stored.
             LOAD R₁ 0              ; Register R₁ ranges from 0 up to n.
             STORE R₁ [sum]         ; Abuse register R₁ to set RAM[sum] to 0.
sum_loop:    LOAD R₀ base_address   ; Calculate the address of the integer that
                                    ; must be added.
             ADD R₀ R₁             ;
             LOAD R₀ [R₀]          ; Load the next value into R₀.
             ADD R₀ [sum]         ; Add it to the partial sum.
             STOR R₀ [sum]        ; And store the result back in memory.
             ADD R₁ 1             ; Increment register R₁.
             LOAD R₀ R₁
             SUB R₀ [array_size]   ; Compare the counter with dim_n.
             BNE sum_loop          ; Iterate while not all n have been added.
             ...                   ; Now, sum is available for use.
```

Arrays can have more than one dimension. For a two dimensional array with $n \times m$ elements, generally the value at position (i, j) is stored at $base + (nj + i)s$ where s is the size of an array element.

5.4.2 Stacks

A very important data structure is the stack. A stack is nothing more than a part of the memory where data is added and removed at one end. There is one register or memory address that points to the top of the stack, which is called the stack pointer. Stacks can grow upwards in memory, where the stack pointer maintains the highest address, or they can grow downwards with the stack pointer maintaining the lowest address.

As pointed out in the previous chapter, every program has its own execution stack that is used to deal with interrupts and return addresses of calls to subroutines, and which can be used for other purposes as well. Recall that the execution stack in our processor grows downwards.

As an example we provide in Figure 5.1 another user defined stack, one that is different from the execution stack. As it is not necessary that the stack grows downward, we let this stack grow upwards increasing the stack pointer when adding elements. Also contrary to the execution stack, we let the stack pointer point to the first empty position above the stack. Other choices are possible, but it is important to agree on the implementation details, and to document such choices properly.

Increasing the stack can be done by one word at a time or by allocating a larger space adding the number of words that are needed to the stack pointer. Placing a single value on top of the stack – by incrementing/decrementing the stack pointer and modifying the value at the pointed to address – is commonly referred to as *pushing* the value. Similarly, removing a value from the stack is known as *popping* it.

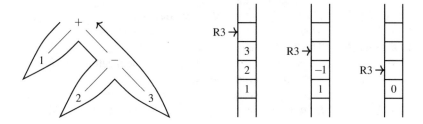

Fig. 5.1 Evaluation of $1 + (2 - 3)$; a parse tree and three stack configurations

One of the many applications of a stack is the systematic evaluation of expressions. Suppose we want to write code to evaluate an expression, say $1 + (2 - 3)$. As long as the expression is small, it is not too hard to figure out the right assembly instructions for the evaluation. But it is far better to design a general scheme for this type of evaluation that can systematically be applied to any expression. For this purpose, we establish some rules on the evaluation of expressions.

- Before evaluating any operation, such as $+$, the arguments are put on the stack from left to right.
- After evaluating an operation, the result is put back on the stack.

The code for evaluating an expression can systematically be derived from the parse tree of the expression. This is depicted on the left in Figure 5.1 for $1 + (2 - 3)$. The parse tree is traversed depth first from left to right. When arriving at a node of the parse tree that contains a number, the code that is written puts this number on the stack. If a node is visited with an operator, of which all sub nodes are visited, it is guaranteed that the arguments of the operation are on top of the stack, and the only code that must be written is to remove the arguments from the stack into registers, carry out the operation, and put the result back on the stack. The code to evaluate the expression $1 + (2 - 3)$ is given below.

```
LOAD R₀ 1      ; Put the value 1 on the stack.
STOR R₀ [R₃]   ; Recall R₃ points to an empty spot on the stack.
ADD R₃ 1       ; Increase the stack pointer.
LOAD R₀ 2      ; Put the value 2 on the stack.
STOR R₀ [R₃]   ; R₃ points to an empty spot on the stack.
ADD R₃ 1       ;
LOAD R₀ 3      ; Put the value 3 on the stack.
STOR R₀ [R₃]   ;
ADD R₃ 1       ;
SUB R₃ 1       ; Start calculating minus. Move the stack pointer
               ; to the second argument.
LOAD R₁ [R₃]   ; The second argument is stored in R₁.
SUB R₃ 1       ; Move the stack pointer to the first argument.
LOAD R₀ [R₃]   ; The first argument is stored in R₀.
SUB R₀ R₁      ; Calculate the subtraction and store the result in R₀.
STOR R₀ [R₃]   ; Store the result on the stack.
ADD R₃ 1       ; Increase the stack pointer to the first empty spot on the stack.
SUB R₃ 1       ; Start calculating addition, with the same sequence of
               ; instructions as for subtraction.
LOAD R₁ [R₃]   ; The second argument is stored in R₁.
SUB R₃ 1       ; Move the stack pointer to the first argument.
LOAD R₀ [R₃]   ; The first argument is stored in R₀.
ADD R₀ R₁      ; Calculate the addition and store the result in R₀.
STOR R₀ [R₃]   ; Store the result on the stack.
ADD R₃ 1       ; Increase the stack pointer to the first empty spot on the stack.
...            ; The result of the calculation is now available on the stack.
```

Note that there are a number of places where the code can be optimised but we have intentionally not done this in order to make the structure of the operations clear. In Figure 5.1 three configurations of the stack are depicted. The first one represents the stack directly before the subtraction is calculated, the second one represents the stack when the addition must be calculated, and the third one represents the final stack.

The use of stacks is of great importance when implementing many algorithms. Many processors provide instructions which can push and pop register values in a single instruction. As it is often convenient to refer to values lower on the stack without manipulating the value of the stack pointer the indexed addressing extension (see Section 4.7) of the simple processor can be used to simplify code.

As all memory used by processors is finite it is not possible to keep pushing values onto the stack. When the stack becomes too large it will either begin to overwrite memory in use by other parts of the program or it tries to access memory that is not there. Both cases are highly undesirable. Therefore processors ordinarily provide a mechanism whereby the size of the stack can be limited. When the stack exceeds this limit it is referred to as a *stack overflow*. Commonly, this triggers a software induced interrupt, such that the program (or even the operating system) can respond adequately to the issue.

5.4.3 Linked lists

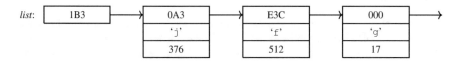

Fig. 5.2 A linked list with each element containing a letter and a number

Another important elementary data structure is the linked list. A linked list is a sequence of blocks at arbitrary places in memory where each block contains the address of the next block. This address is called the *pointer* to the next block. A pointer is any variable or memory location that holds the address, or reference, to a data item, rather than the item itself.

In Figure 5.2 each block in memory consists of three words. The upper word, denoted in hexadecimal notation, contains the pointer to the next block. The two other words consist of a character and a number as the relevant data. There is one fixed address containing the pointer to the first element of the list. This address is called the head of the list.

The last pointer of the list has value 000 to indicate the end of the list. This value can be chosen at will, but the use of the value 0, often referred to as the *null*-pointer, is a common choice. Of course, when using the null-pointer in this way, safeguards should be taken to prevent the storage of a block of memory that is part of the list at address 0 as this will lead to confusion.

Suppose we want to insert an element in a linked list. We assume that R_0 holds the address of the first element e_1 of some linked list. The register R_1 contains the address of a block e_2 of three words of memory that must be inserted in the list. The code to put list element e_2 directly after e_1 is as follows:

LOAD R_2 [R_0] ; Put the address of the next element of e_1 in R_2.
STOR R_1 [R_0] ; Make e_2 the next element of e_1.
STOR R_2 [R_1] ; Set the old next element of e_1 to become the next element of e_2.

To remove an element e_i from a linked list in constant time, we need to know the address of the element e_j that contains the address of e_i as we want to let e_j refer to the element directly after e_i. Sometimes this is inconvenient as the address of e_j is not always available. In a *doubly linked list* it is possible to remove an element e_i from the list by only knowing the address of e_i, as in a doubly linked list each element contains the address of the next and of the previous element in the list. Removing the element e_i consists of letting the previous element of e_i in the list point to the next element of e_i, and the next element to the previous element.

A linked list has the major advantage that elements in the list can be inserted and removed from the list at any place in constant time. Moreover, it does not require a contiguous block of memory to store all the elements as in arrays. Note though that keeping track of the memory that becomes available after a list element has been removed is non-trivial, and can lead to small gaps of free memory that are not easily reused. To overcome this, often the unused elements of a list are kept in a separate *free* list ready to be used again.

Exercise 5.4.1. Write a program that copies the contents of one array to another. The array to be copied starts at the address *source_start* and has a length of *source_length*. The second array starts at *dest_start* and has a length of *dest_length*. If the second array is shorter than the first, only copy as many elements as fit in the second array.

Exercise 5.4.2. Consider the following expression: $(e_1 * (e_2 - e_3)) * (e_4 + e_5)$. The different e values can be considered as constants. Write a routine that implements, according to the outlined parse tree method, the evaluation of this expression. The final result should be available from the top of the stack. Assume that an assembly instruction MUL R_i R_j is available to implement the multiplication. Perform obvious optimisations on the code.

Exercise 5.4.3. Write assembly code to remove the element directly behind an element e_1. If there is no next element, i.e., the null pointer is used for next element of e_1, nothing is removed. You can assume that R_0 contains the address of e_1.

5.5 Memory layout

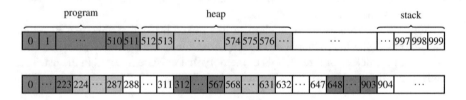

Fig. 5.3 Two memory layouts. The bottom layout has multiple programs loaded

In principle there are no restrictions on how memory is used, but in general it is a good idea to do this in a structured way. In this section we describe the manner in which this is commonly done.

A program consists of code and data. The region of memory where the assembled machine code is stored is called the *code segment* or the *text segment*. In Figure 5.3 the code segment is put at the beginning of the memory in the upper memory layout.

Data generally consists of the program stack and all other data. The stack is put in a section called the *stack segment*. As the stack is growing down, it is wise to put it at the end of the memory such that it has room to grow.

The remaining data is put in data segments of various kinds. Global variables are placed in the *data segment*. These are initialised by the compiler and loaded into memory along with the program. There can also be space for variables that the compiler cannot initialise, for example an incoming 16-bit data value, of which the value is not known until execution. These are stored in the *bss segment*. The abbreviation bss comes from *block started by symbol*, a pseudo assembly instruction indicating the start of uninitialised memory for the IBM 704, introduced in 1954. Data that is dynamic in size, e.g., linked lists, or arrays that grow and shrink, is placed in the *heap* segment. Allocation and deallocation of space on the heap is a frangible matter; programming languages often provide separate libraries for the administration of room on the heap.

Note that both the stack and heap can grow and shrink. If not carefully observed they may collide and the stack may damage the data on the heap or vice versa. In general this leads to unpredictable behaviour of the program, the root cause of which can be very hard to determine.

Although the separation in segments described above is common, there are no strict rules on how memory must be used and more elaborate schemes are conceivable. When multiple programs run at the same time on the processor, each program may have its own code segment, heap and stack. This situation is outlined in the bottom memory layout in Figure 5.3.

As it is cumbersome to have code, data and stack segments of a fixed size, modern hardware is designed in a such a way that the segments can grow arbitrarily and be dynamically located in memory. This is explained in Chapter 7. The operating system generally takes care of assigning and initialising the various segments. In particular the operating system loads the program in the code segment, loads the static data segment, initialises the stack pointer and the heap administration, and calls the program.

5.5.1 Allocation dependence

To execute a program it first has to be loaded into memory. For the first computers the programmer decided at which fixed address the program had to be put in memory. Similarly, the data segment and the stack had fixed positions. The advantage of this approach is its simplicity.

There is however a huge disadvantage that made this method fall out of favour. When only one word is occupied in the fixed addresses ranges where the code, the data or the stack has to be put, the program cannot be run.

A solution is to reassemble the program such that it can be executed at another location or store the data at another place. Or one can design a special loader which adapts the program that must be executed such that it can be run at another than the originally intended location. This means that the loader must identify all relevant addresses in the program and point them to the right relocated positions.

5.5.2 Relocatable code and data

The approaches discussed above are rather cumbersome as it is not straightforward
to make all the required changes in a program in order to relocate it without error.
The solution is to make the program and the data inherently *relocatable*.

For relocatable code it is sufficient that all jump instructions are relative. It does
not matter anymore where the code is loaded in memory as all jumps are calculated
as an offset to the current value of the instruction pointer. This is the reason why
the instruction set of our simple processor only contains relative branch instructions
and does not allow for branching to absolute addresses.

In order to make the data relocatable the assembler will produce a list of the absolute addresses used in the program. At the time of writing a program the absolute
addresses are usually relative to a base address, e.g. 0. When the program is loaded
into memory the operating system consults the list and adjusts all the absolute addresses in the machine code according to the base address where the program and
data are actually loaded.

As all operations on the stack are relative to the top of the stack, the stack by
itself is a relocatable data structure and no special measurements are required.

Note that many computers have different memory capacities. When code is relocatable programs can be run at any spot in memory and the same holds for the data.
In such case multiple programs can be loaded into memory at the same without being in conflict with one another (see the lower layout in Figure 5.3). An example of
this might be multiple programs that need to be run concurrently. As a special case
a single program can be run multiple times, at the same time, each instance with its
own data segment and its own stack, but sharing the program code.

Exercise 5.5.1. Create a program that stores three initial values in variables in the
global data segment. Afterwards, in a loop, increment each of these global variables
in turn. Assume that the pointer to the start of the global data segment is available
in R_2 when the program starts. Use EQUs to define names for the variables. (Hint:
relative indirect addressing instructions may be used to simplify the program.)

Exercise 5.5.2. The branch instructions for the simple processor only allow for relative jumps. If a programmer decides to use a hybrid approach, whereby a part of
the program is placed at a fixed address, how would it be possible for him or her to
make a branch to a fixed address?

5.6 Subroutines

Higher-level programming languages use procedures, functions or methods as a
means to reuse code. In assembly code this is also possible using *subroutines*. The
availability of subroutines is essential to write complex programs.

In this chapter we have used branch instructions such as BRA and BEQ to jump
to other parts of the program. Jumps allow us to branch to another part of our pro-

gram, but they do not facilitate the jumping back to the *calling code*, i.e. to the instruction after the one that made the jump. When calling a subroutine, it is desired that after the subroutine is finished, the instruction directly following the call to the subroutine is executed. The branch to subroutine instruction (BRS) and the return from subroutine (RTS) have been designed especially for subroutines by storing the address directly after the BRS instruction on the program stack when the subroutine is called, and by setting the instruction pointer to the value at the top of the stack when the instruction RTS is executed.

There are other ways to store the return addresses of subroutines, for instance by storing the address of the next process in a register or a specific memory address. This has the disadvantage that it is not possible to call a subroutine within itself. The problem can be overcome by maintaining a separate data structure such as a user stack or list of return addresses. But this is often cumbersome. The BRS and RTS instructions are very convenient and therefore we restrict our explanation of subroutines to the approach using these instructions.

5.6.1 Saving the return address

Figure 5.4 shows a typical use of a subroutine on the left. There is a main program *Main* and a subroutine A. The subroutine can be located in memory before or after the code of the main program but in Figure 5.4 it is drawn besides the code of the main program for convenience. The grey arrows indicate the main program structure. The execution flow is indicated using the thin arrows.

The main program calls subroutine A twice. Note that both calls of A on the left in Figure 5.4 occur at different addresses and therefore the addresses to which the program must jump after executing subroutine A are also different. These return addresses are stored on the program stack.

Calling the subroutine is done using the instruction BRS A where A is the relative address of subroutine A. When BRS A is executed, the instruction pointer already points at the instruction after the BRS instruction. The instruction pointer is put on the stack and the execution proceeds within subroutine A. At the end of subroutine A, the instruction RTS is executed. This has the effect that the value at the top of the stack is moved to the instruction pointer and the stack pointer is incremented by one. This means that the execution continues with the instruction directly after the instruction BRS A that caused the call to the subroutine. Note that subroutine A must ensure that at the end of subroutine A the stack pointer is the same as when it was called, and that the return address on the stack has not been changed.

As the program stack is used to store return addresses, it is possible to make *nested* subroutine calls. Every time a subroutine is called the return address is pushed on top of the stack. This is depicted in Figure 5.4 on the right. Program *Main* calls subroutine B and puts the return address on the stack. Within subroutine B subroutine C is called and the return address is put on top of the stack, above the first return address. When returning from C the first address is popped from the

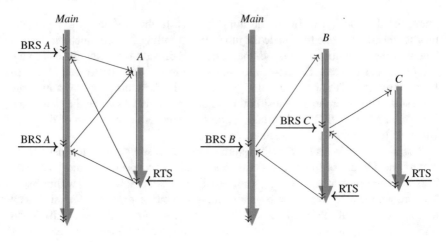

Fig. 5.4 Execution flows when calling subroutines

stack. When *B* terminates the return address back to the program *Main* is now again at the top of the stack.

Note that as long as the stack does not become full, an arbitrary number of subroutines can be called, nested within each other. It is even possible to call a subroutine within itself. Using this mechanism a recursive function can be implemented, i.e. a function that recursively invokes itself.

In the exposition above, the register that refers to the top of the stack is omitted. The precise instructions are BRS R_i *label* to branch to a subroutine and RTS R_i to return from a subroutine. We use R_3 as the register pointing to the stack. Remember that *SP* is another name for R_3.

The next piece of assembly code shows the typical use of a subroutine. In this concrete case the subroutine adds up two values stored at two fixed addresses in memory, and it delivers the result again in a global variable. Transferring parameters via such fixed addresses is simple, but it is not very desirable, because, for instance, it does not permit processes to run in parallel.

```
            EQU global1 100    ; Arbitrary global variables.
            EQU global2 101    ;
subroutine:                    ; Adds [global1] and [global2]. Returns the
                               ; result in global2. Changes register R0.
            LOAD R0 [global1]  ; Load the value of the first global variable.
            ADD R0 [global2]   ; Add the second value.
            STOR R0 [global1]  ; Save the calculated value in the first global
                               ; variable.
            RTS SP             ; The simple subroutine is done and it returns.
main:       ...
            BRS SP subroutine  ; Branch to the subroutine.
            ...
```

When using subroutines a number of conventions need to be respected. As already mentioned, the subroutine must ensure that the stack pointer has the same value when the subroutine terminates as it had when it was called. Moreover, when the subroutine terminates the return address must be on the top of the stack.

Furthermore, the subroutine may use registers, which means that it can arbitrarily change their values. Both the caller of the subroutine and the subroutine need to agree on which registers can be overwritten. It is a good habit to explicitly indicate at the beginning of a subroutine which registers can be changed.

Alternatively, the use of registers in subroutines can be defined as a program wide convention. For example, all the registers (except the stack pointer) may be freely used by a subroutine which makes the caller responsible for saving them when the subroutine is called. Alternatively, subroutines can be responsible for preserving all values for the registers. Typically, such register values are then pushed on the stack immediately after the subroutine is called. The register values are popped back into the registers directly before the subroutine terminates, leaving the stack in exactly the same shape as prior to the subroutine call.

5.6.2 Returning values

A subroutine can calculate a value that must be returned to the calling program. There are two main approaches to returning a value upon function termination. It is either left in a specified register or a specified address.

Returning a value via global addresses has already been shown in the assembly code above. Passing it via registers is just as straightforward, and shown below. Note that if the results are large then multiple registers can be used the return a result.

```
            EQU global1 100   ; Arbitrary global variables.
            EQU global2 101   ;
reg_return:                   ; Adds [global1] and [global2].
                              ; Returns the result in register R_0.
                              ; Changes no additional registers.
            LOAD R_0 [global1] ; Load the values at global1.
            ADD R_0 [global2]  ; Add the value of global2.
            RTS SP            ; This subroutine is done and it returns its result
                              ; in register R_0.
main:       ...
            BRS SP reg_return ; Branch to the subroutine.
            ...
```

The result of a subroutine can also be passed back via the stack at a position above the return address of the subroutine. As the stack grows downward, the return value is placed at a position on the stack that is still valid after the subroutine returns.

The calling code has to explicitly make room for the return value on the stack prior to calling the subroutine. This can be done by simply decreasing the stack pointer. The subroutine writes the return value to this position in the stack before executing the RTS instruction. The calling code reads the return value from the top of the stack and increments the stack pointer to bring the stack back into its original shape.

Note that calculations with the stack pointer in the subroutine are done in a separate register, in this case R_1. The reason for this is that the stack pointer must not be changed to a value beyond the top of the stack. Interrupts may occur at any time and these may arbitrarily change any memory location beneath the value indicated by the stack pointer.

The following example of assembly code shows how a result may be returned via the stack.

```
              EQU global1 100      ; Arbitrary global variables.
              EQU global2 101      ;
              EQU return_address 1 ;
stack_return:                      ; Adds [global1] and [global2].
                                   ; Returns the result on the stack directly
                                   ; above the return address.
                                   ; Changes registers R0 and R1.

     LOAD R0 [global1]      ; Load the value of the global variable
                            ; global1.
     ADD R0 [global2]       ; Add the value at global2.
     ADD R1 SP              ; Move the stack pointer to R1 to calculate
     ADD R1 return_address  ; the address for the result.
     STOR R0 [R1]           ; Put the result at the right place on
                            ; the stack.

     RTS SP                 ;
main: ...
     SUB SP 1               ; Allocate space for return value on stack.
     BRS SP stack_return    ; Branch to the subroutine.
     LOAD R0 [SP]           ; Save the result of the subroutine in R0.
     ADD SP 1               ; Remove the space for the result
                            ; from the stack.

     ...
```

5.6.3 Passing arguments on the stack

Passing arguments to subroutines using fixed addresses or registers can have disadvantages, for instance because the number of available registers is limited. An alternative method is to provide arguments to subroutines by placing them on the stack.

If a calling program wishes to pass arguments on the stack, it must allocate space for them on the stack, store the values of the arguments into the allocated space and then call the subroutine.

When placing multiple values on the stack we use the convention that the first argument has the lowest address in the allocated space and the last argument has the highest address. In this way the indices used to access the stack arguments correspond to the argument order. After a subroutine call returns to the main program the allocated space needs to be reclaimed by increasing the stack pointer.

The following program uses a subroutine to determine whether the product of two numbers is odd. As the product of two numbers is odd iff both numbers are odd, this can be determined by applying the AND instruction to both numbers and AND-ing the result again with 1 to isolate the least significant bit. For brevity of the code we use relative indirect addressing. Observe that accessing the arguments within the subroutine requires a correction of 1. This is due to the return address that is put on the stack when calling the subroutine.

```
        EQU arg0 0                    ; Relative stack address of the first argument.
        EQU arg1 1                    ; Relative stack address of the second argument.
multiplic_is_odd:                     ; Checks whether the multiplication of the
                                      ; arguments is odd.
                                      ; The two arguments are passed on the stack.
                                      ; Returns the result in register $R_0$.
                                      ; Changes no additional registers.
        LOAD $R_0$ [SP + arg0 + 1]    ; Load the first argument from the stack.
        AND $R_0$ [SP + arg1 + 1]     ; Apply the AND to both arguments.
        AND $R_0$ 1                   ; Throw away all bits except least significant one.
        RTS SP                        ; Register $R_0$ is 0 if the product is even and 1
                                      ; if it is odd.
main: ...
        SUB SP 2                      ; Make room for both arguments.
        LOAD $R_0$ 1                  ; Load the value for the first argument.
        STOR $R_0$ [SP + arg0]        ; Store this value on top of the stack.
        LOAD $R_0$ 2                  ; Load the value for the second argument.
        STOR $R_0$ [SP + arg1]        ; Store this value below the top of the stack.
        BRS SP multiplic_is_odd       ; Branch to the subroutine.
        ADD SP 2                      ; Deallocate space used for the arguments.
        ...
```

For some arguments it is preferred to use the stack and for others passing them in registers is the better option. Therefore, in actual assembly programs a mixture of passing arguments on the stack and in registers is often used.

The collection of decisions made on how the registers can be used by subroutines, how arguments are passed, and how the return value is handled constitute the calling convention. In order to keep the complexity of programs to a minimum, it is wise to define exactly one calling convention and to apply it, without exception, throughout a program.

5.6.4 Local variables

As already mentioned, a subroutine may only have permission to overwrite a limited number of registers. But it may be that a subroutine needs to store more intermediary results than there are registers available. It could assign some fixed memory addresses to store these results, but this makes it impossible to call the subroutine within itself, as the second instance of the subroutine may inadvertently modify the same fixed addresses that the first instance of the subroutine is using.

The stack is ideal to overcome this problem. A subroutine can assign extra space on the stack to store intermediate results. Typically, a subroutine saves the contents of all the registers it wants to use on the stack when it is called. Then, immediately before the routine terminates, it moves these values from the stack back into the registers. In this way the calling program will never notice that the contents of the registers have been changed within the subroutine.

If the subroutine requires the use of more memory for its intermediate results than there are registers available, it can reserve more space on the stack. As these results are constrained to the current subroutine they are known as *local variables*.

In the example below a subroutine is provided to calculate the summation $\sum_{i=n}^{m} i$. The arguments n and m are passed in R_0 and R_1, respectively. The result is returned in register R_0. Register R_2 is both used for adding up terms and for checking if the summation is done. As we require the subroutine to preserve all register contents with the exception of R_0, we save the content of register R_2 on the stack. Furthermore, we use an additional local variable *sum* on the stack to store the (partial) sum. As the result is transferred in register R_0, we are free to modify it, and use it to store the running variable i in the summation.

The code to branch to the summation subroutine is not present in the assembly code below. Observe that first, the return address is stored on the stack, and subsequently, space for local variables is located. Therefore, we do not have to compensate the addresses, unlike the previous example where the arguments are passed on the stack.

```
      EQU save_R₂ 1 ; A word on the stack to save register R₂.
      EQU sum 0     ; The relative place on the stack for the local
                    ; variable sum.
summation:          ; Calculates ∑ⁱ₌ₙ i.
                    ; The arguments n and m are passed in R₀ and R₁.
                    ; Returns the result in register R₀.
                    ; Changes no additional registers.
```

```
         SUB SP 2                    ; Make space to save R2 and the local variable
                                     ; sum.
         STOR R2 [SP + save_R2]     ; Save the value of R2 on the stack.
         LOAD R2 0                   ; Initialise the summation to 0.
         STOR R2 [SP + sum]         ; Save this value to the local variable on the stack.
loop:    LOAD R2 R0                  ; R0 is the current i, initially equal to n.
         SUB R2 R1                   ; R1 was the argument m passed to the function.
         BMI return                  ; If n − i is negative all terms have been added.
         LOAD R2 [SP + sum]         ; Load the current sum.
         ADD R2 R0                   ; Add a new term to sum.
         STOR R2 [SP + sum]         ; Save the new sum to the variable on the stack.
         ADD R0 1                    ; Increment i.
         BRA loop                    ; Continue adding up terms.
return:  LOAD R0 [SP + sum]         ; Load the final sum into R0 as return value.
         LOAD R2 [SP + save_R2]     ; Restore the value of register R2.
         ADD SP 2                    ; Release the local storage on the stack.
         RTS SP;
```

Exercise 5.6.1. When returning values on the stack, why should the caller, and not the called subroutine, allocate space on the stack?

Exercise 5.6.2. Write a function to sum three arguments that are passed on the stack. The return value must be placed on the stack. Also give the code that calls this function. Use the convention that none of the registers can be overwritten by the subroutine.

Exercise 5.6.3. Write a function that calculates the value of the quadratic formula $f(x) = a * x^2 + b * x + c$. Calculate the product terms first, assuming a MUL R_i R_j instruction exists, and store them in local variables. The coefficient arguments are passed on the stack and the parameter x is passed in R_0. The result should be available from R_0 and this is the only register that can be modified.

Exercise 5.6.4. Again write a function that calculates the value of the quadratic formula. This time use the function from Exercise 5.6.2 to calculate the sum of the terms. The arguments and the result should be passed in the same manner as in the previous exercise.

Exercise 5.6.5. In the examples above the result is often passed back via a dedicated position on the stack. Is it possible to use one of the positions on the stack reserved for the arguments to return the result of a subroutine?

5.7 Interrupt routines

In Section 4.9 a simple interrupt mechanism is described. Interrupts are signals that can occur at any moment and that request the processor to temporarily execute a special part of the code, generally called an interrupt handler.

We distinguish between two different types of interrupts. The first is caused by external hardware requesting that the processor take notice of some event. This might be a keyboard telling the processor that a key has just been pressed. These *hardware interrupts* usually occur asynchronously, that is, a sender notifies the processor of the event and does not wait for a response (e.g. whether the event was actually handled or not).

The other type is known as a *software interrupt*. Such an interrupt is generated during normal code execution when some exceptional event occurs. This event might be an overflow occurring during an arithmetic operation, the stack reaching a limit or data being written in protected memory. Our simple processor does not have the ability to generate such software interrupts, but it would not be difficult to add the necessary hardware to provide it with such capabilities.

Most processors also have the ability to trigger interrupts by executing special *trap* instructions during normal execution. Such instructions can be used to check for errors in calculations if the processor does not automatically do so (and most don't). Software interrupts are also used as alternatives for the branch to subroutine instruction with extra features such as changing the security level of the program execution.

5.7.1 Interrupt handlers

The code that runs when an interrupt occurs is known as an *interrupt handler*. When an interrupt occurs the processor saves its current execution context and starts executing the appropriate interrupt handler.

Care should be taken to ensure that the interrupt handler completes execution in as little time as possible as it is desirable that the handler is finished before the next interrupt comes. Often the interrupt handler only prepares some elementary data so that the main program can process the interrupt when it has time to do so.

In Section 4.9 it was explained how the processor dispatches an installed interrupt handler. Upon an interrupt indicating that it needs to be handled, the processor finishes executing the current instruction. It then saves the execution context by writing both the IP and CC registers to the stack, where it takes R_3 as the stack pointer. After saving the flags and the return address the processor will immediately jump to the code of the interrupt handler. The processor does not save other register contents to the stack. However, all register contents must be preserved so that, following completion of the handler routine, the main program can resume execution. If the handler uses registers without restoring them, then it loses transparency with respect to any executing code, as during execution of such code the content of registers can arbitrarily change when an interrupt occurs.

Therefore, at the start of the handler routine a copy of all the used register contents is made. The values are then restored at the end of the routine. As interrupts can occur within interrupts, the only safe place to store the register values is the stack. In the example below, only one register needs to be saved, but it is common that an interrupt routine starts by saving the contents of all registers, except the stack pointer, on the stack. At the end of the interrupt handler, directly before the return from interrupt (RTI) instruction, all the values must be restored into the registers in reverse order. When the RTI instruction is executed, the execution of the interrupt handler terminates by restoring the ALU flags and the stack, and by jumping back to the interrupted location in the main program.

The following fragment of assembly code shows an example of a simple interrupt handler. Its task is to read a value provided by external hardware, store it in some fixed memory location and set a flag to indicate that the main program must handle this value. The hardware might be a keyboard and the interrupt could indicate that a key press happened and its value can be read. Note that this handler only uses register R_0 and therefore it is the only register that needs to be saved explicitly on the stack.

```
               EQU global_var 100       ; Variable used to communicate with the
                                        ; main program.
               EQU global_signal 101    ; Flag to indicate that the variable has
                                        ; been updated.
intr_handler:  SUB SP 1                 ; Create space on the stack for register R0.
               STOR R0 [SP]             ; Save R0 to the empty space on the stack.
               IN R0                    ; Load the externally provided value.
               STOR R0 [global_var]     ; Store the provided value.
               LOAD R0 1                ; Set the flag to signal that the global
               STOR R0 [global_signal]  ; variable has been updated. The main
                                        ; program resets the flag.
intr_exit:     LOAD R0 [SP]             ; Restore register R0 from the stack.
               ADD SP 1                 ; Deallocate space from the stack.
               RTI                      ; Restore the flags and return to
                                        ; the main program.
```

Observe that the code of an interrupt handler is similar to that of a subroutine in that it does not have arguments nor a return value, it cannot change the value of any register, and it requires an RTI instruction instead of an RTS instruction to terminate.

5.7.2 Installing handlers

Generally, the address where the handler must be located is in some table, or in special hardware registers that can be set by the programmer or the operating system. This allows for the interrupt handler to be located anywhere in memory. If there are various kinds of interrupts, the *interrupt vector table* has multiple entries.

Up till now we have not described the mechanism that our simple processor is using to install interrupt handlers. Below we describe one way in which this could work. To install an interrupt handler on the simple processor we simply place its execution address at the correct position in a fixed position lookup table. For example, the interrupt lookup table could fill the memory from address 32 up to address 64.

The interrupt handlers are installed during program initialisation. The following example demonstrates the installation of the previously defined handler at address 48. First the address of the handler as part of the code segment is calculated. For the purposes of this example it is assumed that R_2 holds the first address of the code segment.

EQU intr_table_addr 48	; Address in the lookup table for keyboard ; hardware interrupt.
main: LOAD R_0 intr_handler	; Loads the address of the handler as if ; the code segment starts at address 0.
ADD R_0 R_2	; Add up the offset of the handler with the ; actual start of the code segment.
STOR R_0 [intr_table_addr]	; Store the actual address of the handler in ; the table.
LOAD R_0 0	; Set the default value for the global flag
STOR R_0 [global_signal]	; as part of the initialisation.
. . .	

As it is not always desirable to have the main program interrupted by handlers, most processors also provide a mechanism to disable and enable handlers for interrupts. A programmer might decide to turn off all interrupt handling or only the low-priority ones if the main program has entered a time-sensitive part of its execution. In the same way, interrupts can be switched off during the execution of an interrupt handler. Processors with support for enabling and disabling of interrupts do so by setting flags in a special interrupt masking register. An interrupt only occurs if its mask is not set.

5.7.3 An example: displaying keyboard strokes

To conclude the keyboard interrupt example we look at what the remainder of the main program might look like. The above handler only stores the value it reads from the external device and it sets a flag in memory to indicate that the main program should process this value. To flesh out the keyboard interaction example, we can assume that the received value is an ASCII character.

Suppose that a simple display only capable of showing 16 characters on a single line is connected to the processor. To communicate with this display two hardware addresses are available, one for writing a character to and the other for writing a position on the line. When a character is written to the former the display will refresh and show the new character at the position that was in the latter.

We take care to only write displayable characters to this display and cycle round to the first position of the display when the line is full. We support only one non-printable character, the ASCII line feed (newline) with decimal value 10. When this value is read, the display is cleared by printing spaces to all its positions.

The following main program loop brings all this together. It does not contain the initialisation of the interrupt table.

```
        EQU display_char 23       ; Special address used to write a character.
        EQU display_pos 24        ; Special address used to indicate position
                                  ; of a character.
        EQU max_position 15       ; Maximum position for a display character.
loop:   LOAD R0 [global_signal]   ; Load the signal value.
        BEQ loop                  ; If the signal is 0 then there is no new character.
        LOAD R0 [global_var]      ; A new character available, load its value.
        LOAD R1 R0                ; Copy the value to make a comparison.
        SUB R1 10                 ; Check if the character is the ASCII line feed.
        BEQ clear_line            ; Jump to section to clear the line.
        LOAD R1 R0                ; Copy the value again to do a comparison.
        SUB R1 32                 ; Values under 32 are non-printable.
        BMI loop                  ;
        LOAD R1 R0                ; Copy again.
        SUB R1 126                ; Values over 126 are non-printable or invalid.
        BPL loop                  ;
        LOAD R1 [display_pos]     ; Load the position of the previous character.
        ADD R1 1                  ; Increment the position.
        AND R1 15                 ; "Wrap around" to position 0 if value became 16.
        STOR R1 [display_pos]     ; Write the character position to the display.
        STOR R0 [display_char]    ; Write the printable character to the display.
        BRA reset_signal          ; Jump to final part of loop.
clear_line:
        LOAD R0 32                ; Load the ASCII space character to clear the line.
        LOAD R1 max_position      ; Load the final character position.
clear_loop:
        STOR R1 [display_pos]     ; Write the character position to the display.
        STOR R0 [display_char]    ; Write the space character to the display.
        SUB R1 1                  ; Decrement the character position.
        BPL clear_loop            ; Continue the clearing loop unless done
                                  ; with first character.
```

reset_signal:
LOAD R_0 0   ; Load the value to indicate done with processing.
STOR R_0 [global_signal] ; Write the signal value.
BRA loop

This display example is simple, moving the polling on external data to polling on a global variable. Still, this might already be useful as the main program already has relatively complex tasks such as clearing the input line, that should not be part of an interrupt handler.

Under more demanding circumstances the single variable that is now used to store the ASCII character should be replaced by a buffer, in the form of an array or list such that multiple keystrokes can be recorded by the interrupt handler. The main program is free to carry out other tasks and only intermittently poll the *global_signal* variable. If the variable is set then the buffer can be processed.

The main program and the interrupt handler should also monitor whether the input devices are working correctly, by checking their error statuses and responding appropriately.

Most importantly, we would not like to force the main program to continuously monitor whether a keystroke has happened. We want to have a way to only run that part of the main program that deals with keystrokes when a key has been hit. For this we can use multithreading or multitasking, which is the topic of the next section.

Exercise 5.7.1. An interrupt handler often starts with saving all the registers, and restoring them at the end. This could easily be done by the execution unit preventing repeated programming effort. Give a reason why this is generally not done in processors.

Exercise 5.7.2. What happens when the interrupt handler takes a long time? In particular what happens if the next interrupts frequently come when the interrupt handler is not yet finished?

Exercise 5.7.3. Write an interrupt handler that increments a counter whenever an interrupt from a hardware timer occurs. The hardware timer can be instructed to provide an interrupt every millisecond. The counter can be used as an elementary clock. Note that in the small processor the counter is a 16-bit word, and therefore, the clock will go back to 0 approximately every minute. For a more useful clock multiple words are required. In this exercise it suffices to only use a counter consisting of a single word. It is not necessary to write code to initialise the clock variable and install the interrupt handler.

Exercise 5.7.4. Write a handler for the software interrupt that is generated when a division by zero occurs in the program. In this case the error is fatal. Write the message "ERROR" (ASCII: 69,82,82,79,82) to the simple display and enter an infinite loop. Install the handler at address 36 in the lookup table.

5.8 Multitasking and multithreading

Using interrupts allows our simple processor to be transformed, with relative ease, into a machine that can switch between running multiple programs. Each *process*, or program being executed, has its own stack, code and data segments. The main idea of *multitasking* on a machine with a single instruction pointer, one set of registers and one ALU, is that the processor executes each process for a short while and, using timer interrupts, switches to other processes regularly. If this *context switching* occurs frequently, it gives the appearance that the processor runs all the processes at the same time.

Where a single process has different tasks to carry out in parallel, for example, reading from a network and updating a screen, the tasks can be split into *threads* where each thread can be considered a separate process. *Multithreading*, unlike multitasking, gives each thread its own independent call stack yet shares other resources, i.e. threads can access the data of other threads. With multitasking, processes are prevented from accessing data of other processes. This shared memory access between threads is the reason that if a single thread causes an unhandled error or exception, the operating system can end the entire process. With multitasking, if a single process crashes, it should not affect other processes. It is the role of the programmer to determine how a single program can be split into separate threads and to write code that ensures the shared resources are always in a predictable state.

It is the task of the operating system to govern how and when the processor switches between processes or threads. The context switching that occurs for multitasking is generally more complex, and thus slower, than for multithreading, due to the additional data that must be stored regarding the process state. Switching between threads or processes may be supported by processor hardware that, for example, optimises how pipelines and caches are flushed between context switches or by providing multiple register banks that can be activated in turn.

On processors with multiple processor cores, threads and processes can be run simultaneously, but the essential mechanisms to control the multitasking of processes is as we present here.

5.8.1 Timer interrupts and context switching

To give the appearance of processes executing at the same time it is important that the switching between them is based on very short time lapses. To support this an external timer is added to the simple processor. For the purpose of multitasking, the timer is primarily used to regularly provide an interrupt, typically in the order of every millisecond, though this time interval can usually be set by the operating system or scheduler process.

Whenever the timer interrupt occurs, the timer interrupt handler essentially saves all the registers of the currently running process on the stack of that process. Note that the instruction pointer and the flags of this running process are also saved.

The handler then changes the stack pointer to the stack of another process. This stack contains the register values, processor flags and the instruction pointer for that process. These are then pulled from the stack. When the timer interrupt handler executes the instruction RTI, the processor begins executing the instructions of the second process.

So, each time a timer interrupt occurs, the main action of the interrupt handler is to change the stack pointer to the stack of the next process that must be executed. To know which process must be executed next, some data structures must be maintained, which is the topic of the next section.

Timer interrupts can also be used to maintain a software clock. Whenever the timer interrupt occurs, the clock value can be increased. This clock value is then available for other processes to measure time or to determine how long the computer has been running. For any decent operating system the availability of such a clock is paramount.

5.8.2 Data structures for multitasking

To implement multitasking, we require some data structures. For each process we maintain a block of data, called a *PCB* (*process control block*), containing the essential information about a process. This essential information is primarily the current stack pointer and other register contents of this process.

Furthermore, the status of the process, which can be running, waiting or blocked, is stored. If the status is *running* this process is running on the processor. If the process is *waiting* the process is ready to be run. Typically, when a context switch occurs, the running process is made waiting and a waiting process is made running and executed on the processor by making its stack pointer the current stack pointer of the processor. A process can also be *blocked*. This means that the process has no need to be executed on the processor as it stands. This can, for instance, be a dedicated process that is responsible for handling keystrokes, when no keys are struck. Whenever a keystroke interrupt occurs, the keystroke interrupt handler will put the keystroke in a buffer and the operating system will change the blocked process' status to waiting. This method ensures that a process will only be run on the processor when needed thereby avoiding busy waiting.

As the queue and the process control blocks are not part of the data of the processes, these are stored in a memory segment for *system variables* (see Figure 5.6). In this figure, it is also indicated how a running and a waiting process can reside in memory.

To find the waiting processes, the process control blocks of all waiting processes are put into a linked list of waiting processes, see Figure 5.5, called the *wait list*. In order to use it as a first-in-first-out queue, we maintain a pointer to the end of the wait list. Processes that have just been running are put at the end of the wait list, and processes that go from waiting to running are taken from the beginning of it. As is common, we use the value 0 to indicate that the list is empty.

Blocked processes are stored at special places. The keystroke process can be put in a special keystroke process list. When a keystroke occurs the interrupt handler moves this process control block to the wait list. When the keystroke process is complete, it puts itself in the keystroke process list and allows another process to use the processor capacity. Note that inserting the process in the wait list is a very sensitive operation, as an interrupt may occur while this is being performed. Getting such operations correct is extremely difficult. A simple but not always desired solution is to disable interrupts when changing the wait list. Where processes, in particular multithreaded processes, have access to shared data resources, it is important to manage access to those resources by blocking or activating processes. Concepts such as *semaphores* or *mutexes* are often employed. These concepts are outside the scope of this book.

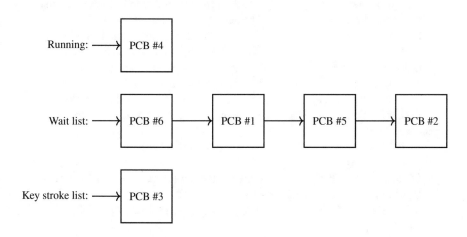

Fig. 5.5 Keeping track of process control blocks

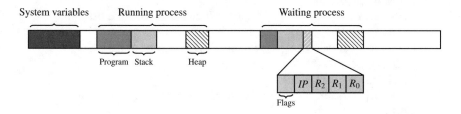

Fig. 5.6 Two processes in memory. The waiting process has its process state stored

Below we illustrate how the timer interrupt handler could be implemented. When the handler is started it saves the registers of the current process on its stack, except if the wait list is empty. In this case no context switch is needed, and the interrupt handler only uses and saves register R_0.

Subsequently, the interrupt handler puts the process control block of the running process at the end of the wait queue, stores the stack pointer in the process control block, and sets its status to waiting. Then the first process control block is taken from the front of the wait list and its status is made running. The crucial subsequent step is to change the stack pointer of the processor to the stored stack pointer of the process that is to be run.

To finish the context switch the registers for the process are restored and a return from interrupt is performed.

```
        EQU running_proc ...          ; The address of the current PCB.
        EQU wait_list ...             ; The address with the pointer to the wait list.
        EQU last_wait_list ...        ; The address of the last element of the wait list.
        EQU next 0                    ; The offset in the list to the next list element.
        EQU status 1                  ; The offset in the PCB to the status of the process.
        EQU stackpointer 1            ; The offset to the saved stack pointer.
        EQU running_status 0          ; Value indicating that a process is running.
        EQU waiting_status 1          ; Value indicating that a process is waiting.
        EQU blocking_status 2         ; Value indicating that a process is blocked.
context_sw_hndlr:
        SUB SP 1                      ; Save register R0.
        STOR R0 [SP]                  ;
        LOAD R0 [wait_list]           ; Only switch out this process if the wait list
        BEQ finish_context_switch     ; is non-empty.
        SUB SP 2                      ; Additionally save registers R1 and R2.
        STOR R1 [SP + 1]              ;
        STOR R2 [SP]                  ;
        LOAD R1 [running_proc]        ; Save the stack pointer in the current PCB.
        STOR SP [R1+stackpointer]     ;
        LOAD R2 waiting_status        ; Set the status of the current process to waiting.
        STOR R2 [R1+status]           ;
        LOAD R2 0                     ; Value to indicate the end of a list.
        STOR R2 [R1+next]             ;
        LOAD R2 [last_wait_proc]      ; Put the PCB at the end of the wait list.
        STOR R1 [R2+next]             ;
        STOR R1 [last_wait_proc]      ;
        LOAD R1 [R0+next]             ; Remove the first PCB from the wait list.
        STOR R1 [wait_list]           ;
        LOAD R1 running_status        ; Set its status to running.
        STOR R1 [R0+status]           ; R0 points to the new process.
        STOR R0 [running_proc]        ; Designate this process as "running."
        LOAD SP [R0+stackpointer]     ; Put the stack pointer of the new process in the
                                      ; stack register.
        LOAD R2 [SP]                  ; Restore the registers R2 and R1 of the new
```

```
        LOAD R₁ [SP + 1] ; process.
        ADD SP 2          ;
finish_context_switch:
        LOAD R₀ [SP]      ; Restore register R₀ of old/new process.
        ADD SP 1          ;
        RTI               ; Return from interrupt.
```

Creating a new process involves creating a process control block along with a specially prepared stack. The stack needs to have the address of the initial instruction of a process at the correct place as this is used by the RTI instruction to start the execution of the process. Assuming that the processor flags can be restored from an arbitrary value and that the state of the registers does not matter for the starting process, all that is necessary is to make sure that the new stack pointer points far enough ahead such that the context switch will read the correct return address value. The process state in the process control block is initialised to waiting and can then be added to the wait list.

There are many more aspects to processes that we will only mention very briefly as they fall under the realm of *operating systems*. Processes can be given different priorities, making special wait lists for every priority. It is often desirable to maintain within the process control block how long a process has been running. It is convenient to be able to identify all processes such that they can, for instance, be listed using a command such as *ps* or *top* on the Linux, Unix and macOS operating systems, requiring all process control blocks to be put into one overall list of all processes. Often the used memory blocks, security rights, accessed and accessible resources are also stored in process control blocks, which become very complex, but very important objects in facilitating multitasking.

Exercise 5.8.1. Write a main program that installs the context switch handler context_sw_hndlr, sets itself as the current process, adds a process (starting from an arbitrary subroutine) to the wait queue, and initialises the timer. Use an arbitrary timer interval, assume the address range 1000 - 2000 is available for system variables, and pick an arbitrary piece of memory for the stack of the new process.

5.9 Summary

In this chapter we explained how to write assembly programs. We showed how some basic data structures can be constructed, such as arrays, stacks and linked lists. We explained the memory layout, and the advantages of making code and data relocatable.

We showed how subroutines are implemented using the stack, and how arguments and return values can be passed back and forth via registers or the stack. We demonstrated how interrupt handlers are implemented, for instance to deal with incoming data or timer interrupts. We also showed how parallel processing can be implemented by letting the processor divide its time across multiple programs, giving the appearance of simultaneous execution.

Chapter 6
Compiling higher-level languages

As you may have noticed, programming in assembly can be time-consuming and error-prone, so to make programming easier higher-level languages have been developed. These languages abstract away the details of particular processors and allow for the expression of common operations in a more concise and comprehensible manner. Typical early examples of higher-level programming languages are Fortran, Cobol, Algol 60 and Lisp. These days C/C++, Java and Python are the most popular languages. There are more than 1000 programming languages in existence and this number is quickly growing.

The introduction of higher-level programming languages did not resolve the problem that programming can be error-prone. Programs in higher-level languages tend to become large and complicated as well, where systems consisting of hundreds of millions of lines of code are no exception. To combat the ensuing complexity, new *domain-specific languages* are developed that allow for more compact descriptions of the desired behaviour of a computer by using knowledge of the application domain. Classic examples are HTML (HyperText Markup Language [26]) for the design of web pages, SQL (Structured Query Language [14]) to query relational databases and BPEL (Business Processes Execution Language, [33]) to connect business processes with web services.

Such higher-level and domain-specific languages need to be executed by a computer. There are essentially two ways to do this. The first one is by using an *interpreter*, which is a program that acts as a computer that can directly execute the higher-level program. The other way is to use a *compiler* that translates the higher-level program to the assembly code for a particular processor and have the processor execute this assembly code. Some languages use a mixture of a compiler and an interpreter. In such cases the higher-level language is translated to an intermediate language which is subsequently interpreted. For instance, programs in Java are often compiled to Java byte code that is interpreted using the Java virtual machine.

The advantage of an interpreter is that it can execute a program without any preprocessing step, which often is faster than if a program is changed, compiled and run repeatedly. The advantage of using a compiler is that the compiled code runs much faster than interpreted code.

J. F. Groote et al., *Logic Gates, Circuits, Processors, Compilers and Computers*,
https://doi.org/10.1007/978-3-030-68553-9_6

In this chapter we show the essence of building a compiler. We provide a simple programming language and we describe how to construct a compiler that translates programs in this language to the assembly code for our simple processor. An interpreter can be built in a similar way, but instead of generating assembly code instructions, the interpreter executes such instructions immediately.

6.1 A simple higher-level programming language

The language that we define consists of the primary language constructs of higher-level languages. This is sufficient to understand the structure of a compiler. We will briefly mention more complex language constructs, which generally require only slight extensions to be compiled.

A program essentially consists of a number of variables that are manipulated. We use variables of the types **bool**, **nat** and **int** as they all fit in a single 16-bit word. In particular we use one whole word for each boolean, where true is represented by the 16-bit number 1 and false by the 16-bit number 0. The type **nat** contains the positive numbers and **int** the two's complement numbers. Each variable that is used must be declared at the beginning of the program or at the beginning of a function in what is called a *declaration*. Variables only have a local scope, which means that a value of a variable declared in the main program can only be used in a function when passed as a parameter.

The task of the main program is to repeatedly calculate new values for the variables until some desired end result is achieved. The parts of the program that express how such manipulations take place are called program *statements*. The basic programming statement is the assignment, often written as $x := e$ meaning that variable x obtains the value represented by the expression e. The type of x must be equal to or compatible with that of e as otherwise the assignment cannot take place. An *expression* consists of variables and/or constants to which operations, and functions, can be applied. A typical expression involving numbers is $x + 1$. The assignment $x := x + 1$ means that the value in variable x is incremented by 1. Our simple programming language has the operators plus (+), multiplication ($*$) and unary minus ($-$) as the operations on numbers.

For expressions of type **bool** we write 0 and 1 for false and true. Numbers can be compared using the 'smaller than' operator ($<$) and equality ($==$), yielding a boolean. We restrict ourselves to a limited set of comparison operators, as the other operations can be expressed using those given above, and therefore adding them is not very instructive.

There are two operators used to combine boolean values, namely the unary operator **not** and the binary operator **and**. We also allow them to be used on numbers, in which case it is the bitwise inversion and the bitwise and. There is no **or** operation, as it can be expressed using the other operators.

Assignments are combined into programs using various programming constructs. The most elementary control structure is sequential composition, often written as $s_1; s_2$ which indicates that statement s_1 must be executed before statement s_2.

Another important construct is *if-then-else*, where contrary to ordinary programming languages, the else part cannot be omitted. The program **if** e **then** s_1 **else** s_2 **fi** indicates that the program s_1 is to be executed if boolean expression e is true. Otherwise program s_2 is run. There is also a construct to repeat a piece of code, namely **while** e **do** s **od**. It indicates that statement s must be executed as long as the boolean expression e is true.

All programs offer forms of abstraction by allowing the declaration and calling of functions or procedures. A function in our programming language looks as follows:

$$\textbf{function } type\ f(type_1\ x_1, \ldots, type_n\ x_n)\ type'_1\ y_1; \ldots; type'_m\ y_m;\ s\ \textbf{end}.$$

This declares a function f with n arguments where argument x_i has $type_i$. The function delivers a value of type $type$. This resulting value is calculated using the program statements s in which it can use the local variables y_1 up to y_m that have types $type'_1$ up to $type'_m$, respectively. In s there must be return statements of the form **return** e where e is an expression of type $type$. Whenever a return statement is executed, the function returns to the invoking program, yielding the value e.

This gives the full description of our tiny programming language. Just for the sake of illustration, we give two programs in our language. The first calculates the factorial of a given number using a recursive function. The second program calculates the powersum $\sum_{i=0}^{N} X^i$ for the given numbers X and N. It uses a nested while loop and a number of local variables in the function. Note that *result* is just a local variable in the program. Our language has no means to communicate such a result to the outside world.

```
nat result;
function nat factorial(nat n)
    if (n < 2)
    then return 1
    else return n * factorial(n−1)
    fi
end;
result := factorial(7);
```

```
nat result;
function nat powersum(nat X, nat N)
    nat x; nat y; nat z; nat n;
    x := X; y := 1; z := 0; n := N;
    while not n == 0 do
        while (n and 1) == 0 do
            z := z + y; y := y * x; n := n − 1
        od
    od;
    return z
end;
result := powersum(12, 3);
```

Exercise 6.1.1. Write a program with a function *middle* that has three integer parameters and returns the middle value of the three. Apply this function to 1, 3 and −4 and put the result in a local variable *result*.

$$
\begin{array}{rl}
Program ::= & Declarations\ Statement\ `;' \\
Declarations ::= & Declaration\ `;'\ |\ Declaration\ `;'\ Declarations \\
Declaration ::= & VariableDeclaration\ | \\
& \mathbf{function}\ Type\ Function\ `\ ('\ ParameterDeclarations\ `\ )' \\
& \hspace{3cm} VariableDeclarations\ Statement\ \mathbf{end} \\
VariableDeclarations ::= & \varepsilon\ | \\
& VariableDeclaration\ `;'\ | \\
& VariableDeclaration\ VariableDeclarations \\
ParameterDeclarations ::= & VariableDeclaration\ | \\
& VariableDeclaration\ `,'\ ParameterDeclarations \\
VariableDeclaration ::= & Type\ Variable \\
Type ::= & \mathbf{bool}\ |\ \mathbf{int}\ |\ \mathbf{nat} \\
Identifier ::= & [`a'\dots`z'\ `A'\dots`Z']\,([`a'\dots`z'\ `A'\dots`Z'\ `0'\dots`9'])* \\
Number ::= & `0'\ |\ [`1'\dots`9']\,([`0'\dots`9'])* \\
Variable ::= & Identifier \\
Function ::= & Identifier \\
Statement ::= & Variable\ `:='\ Expression\ | \\
& Statement\ `;'\ Statement\ | \\
& \mathbf{return}\ Expression\ | \\
& \mathbf{if}\ Expression\ \mathbf{then}\ Statement\ \mathbf{else}\ Statement\ \mathbf{fi}\ | \\
& \mathbf{while}\ Expression\ \mathbf{do}\ Statement\ \mathbf{od} \\
Expression ::= & Number\ | \\
& `\ ('\ Expression\ `\ )' \\
& Variable\ | \\
& `-'\ Expression\ | \\
& Expression\ `+'\ Expression\ | \\
& Expression\ `*'\ Expression\ | \\
& Expression\ `<'\ Expression\ | \\
& Expression\ `=='\ Expression\ | \\
& \mathbf{not}\ Expression\ | \\
& Expression\ \mathbf{and}\ Expression\ | \\
& Function\ `\ ('\ Expressions\ `\ )' \\
Expressions ::= & Expression\ |\ Expression\ `,'\ Expressions
\end{array}
$$

Table 6.1 The context free grammar of a simple programming language

6.2 Context free grammars and parsing

To build a compiler for a language, the first step is to describe the syntax of the language precisely. This is generally done using a *context free grammar*. The notation for context free grammars is also called *BNF* (*Backus-Naur form*) [5]. The context free grammar for our simple language is given in Table 6.1.

A context free grammar consists of terminals and non-terminals. A terminal is a concrete symbol or keyword that occurs in the program. We write symbols within quotes, such as ';', and keywords in boldface, such as **function**.

Non-terminals represent valid sequences of non-terminal symbols. A typical line in a context free grammar is

ParameterDeclarations ::= *VariableDeclaration* |
                                           VariableDeclaration ',' *ParameterDeclarations*.

This indicates that *ParameterDeclarations* either consists of the symbol sequence represented by a *VariableDeclaration* or, as indicated by the vertical bar, it consists of a symbol sequence that belongs to a *VariableDeclaration* followed by a comma followed by a sequence belonging to the non-terminal *ParameterDeclarations*.

We use the symbol ε for an empty sequence of terminals. So, the non-terminal *VariableDeclarations* can be an empty string. Using square brackets an option is indicated. So, ['a'...'z' 'A'...'Z'] indicates a single upper- or lower-case letter. A Kleene star, *, indicates that the previous non-terminal can be repeated zero or more times. For example, an *Identifier* is characterised by

Identifier ::= ['a'...'z' 'A'...'Z'] (['a'...'z' 'A'...'Z' '0'...'9']) *.

This means that an *Identifier* is a sequence of letters and digits, starting with a letter. Similarly, a *Number* is either 0 or a sequence of digits not starting with a zero.

A program in our simple programming language is characterised by the non-terminal *Program*. Unfolding all non-terminals until only a sequence of terminals is obtained, provides us with a syntactically correct program. An example of a syntactically correct program is the following:

nat x; **function nat** *square*(**nat** y) $y := y * y$; **return** y; **end**; $x := square(3)$; (6.1)

Given a sequence of terminal symbols, we want to know whether it represents a syntactically correct program. For this we must determine whether such a sequence belongs to the sequences of terminals characterised by the non-terminal *Program*. The first task is to identify the different terminal symbols, such as **function** and **return**. This process is called *lexing* and the program carrying this out is called a *lexer*. A lexer uses a deterministic finite state automaton to linearly scan through a text and identify which sequences of letters match terminals.

After lexing, it can be shown how the text matches a context free grammar by constructing a *parse tree*, which is a tree that shows how a non-terminal is built up from a sequence of terminals. This process of constructing a parse tree is called *parsing* and a program carrying out this task is called a *parser*. The parse tree for the program given above in (6.1) is depicted in Figure 6.1.

Exercise 6.2.1. Are the following strings syntactically correct corresponding to the non-terminal *Expression*: $1 + -2$, $1 - 2$, $1 + (2 + 3)$, $1 + 2 + 3$, 1 **and** 2, *true* **and** *false*, **and not** *correct*?

Exercise 6.2.2. Draw a parse tree for the program shown directly before Exercise 6.1.1 containing the function *factorial*.

Exercise 6.2.3. Extend the syntax with division, a print statement and a for loop.

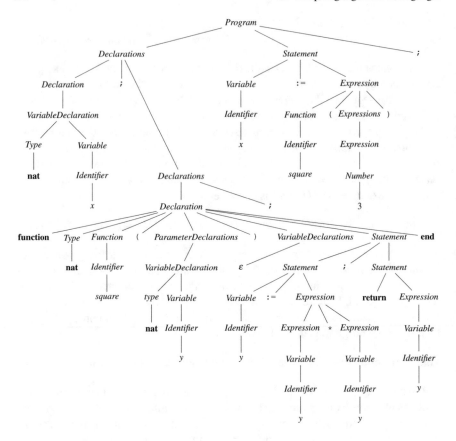

Fig. 6.1 A parse tree of a simple program

6.3 Type checking

A sequence of terminals can be syntactically correct, in the sense that it is properly
characterised by some non-terminal, and still make no sense. For instance, $(1 <
1) + 1$ is a syntactically proper *Expression*, but it makes no sense as we cannot (or
do not want to) add a boolean and a number. The program **nat** y; $x := 3 * 3$; is
syntactically correct, but as the variable x has not been properly declared, we do not
want to accept it as correct.

Type checking is used to check whether the arguments of operators have the
proper type, whether variables and functions have been declared, whether functions
are applied to the right number of elements that have correct types, etc. Generally,
this is done before a program is compiled and in this case it is called *static* type
checking. This is opposed to *dynamic* type checking where the program checks during runtime whether all type checking rules are satisfied. Static type checking leads
to an easier compilation process and faster code. But not all desired properties can

be checked statically, such as whether the stack will not become too large, whether a calculation will lead to an overflow, or whether the program will always terminate properly.

We do not define precisely when a program in our simple programming language is well typed, but we give a number of the main typing rules here.

- For our programs it holds that all variables and functions must be declared when they are used.
- Only the parameters and local variables of a function can be used in that function.
- If predefined and user defined functions are used, they are applied to the right number of arguments with the right type.
- Return statements can only occur in a function and the type of its expression must match the return type of that function.
- The condition in a while loop and an if-then-else is of type **bool**.
- In assignments, the variable on the left side of the assignment has the same type as the expression on the right.
- All functions and all variables in a declaration section have unique names, as have the variables in a parameter list.

As it is somewhat out of scope we do not go into type checking algorithms, and we assume an appropriate algorithm to type check our simple programming language is available. As a result of type checking a program, data about the various objects in the program can be collected and stored such that the compiler can make use of it. We only need to show how many local variables and parameters each function has. Therefore, we require that the type checker implements the following two functions:

variables(f) provides for every function f the number of its local variables.
arguments(f) provides for every function f the number of its arguments.

So, for the function *square* as defined in (6.1) we have

$$variables(square) = 0$$
$$arguments(square) = 1.$$

Exercise 6.3.1. In Exercise 6.2.3 the language was extended with division, a print statement and a for loop. Formulate some static type checking rules for these constructs in natural language.

6.4 Compilation scheme

A parse tree provides us with the general structure of a program and we can use this structure to define the compiler. The basic idea is to generate code for each subtree in the parse tree from the leafs to the root. When generating code for a particular

Expression e	Assembly code $[\![e]\!]_{pos}$	Expression e	Assembly code $[\![e]\!]_{pos}$
n	LOAD R_0 n SUB SP 1 STOR R_0 $[SP]$	v	LOAD R_0 $[SP + pos(v)]$ SUB SP 1 STOR R_0 $[SP]$
$-e_1$	$[\![e_1]\!]_{pos}$ LOAD R_0 0 SUB R_1 $[SP]$ STOR R_1 $[SP]$	**not** e_1	$[\![e_1]\!]_{pos}$ LOAD R_0 1 SUB R_1 $[SP]$ STOR R_1 $[SP]$
$e_1 + e_2$	$[\![e_1]\!]_{pos}$ $[\![e_2]\!]_{pos+1}$ LOAD R_0 $[SP + 1]$ ADD R_0 $[SP]$ ADD SP 1 STOR R_0 $[SP]$	$e_1 * e_2$	$[\![e_1]\!]_{pos}$ $[\![e_2]\!]_{pos+1}$ BRS SP multiplication ADD SP 1
$e_1 < e_2$	$[\![e_1]\!]_{pos}$ $[\![e_2]\!]_{pos+1}$ LOAD R_0 $[SP + 1]$ LOAD R_1 1 SUB R_0 $[SP]$ BCS label LOAD R_1 0 label: ADD SP 1 STOR R_1 $[SP]$	$e_1 == e_2$	$[\![e_1]\!]_{pos}$ $[\![e_2]\!]_{pos+1}$ LOAD R_0 $[SP + 1]$ LOAD R_1 1 SUB R_0 $[SP]$ BZE label LOAD R_1 0 label: ADD SP 1 STOR R_1 $[SP]$
e_1 **and** e_2	$[\![e_1]\!]_{pos}$ $[\![e_2]\!]_{pos+1}$ LOAD R_0 $[SP + 1]$ AND R_0 $[SP]$ ADD SP 1 STOR R_1 $[SP]$	$f(e_1, \ldots, e_n)$	$[\![e_1]\!]_{pos}$ $[\![e_2]\!]_{pos+1}$ $\ldots$ $[\![e_n]\!]_{pos+n-1}$ BRS code_for_f ADD SP $n - 1$
(e_1)	$[\![e_1]\!]_{pos}$		

Table 6.2 The compilation scheme for expressions

subtree we can use the already generated code fragments for the subtrees of this subtree. Consider for instance a statement of the shape $s_1; s_2$. After generating a code fragment for s_1 and a piece of code for s_2, the code for $s_1; s_2$ consists of putting both code fragments behind each other.

Given a program p we denote its translation to assembly code as $[\![p]\!]$. In the same way, $[\![s]\!]$, $[\![e]\!]$ and $[\![d]\!]$ are the assembly code fragments that represent how a statement s, an expression e, and a declaration d are translated.

The stack is used to store all local variables in a program. In order to know where a variable is located, we use a variable positioning function pos that for each local variable or parameter provides its position on the stack, relative to the top of the stack. So, a variable v with $pos(v) = 1$ is located just below the top of the stack.

When the top of the stack is changed, the function pos must also be adapted. For instance, if one extra variable is put on the stack, the distance to the top of the stack of all other variables is increased by one. We increase the values in pos by using the notation $pos + n$ for a natural number n, indicating a new function defined by

Statement	Generated assembly code $[\![s]\!]_{pos}$
$v:=e$	$[\![e]\!]_{pos}$ LOAD R_0 [SP] ADD SP 1 STOR R_0 [SP + $pos(v)$]
$s_1 ; s_2$	$[\![s_1]\!]_{pos}$ $[\![s_2]\!]_{pos}$
return e	$[\![e]\!]_{pos}$ LOAD R_0 [SP] ADD SP 1 + $variables(f)$ STOR R_0 [SP + $arguments(f)$] RTS SP

if e_1 **then** s_1 **else** s_2 **fi**	$[\![e_1]\!]_{pos}$
	              LOAD R_0 [SP]
	              BZE else_label
	              ADD SP 1
	              $[\![s_1]\!]_{pos}$
	              BRA endif_label
	else_label: ADD SP 1
	              $[\![s_2]\!]_{pos}$
	endif_label: ...

while e_1 **do** s **od**	repeat_label: $[\![e_1]\!]_{pos}$
	              LOAD R_0 [SP]
	              BZE endwhile_label
	              ADD SP 1
	              $[\![s]\!]_{pos}$
	              BRA repeat_label
	endwhile_label: ADD SP 1

Table 6.3 The compilation scheme for statements

$$(pos + n)(v) = pos(v) + n.$$

As the function *pos* is used in the translation, we annotate the translation of a program with it, as in $[\![p]\!]_{pos}$. The initial variable positioning function is *pos_init*, which maps each variable to 0. The translation of a program p is given by $[\![p]\!]_{pos\_init}$.

Let us first look at the translation of expressions. For an *Expression* we take the convention that if the compiled code is run, the resulting value of the expression is put on the top of the stack. We also assume that the registers R_0 and R_1 can freely be used.

Using these conventions the translation of expressions is pretty straightforward, as shown in Table 6.2. For instance, the translation of an expression that consists of a constant n simply involves putting the value n on the stack. This can be performed using three assembly instructions, namely putting the value in a register, reserving a space on the stack and putting the value on the stack. An expression that consists of a single variable v can be translated in a similar way, except that we must obtain the value for v from the stack. Using the function *pos* we obtain the value at position $SP + pos(v)$, and put it via register R_0 at the top of the stack.

For an expression of the form $-e_1$, the code to calculate the value of e_1 first needs to be executed, indicated by $[[e_1]]_{pos}$. If this is done, the value is at the top of the stack, and if we then add the code to subtract that value from 0 and to put it back on the stack, we will have generated all the required code for this expression. The code in Table 6.2 does not take into account that an overflow can occur, which occurs when $-e_1$ cannot be represented as a two's complement number. It is wise to add code to check this and raise an exception, or implement another method to handle the error, if an overflow occurs. For simplicity, we leave this out.

In a similar vein the assembly code for the expression $e_1 + e_2$ can be generated. In this case first the code $[[e_1]]_{pos}$ is generated, and if this code is executed, the result is put on the stack. As there is one extra element on the stack, all variables are one position further from the top of the stack, and this means that pos has to be adapted to generate the code for e_2. The code for e_2 is generated by $[[e_2]]_{pos+1}$. After executing this second part of the code the two values to be added are in the top two positions of the stack. The code to add them up, remove them from the stack and put the result back on the stack is straightforward.

The compilation of an expression $e_1 < e_2$ follows the same structure as the compilation of $e_1 + e_2$. The code in Table 6.2 contains a branch instruction to "label:". For each piece of code that the compiler generates all these labels must be unique. But this is not reflected in the table where simple labels are used, for ease of presentation. The result of the evaluation of $e_1 < e_2$ is either false or true; these values are represented by the 16-bit values 0 and 1, respectively. The values e_1 and e_2 can either be of type **nat** (unsigned numbers) or **int** (two's complement numbers). As was indicated in Table 2.3 the comparison must be translated in a different way. In Table 6.2 the compilation for unsigned numbers is given. For two's complement numbers this fragment of code must check whether $N \neq V$. This can be done by replacing 'BCS label' in the table by

```
          [[e_1]]_pos
          [[e_2]]_pos+1
          LOAD R_0 [SP + 1]  ; Load e_1.
          LOAD R_1 1          ; Set R_1 to true.
          SUB R_0 [SP]        ; Calculate e_1 - e_2.
          BPL label1          ; Branch if N = 0.
          BVC label           ; Branch if N = 1 and V = 0; return true.
label1:   BVS label           ; Branch if N = 0 and V = 1; return true.
          LOAD R_1 0          ; Set R_1 to false.
label:    SUB SP 1
          STOR R_1 [SP]
```

Note that this assembly code to check that $N \neq V$ is somewhat clumsy using our simple processor. This is the reason that modern processors have the means to check combinations of flags in their branch instructions.

For an application of a function $f(e_1, \ldots, e_n)$ the caller of the function must transfer the values of the expressions $e_1, \ldots, e_n$ to the function. The rules that determine how this is done are called the *calling convention*. First, all the arguments are put

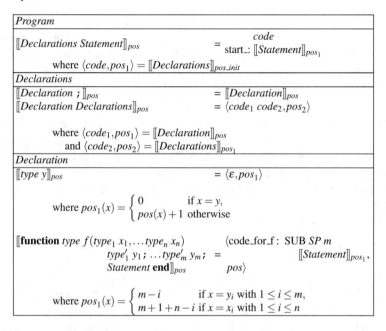

Table 6.4 The compilation scheme for programs and declarations

on the stack. Subsequently, the function is called, and when it returns it leaves the result at the place of the first argument e_1 on the stack. After the branch to subroutine instruction, further instructions are required that will lower the stack pointer by $n - 1$ positions, such that the result of the function application is at the top of the stack.

The compilations of the other expression types are done in the same style, as can be found in Table 6.2. This finishes the description of the compilation of expressions.

We now concentrate on the compilation of statements. The compilation scheme can be found in Table 6.3. For an assignment $v := e$ the translation consists of calculating the value of e, which is stored on the stack. It needs to be obtained from the stack, and stored in the stack at position $SP + pos(v)$ where the variable v resides.

The compilations of the sequential composition, the if-then-else and the while-do constructs are straightforward. Note that in the while-do and the if-then-else statements, the labels must be made unique for every construct that is translated.

The statement **return** e can only occur in the body of a function f. If the compiled code for the expression e is run, its value is at the top of the stack. This result must be put in the position of the first argument of the function f. Furthermore, there can be local variables in the function f. By lowering the stack pointer SP by $variables(f)$, these local variables are removed, and by executing a return from subroutine instruction, RTS SP, the function f returns to the caller of the function.

The elements of a program that still must be translated are the declarations, in particular the functions that are declared in a program. This is encoded in Table 6.4. When compiling a declaration $[\![d]\!]_{pos}$ a pair is returned, namely, the compiled code, and an adapted function pos_1 that incorporates the declaration in the positional function. In symbols

$$[\![d]\!]_{pos} = \langle code, pos_1 \rangle.$$

All local variables are put on the stack. For a declaration of the shape *type y*, with *y* being a variable, there is no code that needs to be generated, but the positional function *pos* is changed into a new positional function pos_1 such that $pos_1(y) = 0$, indicating that *y* is now at the top of the stack, and $pos_1(x) = pos(x) + 1$ for all other variables *x*. This indicates that their positions are one word further from the top of the stack.

For a function declaration

function *type* $f(type_1\ x_1, \ldots, type_n\ x_n)\ type_1'\ y_1; \ldots type_m'\ y_m;\ s$ **end**

the code for a subroutine must be generated. This code consists of the code of the function body *s* that defines the behaviour of the function. This behaviour is translated with the right positional function pos_1 that indicates where the parameters and the local variables of this functions are located. Before the statement *s* is executed, *m* positions must be reserved on the stack for the *m* local variables in the function. Note that these reserved spaces are removed from the stack in the **return** statement.

The translation of the program in (6.1) is given in Table 6.5.

Exercise 6.4.1. Give the translation of the following pseudo code fragment for both the case where *a* and *b* are unsigned numbers and the case where they are integers. Assume that the variables for *a*, *b* and *c* are already located at the top of the stack. Optimise the code by avoiding putting expressions on the stack when possible. Use Table 2.3 to determine the correct flags.

$$\textbf{if } (a \leq b) \textbf{ then } c := b - a \textbf{ else } c := a - b \textbf{ fi};$$

Exercise 6.4.2. Translate the following code. If there are obvious optimisations, such as avoiding putting constants and variables temporarily on a stack, apply them. The arguments and result of function *f* must be passed via the stack. Use EQU to introduce names for offsets on the stack for readability.

$$\begin{aligned}
&\textbf{function int } f(\textbf{int } x_1;\ \textbf{int } x_2)\\
&\qquad \textbf{return } x_1 + x_2\\
&\textbf{end};\\
&\textbf{int } x;\ \textbf{int } y;\ \textbf{int } z;\\
\\
&x := 0;\\
&y := x + 1;\\
&z := f(x + y, y + y);
\end{aligned}$$

code_for_square:	SUB SP 0	; **function nat** square(**nat** y) y:=y*y ; **return** y **end**.
	LOAD R_0 [SP + 1]	; y := y * y.
	SUB SP 1	; Put y on the stack.
	STOR R_0 [SP]	;
	LOAD R_0 [SP + 1]	; Put y again on the stack.
	SUB SP 1	;
	STOR R_0 [SP]	;
	BRS multiplication	; Multiply the top values on the stack.
	ADD SP 1	; Remove one argument from the stack.
	LOAD R_0 [SP]	; Start of the assignment.
	ADD SP 1	;
	STOR R_0 [SP + 1]	; Store y.
	LOAD R_0 [SP + 1]	; **return** y.
	SUB SP 1	; Put y on the stack
	STOR R_0 [SP]	;
	LOAD R_0 [SP]	;
	ADD SP 1	; Remove y from the stack and the local variables.
	STOR R_0 [SP + 1]	; Store the result of square on the stack.
	RTS SP	; End of the function square.
start_:	LOAD R_0 3	; Main program: x := square(3).
	SUB SP 1	; Put 3 on the stack.
	STOR R_0 [SP]	;
	BRS code_for_square	; Calculate square(3).
	LOAD R_0 [SP]	; Get the result from the stack.
	ADD SP 1	;
	STOR R_0 [SP]	; Store the result in variable x.

Table 6.5 The compiled code for the program in (6.1)

6.5 Compiler optimisation

As should be immediately obvious, the generated code in Table 6.5 is far from optimal. For instance by recalling that variable y is stored in register R_0, unnecessary reloading of values into registers can be prevented.

Compilers can make programs much faster by optimising the code. It is not exceptional that such optimisations lead to a speed increase of a factor 10. As the gains are so substantial, compiler optimisation has become an important scientific discipline in itself. We do not go into all the available optimisation techniques. We only mention a few to give an impression of what is typically done.

All compilers apply local optimisations. It is, for instance, determined which values can best be stored in registers, and which values must be stored in memory. Expressions that occur multiple times may be calculated once. Expressions that are not used need not be calculated. Constant expressions can also be calculated once by the compiler such that they do not have to be calculated at runtime.

If the compiler has knowledge about the optimal execution of instructions, it can reorder code, as long as the outcome of the program is the same. This means that the compiler can, for instance, change the order of assignments, when it deems it safe. Often such reorderings are only safe for sequential programs and they are invalid in a parallel context. There are special language constructs, such as barriers and release-acquire instructions, that have been designed to tell the compiler and the processor not to reorder the execution of some instructions.

At a more global level the compiler can reorganise the structure of the code. We give two examples. One is inlining of code. Instead of calling a function explicitly, the body of the function can be 'inlined' at the place of the function call. This avoids the overhead of preparing the stack, jumping to a subroutine, and saving registers in the subroutine. Should the function parameters have known values, the compiler can use these to optimise the code. For instance a statement $x := add(x, 4)$, where *add* is a function adding two numbers with built-in checks for overflows, could be translated using inlining and optimisation by

$$LOAD\ R_0\ [SP + x]$$
$$ADD\ R_0\ 4$$
$$BCS\ overflow\_exception\_handler$$
$$STOR\ R_0\ [SP + x]$$

The compiler replaced the call to the subroutine $add(x, y)$ by its body and replaced the occurrences of variable y by the value 4.

Another common optimisation is the replacement of recursive procedures by a simple loop. This can only be done for limited forms of recursion, often referred to as tail recursion. In such a case, not only are branches to subroutines avoided but use of the stack is almost completely eliminated as well.

Exercise 6.5.1. How would the optimised code for the program in Table 6.5 appear?

Exercise 6.5.2. Translate the following recursive program to assembly code that uses a loop.

> **function nat** *sum*(**nat** n)
>   **if** $(n == 0)$
>   **then return** 0
>   **else return** $n + sum(n - 1)$
> **end**

Exercise 6.5.3. Translate the program in Exercise 6.4.2, optimising the code but still keeping f as a separate function. Also ensure that the variables x, y and z are properly stored on the stack. Use no more than 10 (non-pseudo) instructions. Also optimise the same program with the function f inlined.

6.6 Compilation of other language constructs

Standard programming languages have many more language constructs that need to be compiled. We present some of the most common language extensions as well as different possible semantic interpretations of common constructs such as parameter passing. There are generally multiple possible semantic interpretations of syntactic language constructs, and therefore programming languages should be provided with formal semantics to make it very explicit how the syntax must be understood.

6.6.1 Input/output

A major omission in our simple programming language is the possibility to read and print data. It is actually not too hard to extend the syntax of our language with instructions such as **print** and **readchar** to print a string and to read a character from a keyboard. In Exercise 6.6.1 we extend the compilation scheme of the compiler to make it possible to also generate code for these instructions. Generating code for more complex input and output, for instance for reading and writing more complex data from various devices such as a disk or a network, can essentially be done in the same way.

6.6.2 More complex data types

Programs often have more complex *data types* than the ones we have provided. Typically, there are *primitive* types like floating-point numbers, characters and strings. For operations on such types the compiler needs to generate the right instructions or calls to adequate subroutines.

There are also more complex or *compound* types such as arrays, records or structs, and classes. In order to access an element in an array, the correct array index needs to be calculated. In the same way, finding the right fields in a record or class is a matter of calculating the required offset, which is easy if the compiler knows the structure of such objects. Classes can have static and dynamic methods. Static methods can be called in the same way as ordinary subroutines. For dynamic methods, where the methods can dynamically differ for each object of the type of the class, the addresses of the functions can be stored in each object. When care is taken that each instance of a method uses the same calling convention, the dynamic address of the method can be used to jump to the right subroutine.

6.6.3 Parameter passing

Passing parameters to functions can be done in different ways that can be very subtly different. Our programming language passes the argument by value, often referred to as *call by value*. Consider a function f declared by **function nat** $f(\textbf{nat } y) \ldots \textbf{end}$. When $f(x)$ is called, the value of x is transferred to the parameter y. Any change in y will not be reflected in x.

An alternative is a *call by reference*, which we could denote by

$$\textbf{function nat } f(\textbf{var nat } y) \ldots \textbf{end}$$

as done in the programming language Pascal [18], or by

$$\textbf{function nat } f(\textbf{nat\& } y) \ldots \textbf{end}$$

as written in C++. With a call by reference the variable y is seen as a placeholder for x. Any change in y is reflected in the variable x. This can be used to return part of the result of function f via parameter y to the caller of function f. In general a reference variable can be passed by putting the address of y in x. Whenever y is read or written, the compiler inserts an extra indirection in the assembly code, which ensures that the writing and reading happens in variable x. If large objects such as arrays and records are passed by value, the whole data structure must be copied to the stack. When call by reference is used only a single address is passed as parameter. So, calling by reference avoids copying values onto the stack, which is one of the main reasons for its use.

There are more unusual constructs, such as *call by name*. In this case the name of the variable is used. Consider for instance

$$\textbf{function nat } f(\textbf{name nat } y) \textbf{ nat } x; \textbf{ bool } b; \ldots \textbf{end}$$

where the keyword **name** is used to indicate that y is called by name. Now suppose that the variable x can also exist outside the function f. This is commonly allowed in programming languages, although in our simple language it is forbidden to keep the language simple. When invoking $f(x)$ the string x is used at any place where y occurs in the body of f. Hence, in this case it refers to the locally declared variable x in f. When calling $f(b)$ for some variable b of type **nat**, a type error occurs, because now the variable y in f is equal to b, and hence refers to the local variable b of type **bool** in f. When compiling call by name the compiler needs to keep a representation of the actual names of variables. As call by name is unpleasant to compile and semantically confusing, it is hardly used anymore. It does, however, serve as a good illustration of the creativity in coming up with programming language constructs.

Some languages allow for passing functions as arguments of functions. For instance

$$\begin{aligned}
&\textbf{nat } x; \\
&\textbf{function nat } f(\textbf{nat } y) \ldots \textbf{end}; \\
&\textbf{function nat } g(\textbf{nat} \rightarrow \textbf{nat } h) \ldots \textbf{end}; \\
&x := g(f);
\end{aligned}$$

In this case function g accepts a function of type **nat**→**nat** that requires one argument of type **nat** and delivers a **nat**. If functions of the same type use exactly the same method to pass arguments, such parameter passing can be implemented by passing the address of the function.

A more complex issue is the variables that are accessed outside a function which is passed as a parameter. For instance, assume that in the program above the local variable x can be accessed in the body of f. This is possible in Pascal. In our language, as in languages such as C and C++, this is not allowed. If f is passed as a parameter, it is not easy to calculate the position of x on the stack. A common solution for this problem is to pass the address of the local variable context with each function, similar to what happens for a call by reference. When the variable x is used in f, it is found on the stack via this local variable context.

6.6.4 Classes and objects

In object oriented languages, the objects of a particular class have associated functions belonging to them. These functions are often called *methods*. A method can implicitly be applied to itself; the typical notation is $o.apply(3)$, where o is an object and *apply* is some method with argument 3. Such a method can be translated as an ordinary function, except that it requires one extra parameter, namely its object. This means that in object oriented languages, all methods have one extra argument when translated to assembly code.

6.6.5 Flow control

Programs allow more kinds of statements than those in our simple language. Examples are repeat-until, for-loops, to iterate over a range of elements, and switch statements, which are large if-then-else statements with more than two options for the if. Such constructs can be translated in a very direct and similar vein as the if-then-else or a while loop.

A particularly interesting instruction is the goto statement, which allows the program to jump to an arbitrary place in a program. As goto statements can quickly make code incomprehensible [12], their use is heavily discouraged. But as they occur in certain programming languages, the compiler has to deal with them. The issue with the goto statement is that it allows a line of code in a program to be arrived at from multiple locations. This can make the state of the program and its variables difficult to predict and trace. Where goto jumps can occur between functions, the state of the stack can also become unpredictable.

6.6.6 Exception handling

A relatively modern feature in programming languages is exception handling. If something goes wrong inside a statement, an exception is thrown, which is caught by an appropriate surrounding catch statement that is designed to deal with the exception. The compiler keeps track of where this catching code resides and can generate a jump to this code when desired.

But exceptions can also be thrown inside functions. This is pretty useful because it saves substantially on code that deals with error handling. If such an exception is not caught in the function, the function is terminated, leaving the handling of the exception to the caller of the function. In complex programs, such exceptions can cascade out multiple functions before they are caught.

This means that each function can terminate in two ways, namely with a normal return or via an exception. When a function is called, an extra argument is put on the stack which is the address of a handler the invoked subroutine can call when it wants to return with an exception. This exception handler will then determine whether the exception must be handled inside the calling program or the exception handler of the surrounding program must be called.

Putting the address of an exception handler on the stack is considered a costly overhead, especially because exceptions should be a rare occurrence. As every return address on the stack uniquely determines the address of the associated exception handlers, modern compilers put a lookup table inside the assembly code, which can be used to find an exception handler, avoiding the overhead of putting an extra word on the stack for each subroutine call.

Exercise 6.6.1. An important programming construct is the print statement, which allows for the display of some output on a console. Typically a basic print statement will be along the lines of **print** "The value of x:" x. This causes the string and the value of x to be printed on the screen. Normally, there will also be an expression **read** which delivers input typed on the keyboard. Below these inputs are simplified to make the compilation more concise.

Write assembly code in the style of Table 6.3 for the instruction **print** x, where x is a variable of type nat, and the expression **readnat** that provides the value of the last typed expression on the keyboard. Assume that subroutines *printnat* and *readnat* are available, and that both use register R_0 to transfer the unsigned number that is to be printed or read, respectively.

6.7 Summary

In this chapter we introduced a simple high-level language and showed how it can be compiled to assembly code. We presented the central constructs of programming languages: expressions and statements as well as declarations for variables, functions and parameters. A parser uses a grammar to determine if a text is a syntactically legitimate program, producing a parse tree if this is the case, which can then be further validated by type checking. We compiled parse trees by systematically transforming the parse tree into assembly code. We concluded by highlighting how some other popular high-level features can be compiled.

Chapter 7
Computer organisation

A processor on its own is not particularly useful. It has to be put in an environment to function. The processor within this environment forms a computer or a computer controlled system. On the one hand the environment consists of additional hardware, such as input and output devices, and primary, volatile memory such as RAM along with permanent, secondary memory such as a hard disk. On the other hand standard software is also required to initialise the system and to start carrying out its essential task. If the system is a simple embedded device, e.g. a digital thermometer, such a program is relatively simple. But the system can also be a fully fledged computer, in which case the basic program starts an operating system. The operating system may support multiple programs and users at the same time. It takes care that these users can easily run programs, store and retrieve data from permanent memory and access computer networks. It divides multiple simultaneously running programs over the available memory, preferably in such a way that these programs cannot access the data belonging to each other, or worse cause each other to crash. When multiple processors are available, the operating system also ensures that all of the processors contribute towards running the programs.

This chapter gives an overview of a number of important components surrounding the processor, namely start up software, operating systems, the organisation of main memory, caching and the infrastructure for multiprocessor machines.

7.1 Starting a computer system

When a system is turned on it must be able to start up to execute its primary tasks. For systems without an operating system, such as a digital watch, a microwave or a GPS tracker, the start up procedure is straightforward. The program that such a system must run is stored in non-volatile memory such as *ROM* (*Read Only Memory*) or *EPROM* (*Erasable Programmable Read Only Memory*), which is permanent memory that occupies part of the address space of the processor. This software is known as *firmware*. The processor hardware is configured such that when the sys-

© The Author(s), under exclusive license to Springer Nature Switzerland AG 2021   149
J. F. Groote et al., *Logic Gates, Circuits, Processors, Compilers and Computers*,
https://doi.org/10.1007/978-3-030-68553-9_7

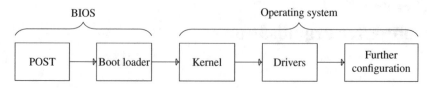

Fig. 7.1 Overview of a typical boot sequence

tem is powered on, the instruction register is set to point to the memory address containing the first instruction to be executed in ROM. The program can make assumptions about the configuration of the system, e.g. the memory available and any external hardware. Should some physical aspect of the system change, for instance the screen of the watch breaks or a button of the GPS tracker stops to physically work, and the software fails as a result, these systems are often cheap enough to replace in their entirety.

As many systems have a similar organisation, it is convenient to initialise the system in a standard way so that this basic software does not have to be rewritten for each device separately. This led to the development of the *BIOS* (*Basic Input Output System*), the *POST* (*Power On Self Test*) and the boot loader. The BIOS is largely being superseded by the *UEFI* (*Unified Extensible Firmware Interface*). This is discussed below.

These basic software components are typically used to start up the following tasks. Initialise the system, determine the hardware configuration, provide a self test, allow the user to vary the way the system is started, and provide an interface to the basic hardware in a system, which makes application software less dependent on the hardware. Such systems are resilient against certain changes in the hardware, such as variations in the amount of random access memory. The BIOS typically determines the amount of memory at start up, and all programs in the system will rely on this figure. The typical start up sequence is depicted in Figure 7.1.

7.1.1 The Basic Input Output System and the Power On Self Test

The *BIOS* (*Basic Input Output System*) is a small firmware program stored in ROM that starts to execute the moment a processor is powered on. Similar to the simple systems discussed above, the first BIOS instruction is located in a predictable memory location such that the processor executes this program first. The BIOS is initially responsible for determining the hardware configuration of the system and for locating the OS kernel that needs to be loaded to primary memory. In many cases the BIOS also has the ability to interface with the monitor and keyboard to allow for basic user interaction though graphics may be restricted and not all keyboard keys may function.

The first stage of BIOS execution is the *POST* (*Power On Self Test*). The Power On Self Test typically checks the integrity of the processor, the available RAM of the system and whether certain hardware devices are connected. The results of the POST are typically visible as the first few messages that appear on the screen when a computer is turned on. Failure of the POST due to broken hardware, missing display devices, no keyboard or faulty memory chips, will lead to error indications and possible abortion of the execution of the boot loader. Successful completion of the POST results in the BIOS executing the boot loader program.

7.1.2 The boot loader

The *boot loader* is responsible for loading the operating system kernel into primary memory, providing information about the hardware configuration of the system and transferring control to the operating system. The boot loader is located at a predictable location in permanent memory, for instance on the first section of the primary hard drive, such that the BIOS knows where to obtain it.

A single-stage boot loader may be able to accomplish this with a single-code file. However, there is often a file size limit for the boot loader and the complexity of modern operating systems means that a multistage boot loader is used where the first stage is only the start for a larger more comprehensive second stage.

Windows, Linux/Unix and macOS have their own boot loaders, but as these programs are software instead of firmware, they can be updated, edited and configured, for instance to allow for the user to choose from loading one of two operating systems. Failure of the boot loader due to corrupt or missing files typically results in the system halting and the BIOS displaying a suitable message to the user.

In many cases execution of the BIOS can be interrupted, typically by pressing a specific keyboard key immediately after power up. The BIOS may have certain configurable options such as date, time and the order in which to check devices for the boot loader program. This configuration is stored in flash memory or volatile RAM that is preserved by a small button battery. If the battery is removed the BIOS reverts to a default configuration. Boot loaders can likewise often be interrupted to allow non-default options to be selected, e.g. to boot the operating system into a 'safe' mode, to reset the operating system to a factory default or to select an alternative boot loader.

During the boot process the processor has full access to the entire memory map in order to allow the POST to access hardware and memory, and also for the operating system to be loaded into primary memory. Once loaded, the operating system is responsible for allowing and preventing access to certain regions of the memory map by subsidiary and user programs. This is covered in more detail in Section 7.2.1.

7.1.3 Unified Extensible Firmware Interface

The BIOS/POST system was initially implemented on 16-bit IBM PCs in the early 1980s and by the 1990s faced limitations. The main reason being that it was tied to the Intel x86 processor family system and not suitable for other platforms. Another reason was that the BIOS and the POST have a limited addressable range of memory ($<1MB$) and they use 16-bit instructions. There are also restrictions on where the boot loader can be stored such that the BIOS can locate it. Many servers and other systems may now be using Peta-byte storage or require fast start-up times. With the BIOS unable to meet these demands, Intel started the development of what became known as the *UEFI* (*Unified Extensible Firmware Interface*). The UEFI, though backwards compatible with the BIOS, offers numerous advantages amongst which it allows for devices to be accessed without starting up the operating system to provide, for instance, networking and high-resolution graphics functionality. Programs can also execute 32 or 64-bit instructions. The UEFI is slowly replacing the BIOS on many desktop systems.

The overall purpose of the UEFI/BIOS/POST system is to ensure that the system hardware is usable and that a valid operating system is then loaded. There are numerous technologies and configurations at play during this process and the entire process is also dependent on the underlying processor and the hardware. For example, many smart phones integrate the BIOS processes within the boot loader firmware whereas desktop systems generally have the boot loader on a special permanent memory device, such as a hard drive, separate from the BIOS.

Exercise 7.1.1. Is it possible to replace the BIOS by a full-fledged operating system including a graphical user interface with windows in ROM? Is this useful?

7.2 Operating systems

Historically a program would be entered into the primary memory using a switch control panel and it could take many hours before it was entered correctly, ready to run. To speed up the process programmers would use coding sheets to detail the instructions and data. These would be given to clerks who would use keypunches to put the instructions onto punched cards. These would then be given to operators who would batch process them sequentially by loading the cards, starting execution, printing the results, resetting the system and loading the next set of cards. Due to the low number of computers, which were mainly found in large corporations and universities, and the high cost of operation, the essential cost of running a program was determined by the time to load and execute, and not by the programming effort.

By the 1950s programs could be prepared on remote terminals onto secondary memory, which was mainly magnetic or paper tape. But the growth in memory capacity and processing speed meant the delay when switching between programs became a significant factor. For each job, the required tape needed to be selected and then loaded into primary memory before the job could commence. *Resident monitor programs* were created to help automate this loading and execution process. These programs are called resident because they sit permanently in primary memory between successive jobs.

Batch processing programs in this manner had several disadvantages. As programs had widely varying running times, operators always had to be on standby. Time was required to prepare programs for batch processing and to run and load them. But above all, programmers wasted a lot of time waiting for their results to return from processing. This was a substantial impetus for the development of time-sharing.

Time-sharing allows a computer to switch between programs. Switching took place as follows. First, the state or *context* of the processor, i.e., the register contents and RAM, were stored. Subsequently, a different program was loaded and executed, and after a period of time this program would be replaced by another. Execution of any program could be stopped and resumed at any time by saving and loading its context to permanent memory. Changing the program that is run by the processor in this way is called a *context switch*. This allowed multiple programs to run simultaneously.

Another advantage was that context switching allowed high-priority tasks to be executed when needed, and let low-priority calculations take place when the computer was idle. This kept the computer employed, even when an operator was not available. Although a context switch was still quite time consuming, the flexibility to postpone a running program and to resume its execution at a later moment was a big step forward.

Context-switching became even more usable when it became possible for programmers to enter their programs directly into the computer from remote terminals and have them executed almost immediately. The compute would divide its time by quickly switching from program to program running a small part of each program in turn. From the perspective of the programmer, the computer was fully at his disposal. This was the start of main frame computing where the computer would serve multiple users simultaneously. The programmer would only notice the presence of other users because the computer was busy with other tasks and therefore slow in executing the programs of the programmer. To divide the time of the computer as fairly as possible among the users, a number of scheduling algorithms to balance jobs of different sizes and priorities were developed.

The growing capacity of RAM led to the possibility of having multiple programs resident in primary memory at the same time, drastically reducing the time of a context switch. But it became possible for any running program to access and modify the data and the program code belonging to other programs. In particular this meant that one stray program could overwrite the data or instructions of another program, making the results of this program unreliable, or crashing it completely. The fact that programs were able to read the data of other programs was initially hardly a concern.

To let programs run simultaneously, and prevent them from corrupting other programs, led to the development of an *operating system* (*OS*). An operating system is an evolution of the earlier resident monitor programs, which control batch or time shared job processing. The *operating system kernel* can be considered to be the core set of functions that an operating system requires in order for it to run. It deals with the core parts of the hardware such as memory and interrupts, and often resides permanently in primary memory. The main tasks of the kernel are

- Memory management.
- Context switching.
- Handling input/output to/from hardware.
- Handling interrupts.

Memory management refers to the supervision of programs to prevent them accidentally changing memory that is currently occupied by the operating system or other programs. Memory management is also used to prevent programs reading or writing directly to hardware devices such as displays and external ports that may be in use by multiple programs.

Operating systems were initially found in multi-user main frames and found their way to desktop systems decades later. Nowadays they are found in many embedded environments as well, such as IoT devices, mobile phones and GPS trackers. The reason is that the existence of an operating system makes programming these devices so much easier that this outweighs the costs of a more capable processor and other hardware.

We do not dive too deep into the subject of operating systems and concentrate on how the operating system integrates with the underlying hardware. From the perspective of programmers, operating systems provide an almost perfect abstraction from the hardware, and many people can spend a lifetime programming computers without ever looking beyond the operating system.

7.2.1 Processor modes

An operating system requires hardware support to ensure that programs do not violate their access rights. This is done by letting a processor operate in various *processor modes*. The exact modes available depend on the architecture of the processor. But the most important modes are the *supervisor mode* and the *user mode*.

In supervisor mode a program can access all memory addresses and hardware devices. When the processor starts, it is in supervisor mode, allowing it to set up the computer system as desired. In particular the BIOS and UEFI run in supervisor mode to determine the parameters of the system and configure it as needed. This also holds for the operating system, including the interrupt service routines, as access to the hardware is often required.

In user mode, a running program can only access limited regions of memory, and generally it has no access to input and output devices. There is a small piece of hardware, called the *MMU* (*Memory Management Unit*) that observes the memory accesses of a program running in user mode. The memory management unit uses a table, which is generally located in main memory, that indicates which parts of memory are allowed to be written and read, and from which parts executable instructions are allowed to be loaded. If a program in user mode tries to violate one of these rules, an exception is generated, giving control to the operating system that can then take appropriate action. It can, for instance, flag a memory violation, or it can decide to assign more memory to the program that caused the violation.

Generally, there are one or more bits in the processor status register that determine which mode the processor is in. If the processor performs a context switch, it preserves the content of the status register, and hence the processor mode. If there are various programs running on a computer, some, such as system services, can be in supervisor mode and others, typically user programs, are in user mode. The operating system makes sure that user programs are started in user mode.

Each running program has its own table of accessible memory. In this way, it can be enforced that programs can only access their own memory space. It is possible to share memory among programs, allowing some programs to read and write certain memory locations, which can be read, or even also written by others. If a number of copies of the same program are running, these programs can share the program code, yet have their own stack and heap.

Programs may want to execute tasks that are not allowed when the processor is in user mode. An example is reading from or writing to memory locations allocated to input and output ports. In such a case the program generates an appropriate software interrupt via a *trap* or *software interrupt* instruction. This calls an appropriate routine in the operating system, which runs in supervisor mode. These routines are known as system calls and are the topic of the next section. The system routine will check whether the calling program has permission for the requested task to be carried out, and if so executes it.

When an exception or a hardware interrupt occurs the effect is the same as with a software interrupt. The processor switches to supervisor mode and performs the required task.

As the operating system puts all interrupt handling routines in place at start up, it can guarantee that when the processor is in supervisor mode only code from the operating system is executed. This gives the operating system full control over what user programs can and cannot do. When the operating system relinquishes control to a user program, it takes care that the mode is switched to user mode.

Within the x86 family of processors found on PCs there is a *real* mode and a *protected* mode. The x86 processors employ the real mode during the boot process. This mode has limited addressing and a small instruction set, enough to locate the operating system kernel on secondary memory and load it into primary memory. Once an operating system is loaded the processor is placed in protected mode which has 4 sub-levels, or rings. Ring 0 is for the kernel and allows complete access to all hardware. The outermost Ring 3 is for user programs and places heavy restrictions on accessing hardware and memory without OS oversight. There are two intermediate rings or levels that allow for a graded access to hardware or memory. In addition to this there are 'negative' rings, -1 and -2. These allow the processor to be placed in a hypervisor state. Hypervisors are programs, which can be firmware, that allow one operating system to emulate or host another operating system.

Within the *ARM* (*Advanced Risc Machines*, previously Acorn Risc Machine) family, described in Section 8.2, there are multiple supervisor and user modes. These are called *privileged* and *unprivileged* modes, respectively. There are also a number of additional modes designed to allow the processor to handle exceptions and interrupts.

Note that this scheme of various processor modes gives the operating system a lot of flexibility in organising protection and security for running programs on a computer. It also puts a heavy responsibility on an operating system designer to avoid security gaps that can allow an intruder to take over control of the computer and access all the data on it.

Different operating systems use the processor modes differently. A Unix operating system running on an x86 processor will only make use of the real mode for the operating system and the protected mode for user programs and device drivers. When discussing these rings from a Unix programming perspective they are referred to as supervisor mode (ring 0) and user mode (ring 3). A Windows operating system on an x86 processor will use rings 1 and 2 to execute device driver software.

7.2.2 System calls

If a program wishes to make use of the functionality of an operating system then it places a *system call*. A system call is a function that is made available by the operating system and each system call has a number. There are over 300 system calls on Unix systems and over 700 on Windows. During the execution of a system call the processor must be in supervisor mode. The only way a user program can change a processor to supervisor mode is by executing specific instructions called traps or software interrupts. Software interrupts, or traps, are similar to hardware interrupts in that normal program flow is halted to allow the trap handler to execute.

The typical flow of an assembly program is to place the system call number in a register and then execute a software interrupt via a trap instruction. Issuing the interrupt puts the processor in supervisor mode. The interrupt handler stores the state of the processor, all relevant registers and the status flags on the stack. The handler function can determine the required system call from the contents of the registers and further code will then ensure the correct system call code is executed. A system call such as opening a file may require further parameters such as the location of the file and the read/write mode of access. These parameters are also placed in registers prior to executing the trap.

Following the completion of the trap handler function, the state of the processor is restored by pulling it from the stack. The processor is changed back to user mode when the return instruction is issued. Processing then resumes in the user program. The exact instruction syntax is dependent on the processor, as are the registers that must be stored on the stack, as the processor can do it automatically or leaves it to the handler.

Below we provide a fragment of a user program that makes use of a system call. The system routine is invoked using the instruction TRAP 0. As we do not have an operating system available, the concrete values are only for the purpose of illustration. When register R_0 is set to 23, the system call will print the string starting at the address indicated in R_1 until it encounters the word 0 that terminates the string. Note that the string to be printed is explicitly put in memory within the program. It is also possible that such strings are put in a separate data section.

```
                    EQU print_string 23    ; print_string is the routine of the OS
                                           ; to print a string.
hello_string:       CONS 72                ; 'H' in ASCII code.
                    CONS 65                ; 'e' in ASCII code.
                    CONS 108               ; 'l' in ASCII code.
                    CONS 108               ; 'l' in ASCII code.
                    CONS 111               ; 'o' in ASCII code.
                    CONS 0                 ; The value 0 is used as an end marker.
                    ...
code:               LOAD R0, print_string  ; R0 indicates that printing is required.
                    LOAD R1, hello_string  ; R1 contains the start of the string.
                    TRAP 0                 ; Execute the trap to invoke the
                                           ; operating system.
                    ADD R1 0               ; Set the flags according to register R1.
                    BMI printing_failed    ; If register R0 is negative, printing
                                           ; was successful.
printing_successful: ...                   ; Here printing was successful.

printing_failed:    ...                    ; Here, printing failed and measures
                                           ; may be required.
```

There are other ways to put a processor in supervisor mode, for example by dividing by 0. The processor cannot determine what the right result is and therefore an exception is generated. The processor is then placed into a supervisor mode and an appropriate handler function within the operating system kernel is executed. The user program has no control over the actions of the operating system in this case. The operating system may simply remove the program from memory to prevent further execution.

If a program issues a system call that attempts to access some part of the system that is restricted then the system call will fail. Examples of this could be trying to open a file for which this program has no access permissions or attempting to read-/write a memory location that is not available. The kernel function communicates the positive, or the failed, execution of the system call by means of a return value from the function. Positive values indicate success, negative values typically indicate a failure. These return values are placed in a specific register that can be read by the user program.

The use of software traps and supervisor/user modes puts a boundary between the user programs and the hardware. This allows operating systems, using relatively simple means, to provide protection such that multiple programs, possibly of multiple users, can run on a computer without essentially disturbing each other. It is only noticeable that other programs are running on the machine because not all machine cycles or all memory is available, and as such it can become slower.

There is of course a price to pay, namely that for relatively simple instructions, such as setting pixels on the screen, or reading data from an input port, a system call is required. This means setting up the registers, performing a trap, determining by the operating system which service is required, checking that the caller has permission for the service, performing the service, and returning the call with appropriate return values. This is a cause of overhead in the sense that it can substantially increase the number of instructions required for such tasks. But given the tremendous protection service operating systems provide, this is a relatively minor price to pay.

Exercise 7.2.1. Can it be expected that a user program has write access to its MMU tables?

Exercise 7.2.2. Throughout time, we see that operating systems offer more and more advanced system calls. Instead of writing single pixels on a screen, they allow for the writing of lines or even complete figures in one single call. Provide two reasons why this is happening.

7.3 Memory organisation

In the previous section it was explained that by using an MMU (Memory Management Unit) it is possible to control the access to memory that programs have. In this section we provide more details about the operation of MMUs and also introduce virtual memory, paging and segments.

As already indicated it is a real problem if programs have unauthorised access to the memory of other processes. But there are two other problems that can occur when multiple programs are using the same stretch of memory. The first one is *fragmentation*. This is the situation where many dispersed parts of memory are in use, and there are a lot of unused 'holes' in between. Memory fragmentation occurs when different-sized parts of memory are used and released repeatedly. If the memory is fragmented it could be that programs requiring a large contiguous block of memory cannot be executed despite the fact that the total amount of free memory is more than sufficient. Without special countermeasures, any memory tends to become fragmented when a computer is running for a while.

Another problem is that programs and the data increase in size. When programs grow, extra RAM has to be acquired. But it can be that adjacent RAM is occupied by another process. This also means that although plenty of RAM is available a program cannot proceed for lack of directly accessible memory at the right place.

Programs typically tend to only be active in a small ranges of contiguous instructions or data at any one time. This is known as *localisation*. As secondary memory such as a disk is much cheaper than directly accessible memory, this naturally leads to the desire to store parts of the program and its data on disk, only loading those parts that are required. Writing programs that dynamically swap the active program and data sections between primary and secondary memory is known as *overlay programming*. This kind of programming is error prone and puts quite an unpleasant burden on the programmer.

7.3.1 Virtual memory

An elegant solution to the issues of fragmentation and localisation was constructed in 1957 by Güntsch[1] who invented the notion of *virtual memory* [15]. The idea is to assume that there is far more memory available than there is directly accessible RAM. This virtual memory is constructed by mapping parts of the virtual memory on primary memory and some less frequently used parts on secondary memory, whilst other parts of the virtual memory that have not been accessed may not exist at all. Whenever the processor requires access to a word in part of the virtual memory that is stored on secondary memory, this part is first loaded into primary memory by the operating system before it can be used. This may require part of the primary memory to be moved to secondary memory to free up space. This process is called *swapping*. When the word resides in virtual memory that has no physical counterpart yet, the operating system assigns some primary memory to represent this part of the virtual memory.

This solution is particularly elegant because a programmer can program as if he or she had the full virtual memory available, and never needs to be concerned with the limited availability of the directly accessible memory. A programmer sees the virtual memory as if it were a large contiguous section of primary memory. It is one of the fine examples of hardware abstractions that modern computers offer.

With virtual memory the addresses issued by the processor are addresses in the virtual memory. Therefore, they are called *virtual addresses*, as opposed to the *physical addresses* that relate to the primary memory. The MMU (Memory Management Unit) also deals with the translation of virtual addresses to physical addresses. The relation between the virtual addresses and the physical addresses is held in a *translation table*, which is stored in primary memory and maintained by the operating system. Whenever the processor requires a virtual address in memory, the MMU translates this using the translation table to a physical address. If the contents at this address are in secondary storage, the operating system stalls the program, swaps this content to primary memory and lets the program continue.

If there was an entry in the translation table for every virtual address, the table would be as big as virtual memory, and then we could have used the table as virtual

---

[1] Fritz-Rudolf Güntsch (1925-2012) was a German computer pioneer who worked on both analog and early digital computers at the Technical University of Berlin.

memory. Therefore, the translation table divides the virtual address space of the
processor into *pages*, which typically have a size in the order of 4096 bytes. Each
of these pages is mapped to an equivalently sized *frame* in either primary memory
or external storage, but it can also be uninitialised.

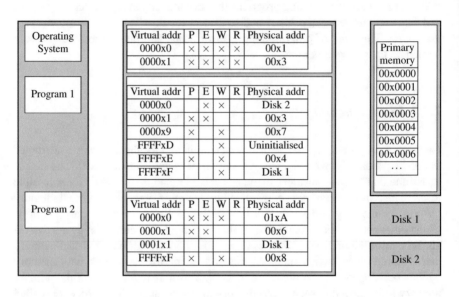

Fig. 7.2 Abstract overview of the translation of virtual addresses to physical addresses

Figure 7.2 illustrates how the virtual address spaces of several programs are
mapped to primary memory. There are three programs running, namely the operating system and two user programs. The three address translation tables are depicted
in the middle. A virtual address consists of a 32-bit word and the page size is 4096
bits large. This means that each page is addressed with 20 bits, or five hexadecimal
numbers. Therefore, in the address translation table an entry is characterised by the
five most significant hexadecimal numbers. A physical address consists of 24 bits
as indicated in the rightmost square in Figure 7.2. This means that a physical page
is characterised by three hexadecimal numbers. These are the numbers in the rightmost column in the tables in the centre. The lower 12 bits of each virtual address
form the offset of the physical address.

It can be seen how the virtual pages are mapped quite arbitrarily on primary
memory. Some of the pages are not present in memory, but located on one of the
two available disks. There is even one page that is not initialised, which means that it
has never been written or read. Note that all programs have an address space starting
from address 0. The MMU takes care that these addresses are mapped to separate
pages of physical memory. Each program can act as if the whole address range is
available without being concerned about other processes.

Within the translation table there is a table with bits that indicate properties
of particular pages. The memory management unit checks these bits to determine

whether certain operations are allowed on a page whenever the page is accessed. The first bit P is the present bit. It indicates whether this page is located in memory. The second bit E is the executable bit, indicating whether the page contains executable code. The writable bit W indicates whether words in this page are allowed to be written. The last bit R is the resident bit indicating that this page must remain in memory and cannot be swapped out. The trained eye can observe the structure of the programs. The stack is typically located at the higher addresses, starting with FFFF. It does not contain executable code, but it can be written. The executable code is typically located at the lowest addresses, and intermediate addresses, such as those in page 0000x9, are typically used for the heap.

There can be more bits in such translation tables. There could have been a readable bit, but we assume that all the pages in the translation table of a particular program can be read by that program. Another bit is the dirty bit that indicates that a page has been changed. If a page has not been changed it does not have to be swapped back to secondary memory which saves time.

The translation tables can be set up such that primary memory pages of different programs are completely disjointed, but it is also possible to share pages among different processes. In this way programs can share their code, or share their data. It is up to the operating system to set this up if such sharing is required.

Paging is very effective for dealing with fragmentation of memory. Whenever a program relinquishes a page of memory, the relevant line is removed from the translation table and the primary memory page can be used by any other program that requires it. The only issue is that if a program requires only part of a memory page, the remainder of the memory on this page cannot be used by any other process and rests unused. This is, however, a small price to pay compared to the substantial advantages of paging. The size of the pages can be decreased to remedy the memory issue, but that would come with the penalty of increased translation tables that require more work to search and maintain by the operating system.

Note that paging is also very effective when it comes to extending the memory of a program. If a program requires more memory, and there are free pages in primary memory or free memory pages on disk, the operating system can assign these pages to this process. So, programs can increase their memory until the computer runs out of primary memory or the swap space on disk, which is the reserved space on a disk to store memory pages, is depleted.

7.3.2 Replacement policies

If the MMU determines that a virtual memory address refers to a page that is not in primary memory then this generates an exception known as a *page fault*. This passes control to the operating system that must load this page into primary memory. But if the primary memory is completely in use, the operating system must determine which page in primary memory must be swapped out. The method of selecting a page to be swapped out, is called the *replacement policy*. There are various replacement policies of which the most important ones are

- *Random.* The page to be removed is selected at random.
- *LRU* (*Least-Recently Used*). The page that has not been used for the longest amount of time is replaced. This strategy follows the principle of locality, which says that some data or parts of a program are used very frequently, and most parts are rarely touched. Hence, the more recently used pages are likely to be used again soon and therefore the least-recently used page is a good candidate for replacement.
- *FIFO* (*First-In, First-Out*). The page that has resided longest in primary memory is removed first.

The least-recently used policy typically works well. But a disadvantage of LRU is that keeping track of which pages have been accessed and when is complex. First-in, first-out is an approximation of LRU which can be implemented with much less overhead. However, it can sometimes lead to pages that are heavily in use being swapped out, after which they almost immediately have to be swapped in again. But as it is hard to predict which pages a program will require, no strategy is perfect in this respect. Remarkably, the random policy, which is quite easy to implement, is not substantially worse than the other strategies, in general.

7.3.3 Translation look aside buffers

To speed up the process of translation a *TLB* (*Translation Look aside Buffer*) stores the results of recent virtual to physical address translations. Virtual addresses issued by the processor pass to the MMU and are first checked against the TLB. If the address is not in the TLB then a *TLB miss* event will be handled in either hardware or software. A hardware solution will result in the CPU hardware automatically executing a *table walk* through the entire translation table. When the page-frame mapping is found it is added to the TLB and the translation re-attempted (which should succeed this time). In a software solution it is the responsibility of the OS to perform the table-walk and add the entry to the TLB. The OS then continues execution of the program from the instruction that caused the TLB miss.

7.3.4 Code, stack, data and other segments

When a stack resides in virtual memory alongside the heap and the program, then certain parts may grow into the memory of another part. For instance, the stack may grow into the heap. In such a case either valuable information is overwritten, or some part, for instance the stack, cannot grow further even though there is still memory available. A solution for this is to give all these objects their own separate virtual

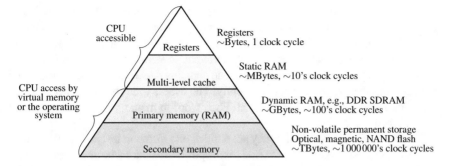

Fig. 7.3 Memory hierarchy with approximate access times and capacities

memories, which are called *segments*. So, a program can have a stack segment, a code segment, a data segment, and even more.

The hardware detects which segment is required. If instructions employ the stack pointer, the hardware knows that the stack segment is required, and when an instruction is fetched, this naturally comes from the code segment. This can be implemented by making a translation table entry for each segment which is selected by the kind of object that is accessed. Within each segment, a page is selected and mapped to primary memory in the ordinary way.

Exercise 7.3.1. How can programs share code or memory using memory translation tables?

Exercise 7.3.2. Suppose a program requires 6 terabytes of memory to run, and the page size is 4096 bytes. How large is the translation table?

7.4 Caches

In the mid 1980s it turned out that the clock frequency of the processor could be increased to make the processor faster, but the clock frequency of dynamic memory lagged behind. Dynamic memory is constructed using small capacitors, as opposed to static RAM, which employs flip-flops. Static RAM is much faster, but as a flip-flop uses more space than a capacitor, dynamic RAM is more suitable for huge memories.

Because of the principle of locality, it is efficient to put frequently used data and code in fast, expensive memory, and less frequently used data in slower memory. This leads to the memory hierarchy shown in Figure 7.3 with the approximate scaling of access times and capacity of the various memory types. What is not shown in the diagram is the cost of the different memory technologies which scales approximately inversely with speed. The memory hierarchy is the result of optimising both total cost and average access speed.

The access time to dynamic RAM is in the order of 100 clock cycles. Most programs use the same code fragments and data repeatedly, while hardly accessing others. This is called *temporal localisation*. Therefore, it makes sense to put high-speed static RAM between the processor and the dynamic RAM. This RAM is called the *memory cache* or *cache* for short. The cache contains those parts of the program and the data that the processor uses frequently. The access time to cache is typically a factor of 10 faster than dynamic RAM. Each word in memory only occurs at most in one place in a cache.

To exploit caches even better they are divided into different levels. A level 1 cache is fast and closest to the processor, and often split into a data cache and an instruction cache. A level 2 cache is available for single processors, while a level 3 or even level 4 cache is often serving multiple processors at the same time. There are various strategies regarding words in memory occurring in multiple caches simultaneously. When they can, they are easier to retrieve, but this is costlier to maintain and also requires more precious cache memory.

When a processor requires data from memory, it checks whether it is available in first level cache. If not, the processor is temporarily halted, and the required memory is loaded into this cache, either from another cache, or from main memory. When writing data to memory an entry can be made in the cache, but the data can also bypass the cache and be written directly to memory. If it is first written in the cache, there are again multiple options. In a *write-through cache* the data is also immediately written to memory. In a *write-back cache* the data is only written to memory when there is some additional necessity.

The write-back policy has two advantages. First, it writes at the speed of the cache and not at the speed of the main memory. And secondly, when data is written back to memory, multiple words can be written back simultaneously. As this is generally supported by memory, this reduces the number of writes to memory.

The main advantage of write-through is that it is easier to implement. Moreover, main memory is always up-to-date as it always has the latest copy of the data.

7.4.1 Placement policies

Besides temporal localisation, there is also *spatial localisation* in the usage of memory. This means that words close together are more likely to be used. Therefore, when moving a word to the cache, it makes sense to also move surrounding words, for instance the next instruction, or values from the same data record, to the cache as well. This is the reason that the smallest unit in a cache, namely a *cache line* consists of multiple words, e.g., a typical size is 64 bytes. A cache line is the unit of data transferred between cache and main memory. There are, basically, three options to organise how blocks of memory can be stored in cache lines, which are called *placement policies*. These placement strategies are illustrated in Figure 7.4.

In a *fully associative* cache, a block of memory can be placed in any cache line. In Figure 7.4 the block in memory on the left can be placed at any line in the fully as-

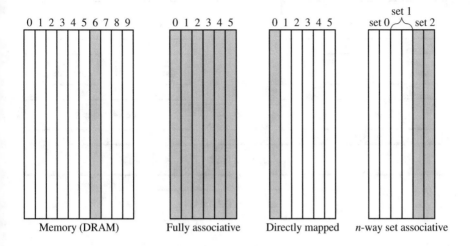

Fig. 7.4 The three main placement policies

sociative cache. Unfortunately, this natural scheme has a huge disadvantage, which makes it unusable in practice. Any cache line in the cache could match this word and therefore, whenever the processor requires a memory word, the whole cache must be searched. This either requires substantial hardware or multiple clock ticks and both are undesirable.

A solution is to use *directly mapped* cache. Each block in memory corresponds to exactly one line in the cache. Typically, the address of this line is calculated by taking the block address in memory modulo the length of the cache. In Figure 7.4 block address 6 is mapped to cache line 0, as is block address 0, block address 12, etc. If the cache line consists of 64 bytes, then addresses from 0 to 63 are mapped to cache line 0, addresses 64 to 127 are mapped to cache line 1, etc.

Determining whether a memory word occurs in the cache is straightforward. The address of the word leads to the cache line by dropping a number of bits from the address, as all sizes are powers of 2. If the address line corresponds to the entry in the cache, the word is found. Otherwise, there is a cache miss, and the word must be retrieved from memory. But directly mapped caches also have a disadvantage. If a program repeatedly accesses different addresses corresponding to the same cache line, the cache line is replaced repeatedly. This can typically happen when accessing a regular data structure. An example is matrix multiplication. Matrices of certain dimensions may cause the multiplication algorithm to jump from address to address all belonging to the same cache line, making multiplication slow, while matrices of other, especially larger, dimensions do not have these problems and are fast.

To alleviate this problem the *n-way set associative* cache has been invented, where *n* is a small power of 2. Here, each block in memory has a corresponding set of *n* cache lines where it can be stored. A 1-way set associative cache is the same as a directly mapped cache. In Figure 7.4, memory block 6 typically corresponds to

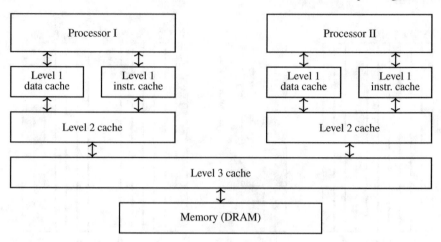

Fig. 7.5 Basic architecture of a shared memory multiprocessor

the set containing line 4 and 5 in the cache. In order to avoid conflicts in the cache as much as possible, each memory block has its own set of n cache lines spread out over the cache. When the processor requires a certain word via an n-way set associative cache, n addresses have to be searched simultaneously, which for restricted n is doable.

With fully or partially associative caches there is the question as to which cache line must be discarded when a new entry must be read from memory. The same replacement strategies apply as with virtual memory, namely random, LRU (Least-Recently Used) and FIFO (First-In, First-Out).

Exercise 7.4.1. If multiple programs are running on one processor, switching from one process to another by changing the stack pointer is rather fast. But due to the cache, such context switches can become sluggish. Why?

Exercise 7.4.2. If, in a directly mapped cache, memory addresses are repeatedly visited that map to the same cache line, the cache line must be refreshed at each access. If a 2-way set associative cache is used and consecutive memory addresses $a_1, a_2, \ldots, a_n$ are visited that map to cache line l and some other cache line l_{a_i}, which is different for each a_i, how many refreshes of cache line l are taking place? Answer this for the random and LRU replacement strategies.

7.5 Multi- and many-core processor machines

When increasing the clock of a processor, it requires disproportionately more energy to function. As only limited heat can be dissipated, this prevents an increase in the speed of processors by simply increasing the frequency of their clocks. The solution to making processors more powerful is therefore not to increase the frequency, but to increase the number of processors.

There are essentially two kinds of multiprocessors, multicore and many-core. *Multicore processors* have a limited number of separate powerful processor cores, typically two or four but potentially up to dozens. All processors can access the same memory, and therefore such processors are also referred to as *shared memory multi-processors*. By combining multiple multicore processors, computers with hundreds of processors, all accessing the same memory, can be made. Groups of processors typically share a level 3 cache, whereas a level 1 cache is generally restricted to a single processor. This is depicted in Figure 7.5.

A major problem in such machines is to keep the view on the caches consistent from the perspective of the different processors. This is called the *cache coherence problem*. When one processor, say processor I in Figure 7.5, writes a value v at address a to its level 1 or level 2 cache, and processor II reads directly afterward at address a, then it is expected that processor II reads value v. However, value v may not have reached the memory, and therefore, without special countermeasures, processor II may read an older value from address a. Caches have a *cache coherency protocol* to inform other caches of addresses that have changed.

There are two classes of cache coherence protocols, snoop and directory. The idea of snoop protocols is that every processor broadcasts memory- and cache-related messages such that other processors snoop these messages and hence know about read and write accesses. This solution works perfectly fine for buses, but when the number of cores increases, broadcasting becomes too expensive. Directory based protocols have a central component keeping track of where references are cached. When reading or writing, a processor first asks the directory which then handles the hit or miss.

The second approach to multiprocessors is found in the realm of GPUs (Graphics Processor Units), that were originally designed to quickly calculate high-quality pictures on the screen. As most of these calculations are very similar, it makes sense to have numerous relatively simple processors available, typically in the order of thousands. These are sometimes referred to as *many-core processors*. As it stands, many-core processors are increasing in speed faster than shared memory multiprocessors. This makes them interesting for a wider range of applications than just graphics processing.

As it is less convenient to let each processor run its own program, such systems often use a *SIMD* (*Single Instruction Multiple Data*) architecture. This means that groups of processors all run the same program on different data. When, for instance, an if-then-else is being executed, some processors have to execute the *then* part, and some the *else* part. This is implemented by letting all processors run both the then and else parts, but the first group only stores the results in the then part, and the second group stores the results solely in the else part.

Multi-core processors also use local caches, global caches and main memory. Because it is much harder to keep all caches in many-core systems synchronised, memory consistency is often abandoned in such systems. Such systems are referred to as weak-memory models. When reading data from memory, the data read can be the last datum written, but it can also be the one before last, or even older. If it is important that data are written before they can be read, an explicit *barrier instruction* can be used. This guarantees that all data are consistent in memory, before the next instruction is executed; but these synchronisation barriers slow the processors down substantially, which discourages their use.

Exercise 7.5.1. Many-core processors execute a larger number of instructions per second than multicore systems. Still, multicore systems are far more widely used. What are reasons for this?

Exercise 7.5.2. Consider two programs $x := 1; y := 1$ and $y := 2; x := 2$. In a weak memory model, would it be possible that after running this program $x = 1$ and $y = 2$?

7.6 Summary

We explained how a processor gets integrated with other hardware to make it into a computer. On startup, firmware initialises hardware and runs a boot loader which in turn starts an operating system. The kernel of an operating system runs in supervisor mode. Processes, isolated from one another, make system calls, asking the kernel to perform tasks. We explained how using virtual memory it can appear to each program that it has unique access to the full memory space, which can be larger than the physically available RAM. We discussed caching as a way of mitigating the latency of storing data in RAM and on disk. Finally, we briefly touched upon processors which have multiple processor cores on board.

Chapter 8
The Raspberry Pi and the ARM processor

The Raspberry Pi is a low-cost experimental platform based on a widely available ARM processor. This chapter describes the main features of the ARM processor and the surrounding hardware of the Raspberry Pi that foster the use of this processor.

8.1 Raspberry Pi overview

The advantages of using standardised processors sparked off an interesting development where companies design processors but leave it to others to manufacture them. An example of this is ARM (Advanced RISC Machine) Holdings. Based in the UK, this company licenses their processor designs to other companies. ARM's RISC processor designs are market dominant in mobile phones and tablets as they offer greater performance per watt than the Intel x86 processors that use a CISC architecture. However, the debate on whether energy consumption is related to the instruction set has not been settled [7].

Broadcom Incorporated, a company with a background in semiconductors for communication devices, utilise ARM processors in their SoC (System On a Chip) solutions. An SoC incorporates a processor and various supporting circuits onto a single silicon substrate. Because all the required circuitry is manufactured on a single chip, SoC solutions are less expensive, less power intensive, lighter and more compact than multi-chip equivalents. The compromise with such SoC systems is often a slower processor speed and the inability to upgrade and extend, e.g., by adding/replacing graphics, audio or other expansions. The development of SoC products stimulated the use of fully fledged computers in all kinds of devices, not only mobile phones. This led to the rise of *embedded systems*, systems with one or more computers embedded within them that control such systems. Because all these devices have the ability to communicate, often wirelessly, over the internet, they are sometimes referred to as the *IoT* (*Internet of Things*).

The *Raspberry Pi* (RPi or Pi for short) originally used the Broadcom BCM 2835, which is a key example of a SoC. Having undergone several evolutions since the

J. F. Groote et al., *Logic Gates, Circuits, Processors, Compilers and Computers*,
https://doi.org/10.1007/978-3-030-68553-9_8

initial release, the RPi has a reputation for being low-cost, functional and strongly supported by the open-source software community. They are widely used in training and education, being the most popular computer besides PCs and Macs.

The onboard ARM processor has multiple processor cores and can run 32 or 64-bit operating systems, the majority of which are based on Linux. There is a wealth of applications available including development tools for various languages. This allows for development in a range of high-level languages such as C, C++ and Python.

The design of the RPi is such that accessing the underlying hardware is relatively straightforward. The block diagram in Figure 8.1 shows the board layout of the Raspberry Pi Version 3 [19]. Notable features include multiple onboard CPUs, RAM, ROM, a micro-SD card reader, graphics, audio, Ethernet, WiFi and Bluetooth, which are implemented by connection through the following interfaces:

- mini-UART (Universal Asynchronous Receiver/Transmitter).
- SPI (Serial Peripheral Interfaces).
- GPIO (General Purpose Input Output) interface.
- DMA (Direct Memory Access) controller.
- EMMC (External Mass Media Controller).
- BSC (Broadcom Serial Controller).
- On-board timers.
- External interrupt connection.

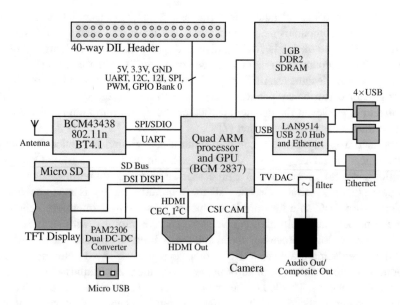

Fig. 8.1 Block diagram of the Raspberry Pi, Version 3

The RPi also has a GPU (Graphics Processing Unit) which can be programmed separately. This is not addressed in this book.

8.2 The ARM architecture

The Raspberry Pi is a computer board containing a processor, primary and secondary non-volatile memory (via an SD card), and a number of interfaces to connect the board with external devices. The processor implements the ARM *architecture*. The distinction is important as there are different vendors and documentation for each aspect. Having covered the device in its surroundings in the previous section, this section covers the processor architecture.

The ARM family around which the RPi is built is a set of RISC (Reduced Instruction Set Computer) architectures. As with all processors, design of the early ARM processors began with the instruction set. This requires, amongst other things, the specification of the number of registers, how data and instructions are to be formatted, what the memory model is and how a processor should handle exceptions. This functional description is now an abstraction over various ARM processors. This high-level abstraction is the *programmer's model* or the *programmer's view* on the system. This is depicted in Figure 8.2 at the top. Within the ARM architecture additional specifications are also made for some lower-level attributes, for example the levels of the cache memory. However, the architecture does not specify the cache size or how the cache controller operates.

The architecture also covers the *ABI* (*Application Binary Interface*). This is the set of conventions and rules that dictate how binary elements, i.e. machine code, and development tools communicate and interact. This covers, for instance, how compiled programs and libraries are stored such that an independent linker can link them together and load the result in memory, ready to be executed. It also indicates calling conventions for subroutines, standard ways of dealing with exceptions and the availability of some standard libraries. This, for instance, allows the development of independent debuggers and profilers.

A core component is the PCSAA (Procedure Call Standard for the ARM Architecture) [4] which determines, for example, the size of words, half-words and other data-types as well as how subroutines should pass parameters. Aspects of the PCSAA are referenced throughout this chapter.

Below the programmer's view there is a layer that explains how the processor works, see the block in the middle in Figure 8.2. This is often called the *microarchitecture*, and it explains how the ARM architecture is implemented in terms of data transfers between registers and buses, see Chapter 4. Such microarchitectures can be very different for different ARM processors. This can, for instance, influence how fast instructions are executed, or how quickly the processor responds to interrupts. Knowledge of this level is only required for programmers who write time-sensitive programs. Most programmers, generally writing software for whole families of processors, do not need knowledge of this level at all.

At the lowest level of abstraction in Figure 8.2, we find the individual sequential and combinatorial circuits that make up the registers and state machines realising the processor. This level is of relevance to neither programmers nor compilers, as it is abstracted away by the levels above it.

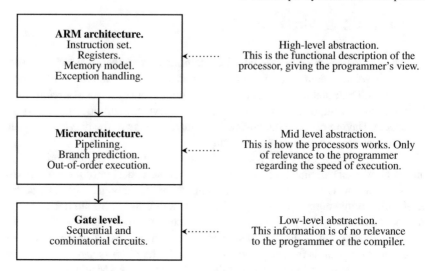

Fig. 8.2 The ARM architecture as an abstraction from processor implementation

8.2.1 ARM architecture instruction sets

The ARMv8A architecture covers multiple instruction sets [3]:

- A64: A 32-bit instruction set using 64-bit registers to handle 64-bit data.
- A32: A 32-bit instruction set using 32-bit registers.
- T32: A mixed 16-bit and 32-bit instruction set used to balance performance and code-size. This instruction set uses 32-bit registers and is called the Thumb instruction set.

These instruction sets are executed when the processor is in a particular *instruction set state*. Processors can readily flip between such states. In state AArch64 the processor has access to 32 64-bit registers, 16 32-bit registers, and the NEON and A64 instruction sets. When in state AArch32 it only has access to the 16 32-bit registers and the A32 instruction set.

The architecture also specifies support for other additional smaller instruction sets that can be present in certain types of ARM processors:

- NEON: An SIMD (Single Instruction Multiple Data) instruction set for parallel computing whereby a single instruction can be applied to multiple items of data simultaneously. Such instructions enable the processor to perform what is called vector processing.
- VFP (Vector Floating-Point): This enables half-, single- and double-precision floating-point arithmetic. For half-precision 16 bits are used, single-precision requires 32 bits and double-precision employs 64 bits.

8.2.2 ARM architecture profiles

Each ARM architecture is further specified into *profiles* depending on how each architecture is to be used:

- Applications (A)-Profile:

  - VMSA (Virtual Memory System Architecture) using an MMU (Memory Management Unit).
  - A64, A32 or T32 instruction sets.
  - Best for systems running full operating systems.

- Real-Time (R)-Profile:

  - Protected Memory System Architecture (PMSA) using an MPU (Memory Protection Unit), which is simpler than a MMU as it does not support virtual memory.
  - A32 or T32 instruction sets only.
  - Best for systems that require fast interrupt handling and predictable execution times, for example medical systems or vehicle control.

- Micro-controller (M)-Profile:

  - PMSA using an MPU.
  - T32 instruction set only.
  - For deep embedded systems that require fast interrupt handling with a compact code base and low-power restrictions, e.g., small sensors and smart home products.

The ARM architecture also specifies a number of optional components that can be integrated with it into one integrated circuit, for example

- An Interrupt Controller which is responsible for presenting interrupts to the processor.
- A System Memory Management Unit which controls processor access to all memory locations.
- A Generic Timer to allow all processors in a system to reference a single clock.
- An Advanced Microcontroller Bus Architecture which specifies the bus protocols used for connecting the different components in a system.

There are numerous implementations and variations of any one architecture. At present there are over 40 processor models implementing the ARMv8 architecture, many of which can switch between the AArch32 and AArch64 instruction set states. It is also the case that various devices implement multiple architectures. For example, a mobile phone may implement different ARM architectures to serve as a CPU, a GPU (Graphics Processing Unit), a network controller and as microcontrollers for other interfaces.

8.2.3 ARM security modes

The ARM architecture offers several security modes. As discussed in Chapter 7 the privileged mode allows for unrestricted access to memory resources, whereas the unprivileged mode places restrictions on the instruction set and access to system resources. The available modes are listed in Table 8.1. Not all modes are available depending on the microarchitecture implementation profile.

Mode	Description
User	unprivileged, restricted access to system resources.
FIQ	privileged, Fast Interrupt reQuest.
IRQ	privileged, Interrupt ReQuest.
Supervisor	privileged, entered from reset.
Monitor	supports the Trustzone security feature. Trustzone is a hardware partitioning of software into secure/non-secure environments [35].
Abort	privileged, entered when data prefetch or abort exceptions occur.
Hypervisor	supports the running of virtual machines.
Undefined	privileged, entered when an undefined instruction exception occurs.
System	privileged, only entered from another privileged mode.
Thread/Handler	privileged modes for use when the processor uses an M-profile architecture.

Table 8.1 ARM processor modes

The processor can switch modes due to external events, exceptions or programmatically. An operating system kernel is typically executed in system mode and user applications execute in user mode. See Section 7.2.2 on system calls for further details.

8.3 Virtual memory (the memory management unit)

The VMMU (Virtual Memory Management Unit) or MMU (Memory Management Unit), see Section 7.3, is responsible for controlling which regions of the available memory devices are accessible by the processor at any one time. It is also responsible for maintaining the attributes of each of those regions of memory. From the perspective of the processor, programmer and compiler, all memory locations are virtual. These addresses are intercepted by the MMU which translates them to physical addresses as can be seen in Figure 8.3.

This section looks at some of the different attributes that can be used to define a block of memory and then moves on to describing how these attributes are stored by the MMU. We also describe the typical memory map of an ARMv8 system.

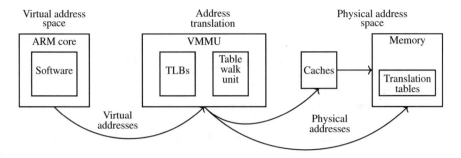

Fig. 8.3 The ARM Virtual Memory Management Unit

8.3.1 Memory attributes

Blocks of addresses are marked within the MMU translation tables as either *normal memory* or *device memory*. Normal memory is most common and describes regions of memory where application and operating system data and code are placed, i.e., what we see as ordinary RAM. There are no side-effects when accessing normal memory. So, the processor implementation may employ techniques to speed up access to these regions. For instance, multiple consecutive accesses may be merged into a single access or data may be prefetched based on previous accesses. Normal memory can also be cached and shared.

Device memory is typically used for physical peripheral devices. For instance, a device address can correspond to a network buffer, where reading a value also removes it from the buffer. Unlike RAM, first writing and then reading from the same device memory address may yield a very different value. Device memory is memory-mapped, cannot be cached, cannot be speculatively accessed and should not contain program instructions.

As shown in Table 8.2, *access permissions* can be allocated to blocks of memory locations according to the current operating mode of the processor. When the processor is executing code in a particular mode the memory can only be accessed according to the flags set. If an instruction attempts to access the memory location outside of the permissions then an exception is generated.

Flag Value	Unprivileged Mode	Privileged Mode
00	No access	Read/write
01	Read/write	Read/write
10	No access	Read only
11	Read only	Read only

Table 8.2 ARM architecture memory access flags

Normally a processor in privileged mode can access resources allocated to a less privileged entity. As shown in Table 8.2, it is always possible for a privileged program to at least read data. However, this may be problematic if applications can trick the operating system into accessing/reading data from protected locations. The ARM architecture can mark memory with a *PAN* (*Privileged Access Never*) flag to prevent this from happening.

It is also possible to mark memory locations with *execution permissions*. The User Execute Never and Privileged Execute Never flags ensure that instructions from that memory location cannot be fetched by programs running in the specified mode.

8.3.2 Memory attributes and the VMMU

Besides the access flags and indicating whether the memory is normal or device, the memory can have a range of other attributes such as such as dirty, cacheable, shared and mapped. It can take up to 8 bits to encode the full attributes of a page of memory. So, the MMU employs a *MAIR* (*Memory Attribute Indirection Register*). The MAIR contains the favoured attributes as a list. It only takes 3 bits to store an index to the list and it is this index that is stored in memory in the translation tables.

The *TLB* (*Translation Look aside Buffer*) holds the results of recent translations and this is consulted first. If no result is found, the *table walk unit* begins looking in the translation tables. The ARM architecture stores data in caches using the physical address. Hence, address translation must occur before a cache lookup can be attempted.

The ARM MMU allows for memory to be divided into pages of either 4 KB, 16 KB or 64 KB. This depends on the specific processor type. The pages or blocks can be further grouped together into sections. These sections have their own access, sharing and execution permissions that override the individual page settings within the group. ARM offers up to four levels of nesting.

If the MMU is disabled then the system can cache all fetched instructions and all addresses have read/write access.

Within the ARM architecture instructions always have little-endianness. The endianness of data accesses is defined by the microarchitecture. Some implementations allow for either big-endian or little-endian data.

8.3.3 The system memory management unit

The MMU of the ARM processor maps the virtual addresses to physical addresses. But in the Raspberry Pi there are other systems that also want to use the memory, such as the graphics processor and the *DMA* (*Direct Memory Access*) system. The direct memory access system can move blocks of data throughout the memory, or it can move blocks to and from input and output devices. It does this independently of the processor and can handle multiple data movements simultaneously.

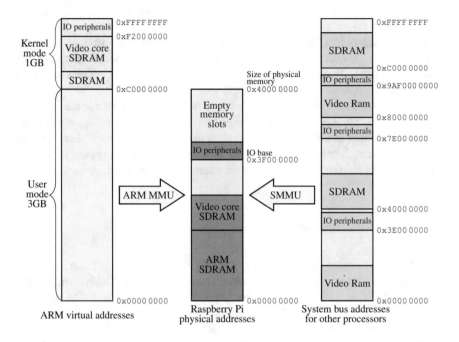

Fig. 8.4 An ARM dual memory map

These other processors need to know which parts of the physical memory they can use. The *SMMU (System Memory Management Unit)* is responsible for mapping the memory requirements of supporting processors to physical memory. For other processor types than ARM, the SMMU is often called the I/O memory management unit. The structure of the memory maps is depicted in Figure 8.4. The virtual addresses of the processor are translated into physical addresses by the MMU. The address requirements of supporting hardware are mapped by the SMMU to physical addresses.

There are various uses of an SMMU. For instance, a graphics processor may only be able to access addresses low in memory. The physical address range available for this graphics processor may be located high in physical memory. The SMMU then translates memory accesses of the graphics card to this high physical address range. Note that the graphics processor is not aware that it uses addresses high in memory. Its virtual view on memory can differ from all other processors on the RPi. They can all 'experience' the graphics RAM at different virtual addresses.

Similarly, a video processor may have multiple blocks of physical RAM to work on, preparing images for multiple screens or preparing one image while the other is displayed. It carries out its operations on one piece of memory, subsequently switches via the SMMU to another, and carries out its next operations there.

Another application is to use more physical memory than a supporting processor can address. Suppose that a DMA processor can only move memory blocks in a small address range, much smaller than physical memory, for instance because its address bus has only a limited number of bits. The SMMU can then map the memory areas that the DMA processor needs to operate on to the required parts of the physical memory. In this way a DMA processor with a limited address range can still be used to operate on the full physical memory.

SMMUs are also used to run operating systems not intended for the hardware structure. The "foreign" operating system may expect, for instance, input/output hardware to occur at different addresses than the actual addresses of these devices. The SMMU can then be configured such that the I/O addresses appear to occur at those places in memory where the foreign operating system assumes they are.

8.4 The ARM instruction set

This section discusses the programmer's model of the ARM using the A32 (32-bit) instruction set, which is the A-profile implementation of the ARMv8 architecture (ARMv8-A). This ARM processor also supports the Thumb instruction set where instructions are either 16 or 32 bits. There is also a 64-bit instruction set for ARM processors. Neither the Thumb nor the 64-bit instruction sets are discussed here.

The ARM architecture follows a *SSEM* (*Simple Sequential Execution Model*). This means that from a programmer's perspective the instructions are executed one at a time and in the order in which they appear in memory. The processor, however, employs pipelining, out-of-order execution and branch prediction. This is in general of no relevance to the programmer unless writing parallel programs.

The instruction set is structured such that all operations can only be performed on values in registers. This means that values first have to be loaded into registers in order to be manipulated. It is not possible to perform such operations on memory locations directly. The only way to change memory is to store the contents of the registers in memory.

There are 16 general registers and one status register available to the programmer in user mode. The general registers are referred to by R_0 until R_{15}. There are two of these registers with a special status, namely register R_{14}, the *link register* and R_{15}, the *program counter*. The last one is comparable to the instruction pointer of the simple processor. The program counter contains the address of the instruction two instructions beyond the instruction that is to be executed next. The link register is used to store return addresses for subroutine calls. All other registers have an equal status. The PCSAA (Procedure Call Standard for the ARM Architecture) convention is commonly used to assign specific roles to these registers as stated below. The PCSAA is addressed further in Section 8.5.

- Registers R_0 to R_3 are *argument* or *scratch* registers. The PCSAA convention prescribes that they are used for passing parameters to, or returning values from, subroutines. During a subroutine call they can be changed and their content is not guaranteed to be preserved after a call.
- Registers R_4 to R_8, R_{10} and R_{11} are *variable* registers, typically used within subroutines to hold variables. Subroutines must preserve the values of these registers such that it is guaranteed that these registers are not changed when calling a subroutine.
- Register R_9 is the *SB* (*Static Base*) register. This is the global base pointer, often containing the base of the data in memory, although its use varies widely. Sometimes, it is just used as another variable register.
- Register R_{12} is the *IP* (*Intra-Procedure call*) register. It is used by the linker and as such the contents should be considered volatile between function calls.
- Register R_{13} is the *SP* (Stack Pointer).
- Register R_{14} is the *LR* (*Link Register*) that stores return addresses. Whenever a subroutine call is made, the return address is put in the link register. It is then up to the subroutine as to whether this return value should be put on the stack or not. Here the simple processor from Chapter 4 and the ARM processors differ in behaviour as the simple processor puts the return address immediately on the stack.
- Register R_{15} is the *PC* (Program Counter). The program counter can be used as a normal register. This means that indexed addressing using the program counter is possible. This is a feature not found in many other processors.

The status register is called the *APSR* (*Application Program Status Register*). It holds the condition code flags: N (Negative), Z (Zero), C (Carry) and V (oVerflow). These status flags behave exactly as in the simple processor, except that with subtraction the carry bit is inverted in the ARM processor.

There are additional system registers in the ARM processor. These become accessible when the processor goes into a security mode other than user mode. There are a total of 43 registers arranged in overlapping banks. The use of these registers and the other modes are not discussed in this book but more detail can be found in [2, 3].

The ARM instruction set that we consider has instructions that are exactly 32 bits long. The instruction format is provided in Table 8.3. It resembles the instruction set of our simple processor, but it has many differences. An overview of the most important instructions is given in Appendix B. In Table 8.3 R_n, R_d, etc., refer to various registers. The letters S, A, U, etc. are bits that can be set to influence the execution of the instruction. Note that up to four registers are mentioned in, for instance, the multiply instruction. And in the store-multiple/load-multiple (STM/LDM) instructions any subset of registers can be involved. There are 16 bits available to indicate such subset.

31	30	29	28	27	26	25	24	23	22	21	20	19	18	17	16	15	14	13	12	11	10	9	8	7	6	5	4	3	2	1	0	Instruction type
Cond	0	0	1	Opcode			S	R_n				R_d				Operand2																Data processing
Cond	0	0	0	0	0	0	A	S	R_d				R_n				R_s				1	0	0	1	R_m						Multiply
Cond	0	0	0	0	1	U	A	S	RdHi				RdLo				R_n				1	0	0	1	R_m						Long multiply
Cond	0	0	0	1	0	B	0	0	R_n				R_d				0	0	0	0	1	0	0	1	R_m						Swap
Cond	0	1	1	P	U	B	W	L	R_n				R_d				Offset															Load/store byte/word
Cond	1	0	0	P	U	S	W	L	R_n				Register list																			Load/store registers
Cond	0	0	0	P	U	0	W	L	R_n				R_d				0	0	0	0	1	S	H	1	R_m						Halfword transfer
Cond	0	0	0	P	U	1	W	L	R_n				R_d				Offset1				1	S	H	1	Offset2						Halfword transfer
Cond	1	0	1	L	Offset																											Branch
Cond	1	1	0	P	U	N	W	L	R_n				CRd				CPNum				Offset										Coproc. data transfer
Cond	1	1	1	0	Op1				CRn				CRd				CPNum				Op2			0	CRm						Coproc. data operation
Cond	1	1	1	0	Op1			L	CRn				R_d				CPNum				Op2			1	CRm						Coproc. register transfer
Cond	1	1	1	1	SWI number																											Software interrupt
Cond	0	0	0	1	0	0	1	0	1	1	1	1	1	1	1	1	1	1	1	1	1	1	0	0	0	1	R_n					Branch and exchange
Cond	0	1	1																						1						Undefined

Table 8.3 The 32-bit ARM instruction format

8.4.1 Instruction groups

The instructions can be divided in four main categories. The first one contains the instructions to move data to and from registers. The second category comprises the logic operations that can be performed on the register values. The third contains the branches, including the branches to subroutines. Finally, there are various miscellaneous instructions of which we only describe a subset.

8.4.1.1 Moving data to and from registers

The instructions to move a single byte/halfword or word to and from memory, as well as between registers, are as follows:

LDR	Instruction for loading a register with a value from memory.
STR	Instruction for storing a value in a register to memory.
MOV	Instruction to load a register with an immediate value or with a value from another register.
MVN	Instruction to load a register with the complement of an immediate or a register value.

The move register instruction MOV can be used to load a value into a register. This value is part of the 32-bit instruction. There are only 12 bits available in the instruction to represent the value. Hence, only a limited range of values can be loaded directly and as it uses the barrel shifter, which we explain below, loading a value into a register is a tricky operation. But this is a common operation and therefore the assembler provides a workaround. It allows for the writing of

$$\text{LDR } R_i, = v;$$

for any 32-bit value v. This pseudo instruction is then translated into one machine code instruction, possibly using one extra word to store v, with the effect that the value v is loaded into register R_i.

The MVN instruction loads a value while inverting all the bits, which is equivalent to applying an xor operation with 0xFFFF FFFF. A number of logic operations also have such a variant.

The ARM processor has remarkable instructions to store or load the contents of any subset of registers. The subset of the registers is indicated by 16 bits in a so-called register list, see Table 8.3. Whenever a bit corresponding to the register is set, that register is also loaded or stored by this instruction. The register values are stored/loaded at subsequent addresses in memory, where the base address is again indicated by a register. For this there are the following instructions:

LDM   Load a subset of all registers from memory.

STM   Store the indicated subset of registers in memory.

There are various uses of these instructions. For instance, when entering a subroutine all registers that are used can be stored on the stack in one instruction. They can also be popped from the stack, including the program counter, saving a separate return from subroutine instruction. Another application is to move blocks of data from one place in memory to another. For instance, the registers $R_0, \ldots, R_8, R_{10}, R_{11}$ can be loaded using one instruction, and with one more instruction they can all be saved at another place in memory. In theory the other registers can also be used for this data transfer, but as they have dedicated purposes, such as the program counter, they may not be available.

There are more advanced loading/storing instructions, such as LDREX (load exclusive) and STREX (store exclusive). After a load exclusive instruction, the accessed memory location is tagged as exclusive to that processor. This memory location cannot be written by any other processor until a STREX instruction is issued on that location by the owning processor. If a processor executes a STREX instruction on an address that is already owned no data is written to memory and, by way of a return value, it is indicated that the attempted store has failed. These instructions are crucial to implementing semaphores and mutex variables, which are both essential for parallel processing and sharing data resources in a multiprocessor system.

The instruction CLREX can be used to clear any exclusive ownership of a memory address by the processor. This is especially used to let exclusive ownership work between various threads running on the same processor. Whenever a context switch occurs, CLREX is used to clear the exclusive ownership of the processor, as any other thread running subsequently on the processor can access this exclussive address. If a thread is allowed to continue its run on the processor, it must reacquire exclusive access to the memory address.

In Appendix B an overview is given of all instructions with more details about their shape. There are instructions to move information between the program status register and normal registers. These can be useful for system programming, but we ignore them here.

8.4.1.2 Logic, arithmetic and compare instructions

There are a limited number of operations that can be carried out on registers. These are given below. Most of these instructions calculate a result on one or two registers and store it in a third register. The comparison instructions TST, TEQ, CMP and CMN do not change any register, except the status register. The MUL instruction multiplies values.

ADD	Instruction to add two register values.
ADC	Instruction to add two registers and the carry bit.
SUB	Instruction to subtract two registers.
SBC	Instruction to subtract two registers with a carry.
RSB	Reverse subtract.
RSC	Reverse subtract with carry.
AND	Instruction to apply the logic bitwise *and* operation.
BIC	The bit clear instruction, which applies a bitwise *and* with the bitwise complement of the second argument.
ORR	The bitwise *or* instruction.
ORN	The bitwise *or* operation with the one bit complements of the second argument.
EOR	The bitwise exclusive or operation.
TST	Apply the *and* operation and update the status flags. Do not store the result.
TEQ	Apply the *xor* operation and update the status flags. Result is not stored.
CMP	Apply a subtraction and set the status flags. Do not store the result.
CMN	Apply an addition and set the status flags. Do not store the result.
MUL	Apply a multiplication.

The ARM architecture does not provide other operations. In particular it does not have a built-in divide instruction, except for one variant of the ARM processor. This means that division has to be implemented in software when we want to use it on the Raspberry Pi.

8.4.1.3 Branching and branch to subroutines

The branch instruction is very simple in ARM. There is essentially only one instruction

B continuation;

meaning that the program must continue at the assembly instruction that is labelled with 'continuation'. In the section on conditional execution (Section 8.4.2), it is indicated that the execution of most instructions can be made dependent on the settings of the flags. This also applies to the branch instruction, allowing for conditional branches.

As the program counter PC is stored in the register R_{15}, standard move instructions can also be used to perform a jump. For instance the instruction

$$\text{MOV } PC, R_0;$$

moves the content of R_0 to PC and hence jumps to the address stored in register R_0.

Subroutines are implemented using the branch link instruction BL. This instruction carries out the jump and puts the address of the next instruction in the link register LR or R_{14}. Only if it is necessary the content of the link register needs to be moved to the stack, for instance if the called subroutine calls another subroutine. Most subroutines start by saving the contents of some registers on the stack. This can be done using the store-multiple instruction, which can store the content of the link register in the same command.

Returning from a subroutine requires the return address to be copied from the link register to the program counter. This can conveniently be done using a move:

$$\text{MOV } PC, LR;$$

When the content of the link register is stored on the stack, restoring the program counter can also be done using a single load-multiple instruction using PC instead of LR as the destination, while at the same time restoring other registers. This means that the ARM does not require a separate return from subroutine instruction, e.g. RTS.

There are two other branch instructions, namely BX, branch with exchange, and BLX, branch with link and exchange. These branch instructions jump to another address and optionally change the instruction set to ARM or Thumb. This allows code written in one instruction set to employ subroutines written in another. For instance, the instruction BX LR moves the content of the LR register to the PC and selects the instruction set based on the least significant bit in LR. This effectively is a return from subroutine, resetting the execution mode back to ARM or Thumb in conformance with the code of the caller. As such this is an even better form of a return than MOV PC, LR. The instruction BLX is the same as BX, except that it also moves the address of the next instruction to be executed to the LR register.

Some ARM processors also supported Java bytecode, which is executed in hardware if the processor is in Jazelle mode. For this purpose there is a special branch instruction BXJ that switches the processor to Java bytecode mode while jumping to a subroutine.

8.4.1.4 Miscellaneous instructions

There are various other instructions of which we describe the most important ones here. The first one is the software interrupt instruction SWI n where n is a 24-bit number. A software interrupt is generally used for system calls. It generates an interrupt causing the processor to go to supervisor mode. This is generally under the control of the operating system. The operating system handles the call, which may require special access to input or output ports, or to specific ranges of memory to which the user process does not have access. The number in the SWI instruction is ignored by the ARM processor, but it can be retrieved by the operating system as an indication of the kind of call that is made. The meaning of this number is therefore defined by the operating system.

Any ARM processor can be provided with optional functionality in the form of co-processors which are then packaged with the processor on the chip. These co-processors provide additional functionality such as floating-point instructions, hardware based debugging facilities, cryptographic instructions and memory management. The MMU is typically a co-processor. The ARM processor has special instructions to cooperate with co-processors.

For parallel and pipeline processing there are *barrier instructions* to prevent re-ordering of instructions. There are atomic swap instructions, which can atomically exchange data in memory with a register. There are instructions to set certain groups of bits in registers and to count how many zeros there are. As these instructions are all less commonly used, we do not explain them here but refer instead to an ARM instruction reference manual [3].

8.4.2 Setting flags and conditional execution

This section deals with the flags in the ARM processor which are used in a very elegant and systematic way in instructions. Essentially there are four flags, exactly the same as for our simple processor: the negative flag N, the zero flag Z, the carry flag C and the overflow flag V.

The meaning is exactly the same, namely N contains the most significant bit of the result of an operation. Z is set if the result is zero. C contains the carry of the result and V indicates whether there was an overflow in the result. There is only one difference, namely with subtraction where the carry flag of the ARM is complemented. This does not happen in the simple processor.

Most instructions do not set the flags by default. This only happens when the letter S is added to the instruction. So, ADD R_0 R_1 does not set the flags and ADDS R_0 R_1 does. The instructions for which the goal is to set the flags, namely CMP, CMN, TST and TEQ, set S by default. So, CMP and CMPS are the same instruction.

Almost all instructions can be conditionally executed depending on the flags. By adding one of the extensions in Table 8.4 to the instruction, the instruction is only executed if the condition in the second column holds. Note that the extensions have been designed such that not only can all flags be tested but also all comparison operations on both signed (two's complement) and unsigned numbers are available. As an example, BEQ means branch if $Z = 1$. And ADDLT means that the addition is only carried out if $N \neq V$.

The extension AL can be added to an instruction to indicate that the instruction must always be executed. But this is equivalent to adding no extension at all. So, ADD and ADDAL both mean add always, while B and BAL both mean jump always.

Suffix	APSR flags	Description
EQ	$Z = 1$	Equal
NE	$Z = 0$	Not equal
CS or HS	$C = 1$	Carry set or unsigned higher or same $\geq$
CC or LO	$C = 0$	Carry clear or unsigned lower $>$
MI	$N = 1$	Negative
PL	$N = 0$	Positive or zero
VS	$V = 1$	Overflow
VC	$V = 0$	No overflow
HI	$C = 1$ and $Z = 0$	Unsigned higher $>$
LS	$C = 0$ or $Z = 1$	Unsigned lower or same $\leq$
GE	$N = V$	Signed $\geq$
LT	$N \neq V$	Signed $<$
GT	$Z = 0$ and $N = V$	Signed $>$
LE	$Z = 1$ or $N \neq V$	Signed $\leq$
AL	Any	Always (suffix normally omitted)

Table 8.4 ARM condition code suffixes

It is very useful that almost all instructions can be conditionally executed, as it can save code and make execution faster. Consider for instance the program

if $x = 0$ **then** $y := y + 1$ **else** $z := z + 2$ **endif**.

If x, y and z are stored in registers R_0, R_1 and R_2, respectively, this can be translated into

```
TST   R0              ; Set the flags in accordance with x.
ADDEQ R1, R1, 1       ; Variable y is incremented if x = 0.
ADDNE R2, R2, 2       ; Variable z is incremented by 2 if x ≠ 0.
```

Observe that this only requires three instructions, which is less than if two explicit jump instructions had to be added. Moreover, as the code does not have any branch instructions, it is easier, and therefore faster, to execute due to the pipelining of the ARM processor.

As an example an arbitrary code fragment showing how the various suffixes can be combined is provided below.

```
CMP    R0, R1        ; Update the APSR flags based on R0-R1.
MOVS   R0, R1        ; Copy contents of R1 to R0 and update the flags.
ADD    R0, R1, R2    ; R0 := R1 + R2 but do not update the flags.
ADDS   R0, R1, R2    ; R0 := R1 + R2 and update the flags.
ADDSCS R0, R1, R2    ; If the carry flag is set then R0 := R1 + R2,
                     ; and update the APSR flags.
```

8.4.3 Arguments and addressing modes

In the previous section, we mentioned the categories of instructions. Here we explain the arguments that instructions can have.

8.4.3.1 Logic instructions and the use of the barrel shifter

We start out with the logic/arithmetic and test instructions as well as the instructions for moving content between registers. Below we use the instructions ADD, CMP and MOV to represent these three categories. They have the general shape

ADD R_d, R_n, *operand* ; $R_d := R_n + operand$.
CMP R_n, *operand*   ; Set the flags based on the calculation $R_n - operand$.
MOV R_d, *operand*   ; $R_d := operand$.

Note that contrary to the simple processor the target register R_d is not automatically also an argument the arithmetic or logic operation.

The operand *operand* can either be an 8-bit value or the content of a register R_m where both can be shifted using a *barrel shifter*. The *barrel shifter* can shift or rotate the input word a number of positions to the left or the right. In Figure 8.5 the position of the barrel shifter just before the ALU is shown. Being positioned in this way, the shift can be performed in the same clock cycle as the ALU operation, which means that the shifts do not take additional computation time.

There are essentially two forms that the shift operation can have. First, it can be an 8-bit constant rotated a specified number of positions to the right or left. Secondly, it can be a register R_m shifted by either a constant number of positions or by the least significant bits of another register R_s.

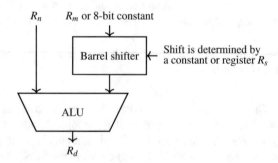

Fig. 8.5 The ARM barrel shifter

In the first situation an 8-bit constant can be rotated $2n$ positions to the right where n is a 4-bit number. This is because in a logic instruction only 12 bits are available to determine this constant. Rotation means that the least significant bit becomes the most significant bit. This type of shift is called *ROR* (*ROtate Right*) or *ROL* (*ROtate Left*). Therefore, numbers can be rotated 0, 2, 4 up to 30 positions. Shifting by an odd number is not possible. The number 101376 is represented by 01100011 (=99) rotated 22 positions to the right, which is equivalent to multiplying by $2^{32-2*11}$. This is depicted below.

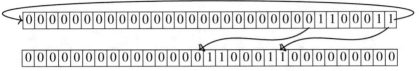

Rotate 11*2 positions to the right (ROR).

Note that only the numbers for which the 1's fit within a byte can be represented this way. The smallest number that cannot be represented is 257. In fact at most 4096 out of the 4 billion 32-bit numbers can be represented in a single instruction.

The assembler checks whether a value can be represented by a rotated 8-bit constant and generates the necessary machine code instruction. Therefore, instructions can use an explicit constant as shown below.

ADD R_d, R_n #101376 ; $R_d := R_n + 101376$.
CMP R_n, #101376   ; Set the flags based on the calculation $R_n - 101376$.
MOV R_d, #101376   ; $R_d := 101376$.

Recall that as it is inconvenient that not every value can be loaded directly into a register, the assembler supports the pseudo instruction LDR R, $= v$ for any value v, which is translated into one or more instructions with the effect that the value v is loaded into register R.

In the second form the barrel shifter is applied to a register R_m. But now there are five different types of shifts and rotations that can be applied. The first one is ROR (ROtate Right) as explained above. In this case the constant is a 5-bit number, which means that all 32 rotations are possible, in particular the number can also be rotated an odd number of positions to the right.

The other four forms are *LSL* (*Logical Shift Left*), *LSR* (*Logical Shift Right*), *ASR* (*Arithmetic Shift Right*) and *RRX* (*Rotate Right eXtended*). These shifts and rotations are best explained graphically, see Figure 8.6. The logical shifts inserts zeros at the empty spots. The arithmetic shift right extends the new number with the most significant bit. This implements divide by 2^n for two's complement numbers using sign extension. LSR implements divide by 2^n for unsigned numbers. The rotate rights use the least significant bit as the new most significant digit, whereas RRX extends the rotation through the carry flag.

We illustrate the use of the shift and rotations by the following examples.

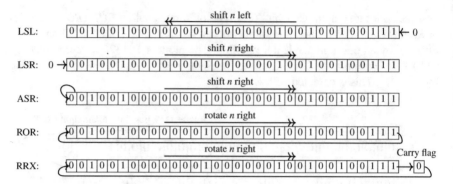

Fig. 8.6 Graphical depiction of various shift operations

ADD $R_d, R_n, R_m,$ LSL #2 ; $R_d := R_n + R_m * 2^2$.
CMP $R_n, R_m,$ RRX R_s ; Set the flags based on the calculation $R_n - v$ where v
                                           ; is the value in R_m rotated n positions right through
                                           ; the carry where n is determined by the least
                                           ; significant bits of R_s.
MOV $R_d, R_m,$ ASR #5   ; $R_d := R_m / 2^5$ where R_m contains a signed number.

8.4.3.2 Loads and stores of a single register

The ARM processor supports essentially one addressing mode for store (STR) and load (LDR) operations, which is register indirect with an index. It has the following form:

LDR $R_d,$ [$R_n, \#offset$] ; $R_d := RAM[R_n + offset]$.
STR $R_d,$ [$R_n, \#offset$]   ; $RAM[R_n + offset] := R_d$.

The offset can either be a number or another register. If the offset is a number it consists of 12 bits and can either be positive or negative. Examples are

LDR $R_d,$ [$R_n, \#2$]   ; $R_d := RAM[R_n + 2]$.
STR $R_d,$ [$R_n, -\#15$] ; $RAM[R_n - 15] := R_d$.

If the offset is a register it can be subtracted or added. Moreover, it can be shifted any constant number of positions using any of the shift and rotations (LSL, LSR, ASR, ROR and RRX) as explained above. Shifting using a register is not possible. Note that the value in the register R_n is first indexed and shifted before it is used as an address. Therefore, this is called *pre-indexed addressing*. Two typical examples are

LDR $R_d,$ [$R_n, R_m,$ LSL #2]   ; $R_d := RAM[R_n + R_m * 2^2]$.
STR $R_d,$ [$R_n, -R_m,$ ASR #15] ; $RAM[R_n - R_m / 2^{15}] := R_d$.

The ARM instruction set provides the option of storing the calculated address back in the register R_n. This is useful, for instance, when storing the contents of a register on the stack and incrementing the stack pointer at the same time. This is called *pre-indexed auto-increment/decrement addressing*. It is activated by putting an exclamation mark at the end of the instruction.

It is also possible to specify that register R_n must be updated after its content is used as an address. This is called *post-indexed auto-increment/decrement addressing*. In this case the change of register R_n is written after the square brackets. As post-indexed addressing is only useful if the answer is stored in the register, it is not necessary to use the exclamation mark.

The first two examples below illustrate pre-increment auto-addressing, and the last two show post-decrement auto-indexing:

$$\text{LDR } R_d, [R_n, \#2]! \qquad ; R_d := \text{RAM}[R_n+2],$$
$$; R_n := R_n+2.$$
$$\text{STR } R_d, [R_n, R_m, \text{LSL } \#2]! \quad ; \text{RAM}[R_n+R_m*2^2] := R_d,$$
$$; R_n := R_n+R_m*2^2.$$
$$\text{STR } R_d, [R_n], -\#15 \qquad ; \text{RAM}[R_n] := R_d,$$
$$; R_n := R_n-15.$$
$$\text{LDR } R_d, [R_n], -R_m, \text{ASR } \#15 ; R_d := \text{RAM}[R_n],$$
$$; R_n := R_n-R_m/2^{15}.$$

8.4.3.3 Loads and stores for multiple registers

The STM and LDM instructions are used to store multiple registers to or load them from memory, respectively. These instructions use one register, called the base register, to indicate the address where the registers must be stored or fetched. This address must be at a word boundary. All registers, except the program counter, can be base registers. The registers that are to be moved are denoted using a set-like notation. E.g., $\{R_0, R_1, R_8\text{-}R_{12}\}$ represents the set containing seven registers, namely R_0, R_1 and R_8 up to R_{12}.

The registers are consecutively stored in a block in memory with the lowest numbered register at the lowest address. The base register can either point to the lowest address of the block, indicated by adding the letter A (ascending) or the highest address, denoted by the letter D (descending). These letters are attached to the STM and LDM instructions. Actually, the base register can also point to one word below or one word above this block, which is explained below.

The STM and LDM are often used to store registers on a stack. Let us assume that the stack grows down in memory. The stack pointer can point to the occupied top of the stack or to the first empty place beyond the top of the stack. These are indicated, respectively, with the letters F (full) or E (empty). If the stack is full, the stack pointer must first be decremented before storing the first register. In the same way, when using the empty scheme, the stack pointer must first be decremented before loading the first register from memory. This scheme works with all base registers.

As an alternative syntax to using ED, FD, EA or FA as an extension to the STM or LDM instructions, one of IB, IA, DB and DA can be used. In this case I stands for incrementing and D for decrementing. B stands for before, and A stands for after. The extension IA is the default. So, LDM becomes LDMIA.

After storing registers on the stack or removing them, it is necessary that the stack pointer is modified. An exclamation mark behind the base register in an LDM or STM instruction indicates that the adapted value of the base register is written back in the base register. This means that after executing the instruction the base register will point to the last, or one word beyond the last, stored register, depending on whether the full or empty scheme is being used. It is unwise to put the base register in the set of registers to be stored or loaded as the behaviour of the LDM and STM instructions is then undefined.

Some examples are provided below, to illustrate the use of STM and LDM.

LDMIA R_{10} {R_0-R_9}   ; Load the block of memory at
                                                        ; RAM[$R_{10}, \ldots, R_{10}+4*9$] into R_0 up till R_9.
STMIB R_{11} {R_0-R_9}   ; Store registers R_0 up till and including R_9 to
                                                        ; RAM[$R_{11}+4, \ldots, R_{11}+4*10$].
STMFA $SP!$, {R_0-R_2, R_4-R_7, LR} ; Push $R_0, R_1, R_2, R_4, R_5, R_6, R_7$ and the link
                                                        ; register onto an ascending 'full' stack and
                                                        ; adapt the stack pointer.
LDMFA $SP!$, {R_0-R_4, R_4-R_7, PC} ; Pull the registers from an ascending stack,
                                                        ; return from subroutine by setting the PC.

As the store-multiple and load-multiple instructions are often used for the stack, there are dedicated instructions PUSH and PULL. PUSH abbreviates STMDB $SP!$ and PULL stands for LDMIA $SP!$. This means that the default stack grows down and the stack pointer points to the first *full* position. Two examples are as follows:

PUSH {R_0-R_{11}, LR} ; Push all registers available to the program onto the
                                    ; stack and save the return address.
PULL {R_0-R_{11}, PC} ; Pull all registers from the stack and return from subroutine.

Exercise 8.4.1. Explain why in the instruction ADD R_d R_n #v less than 2^{12} different values can be generated for v by 8 bits rotated right using 4 bits.

Exercise 8.4.2. How many logic gates are necessary to implement a one-bit shift-left instruction for one 32-bit register? And how many are required to implement a shift register that can either shift one bit to the left or one bit to the right?

Exercise 8.4.3. The pseudo instruction LDR R_i, 0xFFFF FFFF can be translated to one real instruction. Which one?

Exercise 8.4.4. The pseudo instruction LDR R_i, = v can load any value. One possible translation uses pre-indexing relative to the program counter where the value v is stored in the program less than 4096 bytes away. Give assembly instructions that can achieve this. Note that the program counter points 3 instructions beyond the current instruction.

Exercise 8.4.5. Is it a serious restriction that the program counter cannot be used as the base register in an LDM or STM instruction? Would it be a serious restriction if it could not be used in the set of registers to be moved in these instructions?

8.5 The ARM calling convention

In order to align how functions are called and parameters are passed/returned the PCSAA (Procedure Call Standard for the ARM Architecture) has been defined.

The PCSAA states that parameters and return values are typically passed in registers R_0-R_3. When additional arguments are used these should be passed on the stack. Moreover, it states that registers R_4-R_{11} are unchanged when the subroutine returns. This guarantees that when calling a subroutine, these registers do not have to be saved.

On entry to the subroutine any variable registers $R_4, \ldots, R_{11}$ that will be used within the routine are pushed onto the stack. If the subroutine calls other subroutines, the link register LR must also be saved on the stack.

Prior to exiting the subroutine the return values are placed in R_0 to R_3 and the variable register values are restored from the stack. This can include pulling the program counter to return to the invoking program. If the program counter is still in the LR register, a return from subroutine can also be obtained by a MOV PC, LR instruction. If instruction sets must be switched then the instruction BX LR can be used, which causes the processor to jump to the address in the LR register, and which puts the processor in either Thumb or ARM-32 mode.

Below we provide an example of a call to an ARM assembly subroutine. The routine receives two pairs of x and y-coordinates and calculates an approximation of the Euclidean distance between them as a natural number. The coordinates are provided as signed numbers. The subroutine in a higher-level language can be formulated as

> **function nat** *distance*(**int** x_1, **int** y_1, **int** x_2, **int** y_2)
> **return** $\sqrt{(x_2 - x_1)^2 + (y_2 - y_1)^2}$;
> **end**;

According to the standard, the parameters are passed in registers R_0 up to and including R_3. The result is transferred back via R_0. No parameters are passed using the stack.

```
MOV R0, ... ; Prepare parameter x1.
MOV R1, ... ; Prepare parameter y1.
MOV R2, ... ; Prepare parameter x2.
MOV R3, ... ; Prepare parameter y2.
BL distance ; Call the function distance.
    ...         ; Register R0 now contains the calculated Euclidean distance.
    ...         ; The registers R1, R2 and R3 can have arbitrary values.
    ...         ; The registers R4-R11 are the same as before the call to distance.
```

A typical ARM assembly function starts with a label, which should describe its function. It is a good habit to describe the task and the input/output of each subroutine precisely at the beginning of each subroutine. Indicate also the registers that are unchanged. The subroutine for the Euclidian distance could look as follows:

; This subroutine calculates the integer Euclidean distance between points (x_1, y_1)
; and (x_2, y_2). The parameters x_1, y_1, x_2 and y_2 are passed in registers R_0, R_1, R_2
; and R_3, respectively. The result is returned via register R_0.
; The registers R_4-R_{11} are untouched.

```
distance: STMFD SP!, {LR}        ; Push LR on the stack. There are no other
                                 ; registers to be saved as this subroutine
                                 ; only uses registers R0-R3.
          SUB R0, R0, R2         ; R0 := x1 − x2.
          SUB R1, R1, R3         ; R1 := y1 − y2.
          MUL R0, R0, R0         ; R0 := (x1 − x2)^2.
          MUL R1, R1, R1         ; R1 := (y1 − y2)^2.
          ADD R0, R0, R1         ; R0 := (x1 − x2)^2 + (y1 − y2)^2.
          BL integer_square_root ; Call the integer square root library routine.
                                 ; The parameter and the result are passed in
                                 ; register R0.
          LDMFD SP!, {PC}        ; Return from subroutine.
```

Exercise 8.5.1. Would the instruction LDR PC, $[SP, -\#4]$! be a proper alternative for a return from the subroutine *distance*?

Exercise 8.5.2. Can the code of the subroutine *distance* be optimised by removing the STMFD instruction at the beginning, the LDMFD instruction at the end, and replacing BL in the one but last line with B?

8.6 The use of system calls

As discussed in Chapter 7, a system call is implemented by a low-level function that is a core component of an operating system. For programs operating in unprivileged modes that wish to access restricted memory locations, such as hardware device addresses or files, the processor must be placed in a privileged mode. In the ARM architecture this can be achieved by user mode programs executing a software interrupt SWI. All interrupts in the ARM architecture place the processor into a privileged mode.

When an SWI instruction happens, the address of the next instruction to be executed is put in the link register LR, and then the processor switches to privileged mode and calls the software interrupt handler. This handler interrogates the current register values and uses these values to determine which system call to execute. Once the system call has been executed the software interrupt is deemed complete and the processor is placed back to user mode. Execution resumes from the instruction following the software interrupt call, the address of which is in the LR. Should the operating system need to return values to the user program this is done through registers R_0 to R_3. The type of system call can be encoded as a parameter of the SWI instruction, or it can be handed over in a register. This is dependent on the operating system. System calls are very much like normal subroutine calls, except for the security mode switch.

An example of a system call is given below. It is a fragment of a program to put some text on the screen and subsequently stop execution. Register R_7 contains the type of the call, in this case 4 to put text on the screen. In register R_0 the output device is provided. Register R_2 provides the length of the string and R_1 contains a pointer to the beginning of the string.

MOV R_7, #4	; The value 4 is the code to display text.
MOV R_0, #1	; The value 1 indicates that the text must appear
	; on the monitor.
MOV R_2, #19	; The length of the text is 19 characters.
LDR R_1,=*message*	; The address of the string to be printed.
SWI 0	; Execute the software interrupt to print the text.
MOV R_7, #1	; The value 1 indicates the system call to halt
	; the program.
SWI 0	; Execute the software interrupt to halt the
	; program.

.data	; The data section of the program.
message:	
.ascii "Hello lovely world\n"	; The text to be printed.

Exercise 8.6.1. The ARM processor does not do anything with the number n in the instruction SWI n when this instruction is executed. But a software interrupt handler may need to know this number to determine what to do. Write the initial instructions for an interrupt handler that retrieves this number and puts it in register R_4.

8.7 Summary

In this chapter we gave an overview of the Raspberry Pi, and the ARM processor. We also gave an overview of the structure of the MMU (Memory Management Unit) and the SMMU (System Memory Management Unit). The ARM A32 instruction set was described together with the PCSAA (Procedure Call Standard for the ARM Architecture).

Appendix A
An extended instruction set for the simple processor

This appendix contains the instruction set of the simple processor, except that it now has eight registers and it allows for indexed addressing. It also has a multiply and a divide instruction and allows for conditional branches depending on signed number comparisons. The purpose of these extensions is to ease assembly programming for the simple processor.

Registers and condition codes.

Registers: $IP, R_0, R_1, R_2, R_3, R_4, R_5, R_6, R_7$.
Aliases: $GB = R_6, SP = R_7$.
Flags Z: The result of the last binary operation equals 0.
N: The result of the last binary operation is negative.
C: The last addition, subtraction or compare generated a carry-out.
V: The result of the last binary operation is not representable as a two's complement number.

Syntactical categories used in instructions.

Operand Shape		Description
val	A positive or negative number	An immediate value.
disp	A positive or negative number	A relative displacement.
operand	*val*	Immediate value.
	R_i	Register.
	$[R_i + val]$	Register indexed.
	$[R_i + R_j]$	Register register indexed.
	$[R_i{+}{+}]$	Register, post-increment.
	$[{-}{-}R_i]$	Register, pre-decrement.

J. F. Groote et al., *Logic Gates, Circuits, Processors, Compilers and Computers*, https://doi.org/10.1007/978-3-030-68553-9

Binary instructions.

Instruction	Effect	Condition codes set
LOAD R_i operand	$R_i \leftarrow$ operand	Z,N
STOR R_i operand	operand $\leftarrow R_i$	Z,N
ADD R_i operand	$R_i \leftarrow R_i +$ operand	Z,N,C,V
SUB R_i operand	$R_i \leftarrow R_i -$ operand	Z,N,C,V
CMP R_i operand	calculate $R_i -$ operand	Z,N,C,V
MUL R_i operand	$R_i \leftarrow R_i *$ operand	Z,N,C,V
DIV R_i operand	$R_i \leftarrow R_i \div$ operand	Z,N,C,V
MOD R_i operand	$R_i \leftarrow R_i$ mod operand	Z,N,C,V
AND R_i operand	$R_i \leftarrow R_i \wedge$ operand	Z,N
OR R_i operand	$R_i \leftarrow R_i \vee$ operand	Z,N
XOR R_i operand	$R_i \leftarrow R_i \oplus$ operand	Z,N

Branches and returns.

Instruction	Effect
BRA disp	$IP \leftarrow IP + disp$
BRS R_i disp	$RAM[R_i-1], IP, R_i \leftarrow IP, IP + disp, R_i - 1$
RTS R_i	$IP, R_i \leftarrow RAM[R_i], R_i + 1$
BEQ disp	if $Z = 1$ then $IP \leftarrow IP + disp$
BNE disp	if $Z = 0$ then $IP \leftarrow IP + disp$
BCS disp	if $C = 1$ then $IP \leftarrow IP + disp$
BCC disp	if $C = 0$ then $IP \leftarrow IP + disp$
BLS disp	if $Z = 1 \vee C = 1$ then $IP \leftarrow IP + disp$
BHI disp	if $Z = 0 \wedge C = 0$ then $IP \leftarrow IP + disp$
BVC disp	if $V = 0$ then $IP \leftarrow IP + disp$
BVS disp	if $V = 1$ then $IP \leftarrow IP + disp$
BPL disp	if $N = 0$ then $IP \leftarrow IP + disp$
BMI disp	if $N = 1$ then $IP \leftarrow IP + disp$
BLT disp	if $N \neq V$ then $IP \leftarrow IP + disp$
BGE disp	if $N = V$ then $IP \leftarrow IP + disp$
BLE disp	if $N \neq V \vee Z = 1$ then $IP \leftarrow IP + disp$
BGT disp	if $N = V \wedge Z = 0$ then $IP \leftarrow IP + disp$

Pseudo instructions.

Instruction	Equivalent instruction
PULL R_i	LOAD R_i $[SP{+}{+}]$
PUSH R_i	STOR R_i $[{-}{-}SP]$

Appendix B
The ARM 32-bit instruction set

This appendix provides a concise overview of the main instructions of the ARM-32 instruction set. Expressions indicated within curly brackets are optional. E.g., {!} indicates that the exclamation may be added. The bar indicates possible alternatives. IA|IB means that either IA or IB can be chosen.

Registers and condition codes.

Registers: $R_0, R_1, R_2, R_3, R_4, R_5, R_6, R_7, R_8, R_9, R_{10}, R_{11}, R_{12}, R_{13}, R_{14}, R_{15}$.

Aliases: $SB = R_9$ (Static Base), $IP = R_{12}$ (Intra-Procedure call register),
$SP = R_{13}$ (Stack Pointer), $LR = R_{14}$ (Link Register),
$PC = R_{15}$ (Program Counter).

Flags Z: The result of the last binary operation equals 0.
N: The result of the last binary operation is negative.
C: The last addition, subtraction or compare generated a carry-out.
V: The result of the last binary operation is not representable as a two's complement number.

Syntactical categories used in instructions.

Category	Shape	Description
val	A non-negative number	The number may have range constraints.
label	A string	Label is used for relative jumps.
constant_shift	LSL #val	Logical Shift Left.
	LSR #val	Logical Shift Right.
	ASR #val	Arithmetic Shift Right.
	ROR #val	ROtate Right.
	RRX #val	Rotate Right with eXtend.
register_shift	LSL R_s	Logical Shift Left.
	LSR R_s	Logical Shift Right.
	ASR R_s	Arithmetic Shift Right.
	ROR R_s	ROtate Right.
	RRX R_s	Rotate Right with eXtend.

© The Editor(s) (if applicable) and The Author(s), under exclusive license
to Springer Nature Switzerland AG 2021
J. F. Groote et al., *Logic Gates, Circuits, Processors, Compilers and Computers*,
https://doi.org/10.1007/978-3-030-68553-9

Category	Shape	Description
shift	*constant_shift*	Shift by a constant.
	register_shift	Shift by a register value.
operand	#*val*	Immediate values
	R_m, *constant_shift*	Register, optionally shifted by a constant.
	R_m, *register_shift*	Register, optionally shifted by a register.
reglist	{*registers*}	Set notation for registers.
registers	R_i	Single register.
	R_i-R_j	Register range.
	registers, *registers*	Multiple register ranges.

Suffixes. All instructions, with the exception of CMP, CMN, TST and TEQ, can be conditionally executed by adding one of the following suffixes. E.g., the branch instruction B *label* is executed only when $Z = 1$ if it is written as BEQ *label*.

Suffix	Condition for execution	Description
EQ	$Z = 1$	Equal ($=$).
NE	$Z = 0$	Not equal ($\neq$).
CS or HS	$C = 1$	Carry set / unsigned greater or equal ($\geq$).
CC or LO	$C = 0$	Carry clear / unsigned lower ($<$).
MI	$N = 1$	Negative (< 0).
PL	$N = 0$	Positive or zero (≥ 0).
VS	$V = 1$	Overflow.
VC	$V = 0$	No overflow.
HI	$C = 1$ and $Z = 0$	Unsigned higher ($>$).
LS	$C = 0$ or $Z = 1$	Unsigned less or equal ($\leq$).
GE	$N = V$	Signed greater or equal ($\geq$).
LT	$N \neq V$	Signed smaller ($<$).
GT	$Z = 0$ and $N = V$	Signed larger ($>$).
LE	$Z = 1$ or $N \neq V$	Signed less or equal ($\leq$).
AL	Any	Always (suffix generally omitted).

Load, store, move instructions and pseudo instructions.

Instruction	Description
LDR R_i [R_j{,#*val*}]{!}	Load, immediate offset.
LDR R_i [R_j],#*val*	Load, post-indexed, immediate.
LDR R_i [R_j, {$-$}R_k{, *constant_shift*}]	Load, register offset.
LDR R_i [R_j], {$-$}R_k{, *constant_shift*}	Load, post-indexed, register.
STR R_i [R_j{,#*val*}]{!}	Store, immediate offset.
STR R_i [R_j],#*val*	Store, post-indexed, immediate.
STR R_i [R_j, {$-$}R_k{, *constant_shift*}]	Store, register offset.
STR R_i [R_j], {$-$}R_k{, *constant_shift*}	Store, post-indexed, register.
LDM{IA|IB|DA|DB|ED|FD|EA|FA} R_i{!} *reglist*	
	Load-multiple.
STM{IA|IB|DA|DB|ED|FD|EA|FA} R_i{!} *reglist*	
	Store-multiple.

Instruction	Description
MOV{S} R_i *operand*	Move registers.
MVN{S} R_i *operand*	Move registers, negated.
LDR R_i, =*val*	Pseudo instruction. Translation depends on *val*.
PUSH *reglist*	Pseudo instruction for LDMDB *SP*!, *reglist*.
POP *reglist*	Pseudo instruction for LDMIA *SP*!, *reglist*.

Branches. Jumps are also possible by loading a value in the *PC* register directly.

Instruction	Description
B *label*	Simple branch.
BL *label*	Branch and move address of next instruction to *LR*.
BX *label*	Branch and switch instruction set.
BLX *label*	Branch, move address of next instruction to *LR* and switch instruction set.
SWI *val*	Software interrupt.

Logic instructions.

Instruction	Description
ADD{S} R_i R_j *operand*	Instruction to add two registers.
ADC{S} R_i R_j *operand*	Instruction to add two registers and the carry bit.
SUB{S} R_i R_j *operand*	Instruction to subtract two registers.
SBC{S} R_i R_j *operand*	Instruction to subtract two registers with a carry.
RSB{S} R_i R_j *operand*	Instruction to reverse subtract two registers.
RSC{S} R_i R_j *operand*	Instruction to reverse subtract two registers with a carry.
AND{S} R_i R_j *operand*	Instruction to apply the logic bitwise *and* operation.
BIC{S} R_i R_j *operand*	The bit clear instruction, which applies a bitwise *and* with the bitwise complement of the second argument.
ORR{S} R_i R_j *operand*	The bitwise *or* instruction.
ORN{S} R_i R_j *operand*	The bitwise *or* operation on the one-bit complement of the second argument.
EOR{S} R_i R_j *operand*	The bitwise exclusive or operation.
TST R_i *operand*	Apply the *and* operation and update the status flags. Do not store the result.
TEQ R_i *operand*	Apply the *xor* operation and update the status flags. The result is not stored.
CMP R_i *operand*	Apply a subtraction and set the status flags. Do not store the result.
CMN R_i *operand*	Apply an addition and set the status flags. Do not store the result.
MUL{S} R_i R_j R_k	Apply a multiplication.

Appendix C
Syntax of the register transfer language

A register transfer program satisfies the following syntax given by a context free grammar. Terminals are provided in teletype font, e.g., 'Abus' or '!='. A non-terminal, e.g., *Assignment* is written in italics. For a nonterminal X the notation $(X)*$ means that X can occur zero or more times in succession. The notation $(X)?$ means that X is optional. Between the brackets there can be multiple items, as in (, *Assignment*)* which stands for zero or more pairs of a comma followed by an assignment.

RegisterTransferProgram	::= (*RegisterTransfers*)*
BusName	::= Abus | Bbus | Cbus | Dbus | Ebus | Ibus
RegisterName	::= IP | IPB | IR | IR.compl | IR.val | RA | RAB |
	RB | CC | SigmaA | SigmaW | SigmaR |
	RAM[SigmaA] | _
RegisterTransfers	::= *Registers* <- *RegisterExpressions*
Registers	::= *RegisterName* (, *Registers*)*
RegisterExpressions	::= *RegisterExpr* (, *RegisterExpressions*)*
AnnotatedRegister	::= *RegisterName* ((*BusName*))?
RegisterExpr	::= ALU.cc |
	AnnotatedRegister |
	AnnotatedRegister+*AnnotatedRegister* |
	AnnotatedRegister−*AnnotatedRegister* |
	AnnotatedRegister+1 |
	AnnotatedRegister−1 |
	AnnotatedRegister&&*AnnotatedRegister* |
	AnnotatedRegister||*AnnotatedRegister* |
	AnnotatedRegister!=*AnnotatedRegister*

The terminal && represents the bitwise 'and' operator, || stands for the 'or', and != is the xor. Together with addition, subtraction, increment, decrement and pass-through, these represent the operations of the ALU.

A typical register transfer program looks as follows, where the program implements the instruction STOR R_i [R_j]:

J. F. Groote et al., *Logic Gates, Circuits, Processors, Compilers and Computers*,
https://doi.org/10.1007/978-3-030-68553-9

```
SigmaA, IP <- IP(Bbus), IP(Abus)+1
SigmaR <- RAM[SigmaA]
IR <- SigmaR(Bbus)
SigmaA, SigmaW, CC <- RB(Bbus), RA(Abus), ALU.cc
RAM[SigmaA] <- SigmaW
```

Appendix D
Answers to the exercises

This appendix contains short answers for the questions in the main text.

D.1 Answers for Chapter 1

Answer 1.1.1. The two-input multiplexer is written as: $(in_1 \wedge \neg sel) \vee (in_2 \wedge sel)$.

Answer 1.1.2.

in_1	in_2	in_3	out
0	0	0	0
0	0	1	0
0	1	0	0
0	1	1	1
1	0	0	0
1	0	1	1
1	1	0	1
1	1	1	0

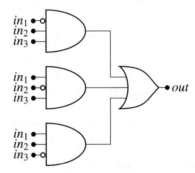

Answer 1.1.3.

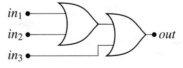

An n input version, using $n-1$ basic gates, can be constructed from a circuit for $n-2$ inputs. Connect an *and/or* gate to the smaller circuit's output and connect the new input to the second input of the gate. Connecting binary gates always yields a full binary tree. Full binary trees have the property that the number of internal nodes (i.e. gates) is one less than the number of leaves (i.e. inputs).

J. F. Groote et al., *Logic Gates, Circuits, Processors, Compilers and Computers*, https://doi.org/10.1007/978-3-030-68553-9

Answer 1.2.1.

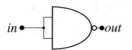   

Answer 1.2.2.

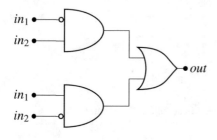   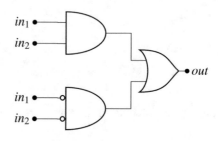

$$in_1 \oplus in_2 = (\neg in_1 \wedge in_2) \vee (in_1 \wedge \neg in_2)\qquad in_1 \leftrightarrow in_2 = (in_1 \wedge in_2) \vee (\neg in_1 \wedge \neg in_2)$$

Answer 1.3.1.

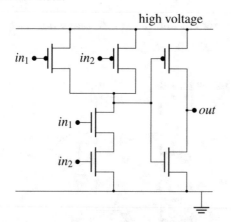   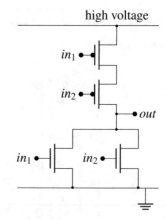

On the left we have an *and* gate constructed by the standard *nand* gate followed by the standard inverter. For reference, on the right we have the standard *nor* gate.

Suppose we replace the pFET at the top of the *nor* gate by an nFET. If we connect the drain of the nFET to high voltage there will be no gate-to-source voltage difference. Similarly, when we connect the source of the nFET to high voltage this will cause the voltage at the source to be at least as high as the voltage at the gate, meaning the transistor will also never be enabled.

Answer 1.3.2. A CMOS buffer gate is just two inverters in sequence. Below, at the left, we have a three input *or* gate. To its right is a CMOS *xor* gate.

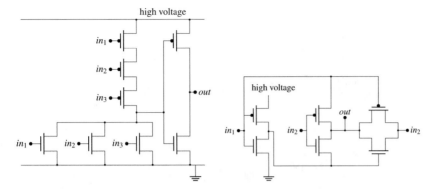

Answer 1.3.3. An output of a gate can safely be connected to multiple inputs as the inputs require a much smaller current than the output of a gate can provide. For this reason it does not damage a gate to connect the output to an input, although the effect may be undefined, for instance by connecting the output of a *not* gate to its input.

Answer 1.3.4.

OE	in	out
0	0	Z
0	1	Z
1	0	0
1	1	1

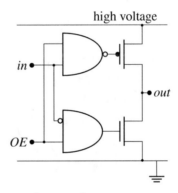

Answer 1.3.5. The gates are a *not* gate, an *and* gate and an *or* gate.

Answer 1.4.1.

$$\neg(in_1 \wedge in_2) \wedge (in_1 \vee in_2)$$
$$\overset{\text{De Morgan}}{=}$$
$$(\neg in_1 \vee \neg in_2) \wedge (in_1 \vee in_2)$$
$$\overset{\text{Distributivity}}{=}$$
$$(\neg in_1 \wedge (in_1 \vee in_2)) \vee (\neg in_2 \wedge (in_1 \vee in_2))$$
$$\overset{\text{Distributivity twice}}{=}$$
$$((\neg in_1 \wedge in_1) \vee (\neg in_1 \wedge in_2)) \vee$$
$$((\neg in_2 \wedge in_1) \vee (\neg in_2 \wedge in_2))$$
$$\overset{\text{Contradiction twice}}{=}$$
$$(0 \vee (\neg in_1 \wedge in_2)) \vee ((\neg in_2 \wedge in_1) \vee 0)$$
$$\overset{\text{Identity element twice}}{=}$$
$$(\neg in_1 \wedge in_2) \vee (\neg in_2 \wedge in_1)$$
$$\overset{\text{Definition of } xor}{=}$$
$$in_1 \oplus in_2$$

Answer 1.4.2.

$$
\begin{array}{ll}
x \vee (\neg x \wedge y) & \text{Distributivity} \\
\stackrel{\text{Distributivity}}{=} & \\
(x \vee \neg x) \wedge (x \vee y) & \text{Excluded middle} \\
\stackrel{\text{Excluded middle}}{=} & \\
1 \wedge (x \vee y) & \text{Identity element} \\
\stackrel{\text{Identity element}}{=} & \\
(x \vee y) &
\end{array}
$$

$$
\begin{array}{ll}
x \wedge (\neg x \vee y) & \text{Distributivity} \\
\stackrel{\text{Distributivity}}{=} & \\
(x \wedge \neg x) \vee (x \wedge y) & \text{Contradiction} \\
\stackrel{\text{Contradiction}}{=} & \\
0 \vee (x \wedge y) & \text{Identity element} \\
\stackrel{\text{Identity element}}{=} & \\
(x \wedge y) &
\end{array}
$$

Answer 1.4.3.

$$
\begin{array}{ll}
(x \oplus y)^D & \stackrel{\text{Def. of } xor}{=} \quad ((\neg x \wedge y) \vee (x \wedge \neg y))^D \\
& \stackrel{\text{Duality}}{=} \quad (\neg x \wedge y)^D \wedge (x \wedge \neg y)^D \\
& \stackrel{\text{Duality twice}}{=} \quad ((\neg x)^D \vee (y)^D) \wedge ((x)^D \vee (\neg y)^D) \\
& \stackrel{\text{Duality}}{=} \quad (\neg x \vee y) \wedge (x \vee \neg y) \\
& \stackrel{\text{Distributivity}}{=} \quad (\neg x \wedge (x \vee \neg y)) \vee (y \wedge (x \vee \neg y)) \\
& \stackrel{\text{Dist. twice}}{=} \quad ((\neg x \wedge x) \vee (\neg x \wedge \neg y)) \vee ((y \wedge x) \vee (y \wedge \neg y)) \\
& \stackrel{\text{Contra. twice}}{=} \quad (0 \vee (\neg x \wedge \neg y)) \vee ((y \wedge x) \vee 0) \\
& \stackrel{\text{Identity twice}}{=} \quad (\neg x \wedge \neg y) \vee (y \wedge x) \\
& \stackrel{\text{Def. of } xnor}{=} \quad x \leftrightarrow y
\end{array}
$$

$$
\begin{array}{ll}
\neg(x \oplus y) & \stackrel{\text{Def. of } xor}{=} \quad \neg((\neg x \wedge y) \vee (x \wedge \neg y)) \\
& \stackrel{\text{De Morgan}}{=} \quad \neg(\neg x \wedge y) \wedge \neg(x \wedge \neg y) \\
& \stackrel{\text{De Morgan twice}}{=} \quad (\neg\neg x \vee \neg y) \wedge (\neg x \vee \neg\neg y) \\
& \stackrel{\text{Double neg. twice}}{=} \quad (x \vee \neg y) \wedge (\neg x \vee y) \\
& \stackrel{\text{Comm., Duality}}{=} \quad ((\neg x \wedge y) \vee (x \wedge \neg y))^D \\
& \stackrel{\text{Just established}}{=} \quad x \leftrightarrow y
\end{array}
$$

Answer 1.4.4.

$x\,y$	$x \wedge y$	$x \vee (x \wedge y)$	$x \vee y$	$x \wedge (x \vee y)$
0 0	0	0	0	0
0 1	0	0	1	0
1 0	0	1	1	1
1 1	1	1	1	1

$x\,y\,z$	$y \vee z$	$x \wedge (y \vee z)$	$x \wedge y$	$x \wedge z$	$(x \wedge y) \vee (x \wedge z)$
0 0 0	0	0	0	0	0
0 0 1	1	0	0	0	0
0 1 0	1	0	0	0	0
0 1 1	1	0	0	0	0
1 0 0	0	0	0	0	0
1 0 1	1	1	0	1	1
1 1 0	1	1	1	0	1
1 1 1	1	1	1	1	1

x y z	$y \wedge z$	$x \vee (y \wedge z)$	$x \vee y$	$x \vee z$	$(x \vee y) \wedge (x \vee z)$
0 0 0	0	0	0	0	0
0 0 1	0	0	0	1	0
0 1 0	0	0	1	0	0
0 1 1	1	1	1	1	1
1 0 0	0	1	1	1	1
1 0 1	0	1	1	1	1
1 1 0	0	1	1	1	1
1 1 1	1	1	1	1	1

Answer 1.5.1.

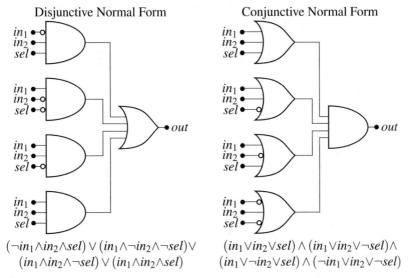

Disjunctive Normal Form

Conjunctive Normal Form

$(\neg in_1 \wedge in_2 \wedge sel) \vee (in_1 \wedge \neg in_2 \wedge \neg sel) \vee$
$(in_1 \wedge in_2 \wedge \neg sel) \vee (in_1 \wedge in_2 \wedge sel)$

$(in_1 \vee in_2 \vee sel) \wedge (in_1 \vee in_2 \vee \neg sel) \wedge$
$(in_1 \vee \neg in_2 \vee sel) \wedge (\neg in_1 \vee in_2 \vee \neg sel)$

Answer 1.5.2. We write $\phi_1 = (\neg in_1 \wedge \neg in_2 \wedge in_3)$, $\phi_2 = (\neg in_1 \wedge in_2 \wedge \neg in_3)$, $\phi_3 = (in_1 \wedge \neg in_2 \wedge \neg in_3)$ and $\phi_4 = (in_1 \wedge in_2 \wedge in_3)$. In the derivation below we use distribution of $\wedge$ over $\vee$ at $(*)$.

$\phi_1 \vee \phi_2 \vee \phi_3 \vee \phi_4 =$
$(\neg in_1 \wedge \neg in_2 \wedge in_3) \vee (\phi_2 \vee \phi_3 \vee \phi_4) \overset{(*)}{=}$
$(\neg in_1 \vee \phi_2 \vee \phi_3 \vee \phi_4) \wedge (\neg in_2 \vee \phi_2 \vee \phi_3 \vee \phi_4) \wedge (in_3 \vee \phi_2 \vee \phi_3 \vee \phi_4).$

We concentrate on the first expression. By absorption $\neg in_1$ subsumes ϕ_2 and therefore ϕ_2 can be left out. At $(**)$ complement absorption is used:

$\neg in_1 \vee \phi_2 \vee \phi_3 \vee \phi_4 =$
$\neg in_1 \vee \phi_3 \vee \phi_4 \overset{(**)}{=}$
$\neg in_1 \vee (\neg in_2 \wedge \neg in_3) \vee (in_2 \wedge in_3) =$
$\neg in_1 \vee ((\neg in_2 \vee in_3) \wedge (in_2 \vee \neg in_3)) =$
$(\neg in_1 \vee \neg in_2 \vee in_3) \wedge (\neg in_1 \vee in_2 \vee \neg in_3).$

In exactly the same way we derive

$$(\neg in_2 \vee \phi_2 \vee \phi_3 \vee \phi_4) = (\neg in_1 \vee \neg in_2 \vee in_3) \wedge (in_1 \vee \neg in_2 \vee \neg in_3)$$
$$(in_3 \vee \phi_2 \vee \phi_3 \vee \phi_4) = (in_1 \vee in_2 \vee in_3) \wedge (\neg in_1 \vee \neg in_2 \vee in_3).$$

Joining these result gives us

$$\phi_1 \vee \phi_2 \vee \phi_3 \vee \phi_4 =$$
$$(in_1 \vee in_2 \vee in_3) \wedge (in_1 \vee \neg in_2 \vee \neg in_3) \wedge (\neg in_1 \vee in_2 \vee \neg in_3) \wedge (\neg in_1 \vee \neg in_2 \vee in_3).$$

Answer 1.6.1.

$a\ b\ c\ d$	$\neg a$	$\neg b$	$\neg a \wedge b \wedge d$	$c \wedge d$	$\neg b \wedge c$	$(\neg a \wedge b \wedge d) \vee (c \wedge d) \vee (\neg b \wedge c)$
0 0 0 0	1	1	0	0	0	0
0 0 0 1	1	1	0	0	0	0
0 0 1 0	1	1	0	1	1	1
0 0 1 1	1	1	0	0	1	1
0 1 0 0	1	0	0	0	0	0
0 1 0 1	1	0	1	0	0	1
0 1 1 0	1	0	0	0	0	0
0 1 1 1	1	0	1	1	0	1
1 0 0 0	0	1	0	0	0	0
1 0 0 1	0	1	0	0	0	0
1 0 1 0	0	1	0	0	1	1
1 0 1 1	0	1	0	1	1	1
1 1 0 0	0	0	0	0	0	0
1 1 0 1	0	0	0	0	0	0
1 1 1 0	0	0	0	0	0	0
1 1 1 1	0	0	0	1	0	1

$c \vee d$	$\neg a \vee c$	$\neg b \vee d$	$b \vee c$	$(\neg a \vee c) \wedge (\neg b \vee d) \wedge (b \vee c)$
0	1	1	0	0
1	1	1	0	0
1	1	1	1	1
1	1	1	1	1
0	1	0	1	0
1	1	1	1	1
1	1	0	1	0
1	1	1	1	1
0	0	1	0	0
1	0	1	0	0
1	1	1	1	1
1	1	1	1	1
0	0	0	1	0
1	0	1	1	0
1	1	0	1	0
1	1	1	1	1

Answer 1.6.2. The maxterm $c \vee d$ is already covered by the maxterms $\neg b \vee d$ and $b \vee c$.

Answer 1.6.3. Consider the input $a = 0$, $b = 1$, $c = 1$, and $d = 1$ for both circuits in Figure 1.18. The disjunctive circuit, $d \vee (\neg b \wedge \neg c)$, outputs 1 while the conjunctive circuit, $\neg c \wedge (b \vee \neg d)$, outputs 0. Therefore, these circuits behave differently on don't care inputs which means they do not define the same boolean function.

Answer 1.6.4.

$$00\ 01\ 11\ 10\ in_1 in_2$$

	0	0	1	0	1
1	1	0	1	0

in_3

The function derived by applying the conjunctive version of the Karnaugh map is the one given in Figure 1.15. Because it is not possible to form larger clusters in the Karnaugh map the derived version is an optimal two-layer circuit for this function.

Answer 1.7.1.

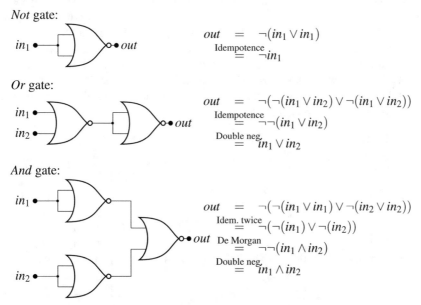

Not gate:

$$out = \neg(in_1 \vee in_1)$$
$$\overset{\text{Idempotence}}{=} \neg in_1$$

Or gate:

$$out = \neg(\neg(in_1 \vee in_2) \vee \neg(in_1 \vee in_2))$$
$$\overset{\text{Idempotence}}{=} \neg\neg(in_1 \vee in_2)$$
$$\overset{\text{Double neg.}}{=} in_1 \vee in_2$$

And gate:

$$out = \neg(\neg(in_1 \vee in_1) \vee \neg(in_2 \vee in_2))$$
$$\overset{\text{Idem. twice}}{=} \neg(\neg(in_1) \vee \neg(in_2))$$
$$\overset{\text{De Morgan}}{=} \neg\neg(in_1 \wedge in_2)$$
$$\overset{\text{Double neg.}}{=} in_1 \wedge in_2$$

Answer 1.7.2. Both the *not* gate and the *buffer* gate are unary functions (have only one input). As it is not possible to define behaviour for multiple inputs with these gates it is not possible to implement the *or* gate, and therefore these gates are not functionally complete.

Answer 1.7.3. We show, by induction on n the number of gates, that the output of a circuit consisting solely of *and* gates is 1 if all its inputs are 1. Base case $n = 0$: an input directly connected to the output is 1 if its input is 1. Now consider the case of an $n + 1$ gate circuit. A particular gate G must produce the output. Assume as an induction hypothesis that all circuits of n *and* gates output 1 when the inputs are 1. The circuits connected to either input of G have at most n *and* gates and hence these circuits output 1 when all inputs of the entire circuit are 1. According to the truth table of G, the output of the entire circuit must be 1.

The proofs for the *or* and the *xnor* gates are completely analogous as their output is also 1 when both inputs are 1. The proof for the *xor* is similar except that the output is 0 when all inputs are 0.

Answer 1.7.4. Let f be any boolean function. By Section 1.5, f can be implemented by a two-layer circuit. Suppose we have the disjunctive normal form of f, i.e. a circuit with a layer of *and* gates feeding into a single *or*. If we place *not* gates on the outputs of the *and* gates, making them into *nand* gates, and *not* gates on the inputs of the *or* gate, this circuit still computes f. By De Morgan, we can replace the *or* with negated inputs by a single *nand* gate. We now have a two-layer circuit implementing f, using only *nand* gates. The proof for *nor* is analogous, but using the conjunctive normal form of f.

Answer 1.8.1. First produce the truth table for the k inputs function. Notice that the output column has 2^k values. Observe that the truth table can be split vertically based on the value of the first input and that this holds recursively for all the subsequent inputs. For each input column in the truth table, going left to right, connect the corresponding input line to the selectors at each level of multiplexers, starting from the rightmost level with the single multiplexer (see Figure 1.21). Take the output values from the truth table and connect them in order to the 2^k inputs from the general multiplexer. Now using the k selectors as the inputs this circuit implements the boolean function defined by the truth table.

Answer 1.8.2.

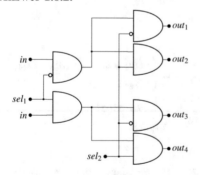

in	sel_1	sel_2	out_1	out_2	out_3	out_4
0	0	0	0	0	0	0
0	0	1	0	0	0	0
0	1	0	0	0	0	0
0	1	1	0	0	0	0
1	0	0	1	0	0	0
1	0	1	0	1	0	0
1	1	0	0	0	1	0
1	1	1	0	0	0	1

D.2 Answers for Chapter 2

Answer 2.1.8. $42 = 32+8+2 = 2^5+2^3+2^1 = \langle 101010 \rangle_2 = \langle (101)(010) \rangle_8 = \langle 52 \rangle_8 = \langle (0010)(1010) \rangle_{16} = \langle 2A \rangle_{16}$.

Answer 2.1.9. $\langle 31 \rangle_8 = \langle (011)(001) \rangle_8 = \langle 11001 \rangle_2 = \langle (0001)(1001) \rangle_{16} = \langle 19 \rangle_{16} = 1 * 16^1 + 9 * 16^0 = 25$.

Answer 2.1.10. Base 9: 260042. Base 12: 77192. Base 15: 31A02.

Answer 2.1.11. Group the ternary digits by two, and translate these pairs directly to their representation in base 9. $220220 = (22)(02)(20) = 826$,
$111111112 = (01)(11)(11)(11)(12) = 14445$,
$22121201010101 = (22)(12)(12)(01)(01)(01)(01) = 8551111$.

Answer 2.2.8. $-27 = -26 - 1 = -[00011010] - 1 = \overline{[00011010]} = [11100101]$.
$-115 = -114 - 1 = -[01110010] - 1 = \overline{[01110010]} = [10001101]$. The number -200 cannot be represented as an 8-bit two's complement number. Using the sign extension rule, two leading 1's for the twos's complement representation of -27 and none for -115 can be dropped.

Answer 2.2.9. If the number $m = [100\ldots00] = -2^{n-1}$ is negated, we obtain the representation $0100\ldots00$ of length $n+1$. Truncated to n bits this again represents m. This does not conflict with Example 2.2.7 as this example silently allows the intermediate result to have a bit representation of $n+1$ bits.

Answer 2.2.10. Assume $\alpha = a_{n-1}\ldots a_0$. We derive $[0\alpha] = -0 \cdot 2^n + \sum_{i=0}^{n-1} a_i \cdot 2^i = 0 \cdot 2^n + \sum_{i=0}^{n-1} a_i \cdot 2^i = \langle 0\alpha \rangle$.

Answer 2.2.11. Observe that there are only two values for a, namely $a = 0$ and $a = 1$. If a is 0 then only the unsigned number representation of its remaining bits contribute to its value. Therefore, its value is non-negative. If the sign bit is 1, the largest value for the number being represented is $-2^{n-1} + \sum_{i=0}^{n-2} 2^i$. We know that $\sum_{i=0}^{n-2} 2^i = 2^{n-1} - 1$. Therefore, numbers with sign bit 1 will always have a negative sign.

Answer 2.2.12. $\langle \alpha \rangle - [\alpha] = a_{n-1}2^{n-1} + \sum_{i=0}^{n-2} a_i \cdot 2^i - (-a_{n-1}2^{n-1} + \sum_{i=0}^{n-2} a_i \cdot 2^i) = a_{n-1}2^{n-1} + a_{n-1}2^{n-1} = a_{n-1}2^n$.

Answer 2.2.13. We have by the definition of two's complement that the smallest value for $[a]$ and $[b]$ is -2^{n-1}. The carry in bit c_{in} is either 0 or 1. Therefore, the sum of the smallest values for $[a], [b]$, and c_{in} is $-2^{n-1} + (-2^{n-1}) + 0 = -2^n$. The largest value for $[a]$, and $[b]$ is $2^{n-1} - 1$ and therefore the sum of the largest values is $2^{n-1} - 1 + 2^{n-1} - 1 + 1 = 2^n - 1$. Conclude $[a] + [b] + c_{in} \in \{-2^n, \ldots, 2^n - 1\}$.

Answer 2.3.3.

1 0 1 1 0 0	Carry bits	
1 0 1 1 1	First operand	$\langle 10111 \rangle = 16 + 4 + 2 + 1 = 23$
1 0 0 1 0	Second operand	$\langle 10010 \rangle = 16 + 2 = 18 \,+$
1 0 1 0 0 1	Binary result	$\langle 101001 \rangle = 32 + 8 + 1 = 41$

Answer 2.3.4.

1 1 0 1 1 0	Carry bits
1 1 0 1 1	First operand
0 1 0 1 1	Second operand +
1 0 0 1 1 0	Binary result

The carry bit is non-zero and therefore the carry-out flag is set.

Answer 2.3.5. The result is 20010. In decimal $2 * 81 + 3 = 165$.

Answer 2.4.4.

$$
\begin{array}{r|l}
1\ 1\ 0\ 0\ 0 & \\
1\ 1\ 0\ 0 & -4 = \overline{[0100]} + 1 = [1011] + 1 \\
1\ 1\ 0\ 1 & -3 = \overline{[0011]} + 1 = [1100] + 1\ + \\
\hline
1\ 1\ 0\ 0\ 1 & -7 = [11001] = [1001]
\end{array}
$$

$$
\begin{array}{r|l}
0\ 0\ 0\ 1\ 0 & \\
0\ 0\ 0\ 1 & 1 \\
1\ 0\ 0\ 1 & -7 \qquad\qquad\qquad + \\
\hline
0\ 1\ 0\ 1\ 0 & -6 = [01010] = [1010]
\end{array}
$$

For both cases no overflow occurs, and therefore the results can be safely truncated to 4 bits.

Answer 2.4.5.

$$
\begin{array}{r|l}
1\ 0\ 1\ 1\ 0 & \\
1\ 0\ 1\ 1 & -5 \\
1\ 0\ 1\ 1 & -5\ + \\
\hline
1\ 0\ 1\ 1\ 0 & -10
\end{array}
\qquad\qquad
\begin{array}{r|l}
0\ 1\ 1\ 1\ 0 & \\
0\ 0\ 1\ 1 & 3 \\
0\ 1\ 1\ 1 & 7\ + \\
\hline
0\ 1\ 0\ 1\ 0 & 10
\end{array}
$$

For both cases an overflow occurs as the carry bits are not equal. The results are too small/too large to fit within 4 bits.

Answer 2.4.6.

$$
\begin{array}{r|l}
1\ 1\ 1\ 1\ 1\ 1\ 1\ 0 & \\
1\ 1\ 1\ 0\ 0\ 1\ 0\ 1 & -27 \\
1\ 1\ 1\ 1\ 1\ 0\ 1\ 1 & -5 \qquad\qquad\qquad\qquad + \\
\hline
1\ 1\ 1\ 1\ 0\ 0\ 0\ 0\ 0 & -32 = [111100000] = [11100000]
\end{array}
$$

$$
\begin{array}{r|l}
1\ 1\ 1\ 0\ 0\ 1\ 0\ 0\ 0 & \\
1\ 1\ 1\ 1\ 0\ 1\ 1\ 0 & -10 \\
0\ 0\ 1\ 0\ 0\ 1\ 0\ 0 & 36 \qquad\qquad\qquad\qquad + \\
\hline
1\ 0\ 0\ 0\ 1\ 1\ 0\ 1\ 0 & 26 = [00011010] \neq [100011010] = -486
\end{array}
$$

As there are no overflows the results are safely truncated to 8 bits. The first result could be truncated to 6 bits by sign extension. Similarly the second result can be truncated from 8 bits to 6 bits.

Answer 2.4.7. We use $\langle c_n\ a_{n-1} \oplus b_{n-1} \oplus c_{n-1}\rangle = a_{n-1} + b_{n-1} + c_{n-1}$ and, to ease notation, define $s = a_{n-1} \oplus b_{n-1} \oplus c_{n-1}$.

$$\overbrace{[\alpha +_{c_0} \beta]}^{\text{length } n+1} = [c_n \ a_{n-1} \oplus b_{n-1} \oplus c_{n-1} \ \gamma] = [c_n \ s \ \gamma]$$
$$= -c_n 2^n + s2^{n-1} + \langle \gamma \rangle$$
$$= s2^n - c_n 2^n - a_{n-1} \oplus b_{n-1} \oplus c_{n-1} 2^{n-1} + \langle \gamma \rangle$$
$$= s2^n - \langle c_n \ a_{n-1} \oplus b_{n-1} \oplus c_{n-1} \rangle 2^{n-1} - c_{n-1} 2^{n-1} + \langle c_{n-1} \gamma \rangle$$
$$= s2^n - (a_{n-1} + b_{n-1} + c_{n-1}) 2^{n-1} - c_{n-1} 2^{n-1} + \langle c_{n-1} \gamma \rangle$$
$$= s2^n - c_{n-1} 2^n - (a_{n-1} + b_{n-1}) 2^{n-1} + \langle \alpha' +_{c_0} \beta' \rangle$$
$$= (a_{n-1} \oplus b_{n-1} \oplus c_{n-1} - c_{n-1}) 2^n + [\alpha] + [\beta] + c_0$$

Answer 2.5.4. The number 116 is represented as 0111 0100 and 123 as 0111 1011. $116 - 123$: $0111 0100 +_1 1000 0100 = 1111 1001$ with $c_7 = 0$ and $c_8 = 0$. Hence, the unsigned number subtraction is invalid and the two's complement subtraction is valid. $123 - 116$: $0111 1011 +_1 1000 0111 = 0000 0111$ with $c_7 = c_8 = 1$. Both the results of the unsigned number subtraction and the two's complement subtraction are valid.

Answer 2.5.5. $1000 1000 +_1 1010 0011 = 0010 1100$ with carries $c_7 = 0$ and $c_8 = 1$. There is an overflow error.

Answer 2.6.1. $0101 +_1 1000 = 1110$. The flag $Z = 0$. So, $0101 \neq 0111$ in both unsigned and two's complement notation.
$1011 +_1 0011 = 1111$ with $C = 1$, $N = 1$ and $V = 0$.
Unsigned: ok. Two's complement: ok.
$1011 +_1 1100 = 1000$ with $C = 0$, $N = 1$ and $V = 0$.
Unsigned: not ok. Two's complement: ok.
$0111 +_1 0111 = 1111$ with $C = 1$, $N = 1$ and $V = 1$.
Unsigned: ok. Two's complement: not ok.
$0111 +_1 1010 = 0010$ with $C = 0$, $N = 0$ and $V = 0$.
Unsigned: ok. Two's complement: ok.

Answer 2.6.2.

	unsigned	two's complement
$\alpha \leq \beta$	$C = 0 \vee Z = 1$	$N = V \vee Z = 1$
$\alpha < \beta$	$C = 0$	$N = V$
$\alpha = \beta$	$Z = 1$	$Z = 1$
$\alpha \neq \beta$	$Z = 0$	$Z = 0$
$\alpha > \beta$	$C = 1 \wedge Z = 0$	$N \neq V \wedge Z = 0$
$\alpha \geq \beta$	$C = 1$	$N \neq V$

Answer 2.7.1. The zero flag can be calculated by taking the negated disjunction of s_0, s_1, s_2 and s_3. Adding a single four-input *nor* gate with Z as output suffices.

Answer 2.7.2. The first carry out of the 4-bit ripple carry adder calculates $FA_{c_1}(a, b) = (c_0 \wedge (a \oplus b)) \vee (a \wedge b)$ in 4 gate delays. The subsequent full adders use this time to calculate $a \oplus b$, and $a \wedge b$ and only need an additional two gate delays to calculate $FA_{c_i}(a, b) = (c_{i-1} \wedge (a \oplus b)) \vee (a \wedge b)$. Therefore, the gate delay for an n-bit ripple carry adder can be expressed as $ripple(n) = 4 + (n - 1) * 2$.

For the look-ahead adder it holds for all i and $0 \leq j < i$ that c_i is the disjunction of conjunctive combinations of g_j, p_j, c_0. As g_j and p_j only depend on the input bits these cause a maximum of 2 gate delays. This leads to a constant gate delay of 4 for the final carry of a look-ahead adder: $lookahead(n) = 4$.

The difference in delay for a 4-bit adder is $ripple(4) - lookahead(4) = (4 + 3 * 2) - 4 = 6$. The difference in delay for a 32-bit adder is $ripple(32) - lookahead(32) = (4 + 31 * 2) - 4 = 62$.

Answer 2.7.3.

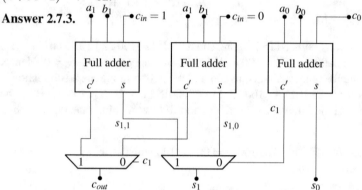

Answer 2.8.1. The 1-bit arithmetic logic unit shown below has the additional operation b for $ALU.op = op_0 op_1 op_2 c_{in} = 011 c_{in}$.

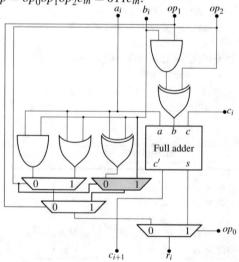

Answer 2.8.2. The overflow flag is used to indicate that the addition of two operands with the same sign resulted in a value of the opposite sign, or that the subtraction of a positive from a negative value resulted in a positive value, or that the subtraction of a negative from a positive value resulted in a negative value. The following two tables indicate the situations when the V flag should be set according to whether $ALU.op$ indicates addition or subtraction. Now a circuit can be constructed without using any internal signals.

a_{n-1}	b_{n-1}	r_{n-1}	V flag after addition	a_{n-1}	b_{n-1}	r_{n-1}	V flag after subtraction
0	0	0	0	0	0	0	0
0	0	1	1	0	0	1	0
0	1	0	0	0	1	0	0
0	1	1	0	0	1	1	1
1	0	0	0	1	0	0	1
1	0	1	0	1	0	1	0
1	1	0	1	1	1	0	0
1	1	1	0	1	1	1	0

Answer 2.9.1. Let $a = \langle a_2 a_1 a_0 \rangle$ and $b = \langle b_2 b_1 b_0 \rangle$ be two (unsigned) 3-bit numbers. The circuit below implements 3-bit long division for b/a. The resulting quotient is given as $quot(b,a) = \langle \neg N_0 \neg N_1 \neg N_2 \rangle$ where N_i is the flag indicating a negative result for a subtraction in a subtraction unit. The remainder of b/a is $rem(b,a) = \langle r_2 r_1 r_0 \rangle$. The subtraction units can be implemented by full 3-bit ALUs (or by more efficient means).

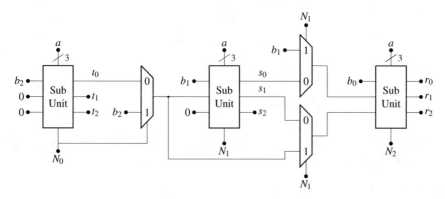

Answer 2.10.1. We prove $[\overline{a}\alpha]_{\bar{1}} = -[a\alpha]_{\bar{1}}$ as the first bit of the bit sequence α has a special role. Furthermore, we assume $\alpha = a_{n-2}\ldots a_0$. First, we consider $a = 0$.

$$[0\alpha]_{\bar{1}} = [1\overline{\alpha}]_{\bar{1}} = \langle \overline{\alpha} \rangle - (2^{n-1}-1) = \sum_{i=0}^{n-2} \overline{a_i} 2^i - (2^{n-1}-1) =$$
$$\sum_{i=0}^{n-2}(1-a_i)2^i - (2^{n-1}-1) = \sum_{i=0}^{n-2} 2^i - \sum_{i=0}^{n-2} a_i 2^i - (2^{n-1}-1) =$$
$$(2^{n-1}-1) - \sum_{i=0}^{n-2} a_i 2^i - (2^{n-1}-1) = -\sum_{i=0}^{n-2} a_i 2^i = -\langle \alpha \rangle = -[0\alpha]_{\bar{1}}.$$

Next we consider $a = 1$.

$$[\overline{1}\alpha]_{\bar{1}} = [0\alpha]_{\bar{1}} = \langle \overline{\alpha} \rangle = \sum_{i=0}^{n-2} \overline{a_i} 2^i = \sum_{i=0}^{n-2}(1-a_i)2^i =$$
$$\sum_{i=0}^{n-2} 2^i - \sum_{i=0}^{n-2} a_i 2^i = (2^{n-1}-1) - \sum_{i=0}^{n-2} a_i 2^i =$$
$$-(\sum_{i=0}^{n-2} a_i 2^i - (2^{n-1}-1)) = -(\langle \alpha \rangle - (2^{n-1}-1)) = -[1\alpha]_{\bar{1}}.$$

Answer 2.10.2.

	unsigned	two's complement	sign and magnitude	one's complement
1010	10	−6	−2	−5
0101	5	5	5	5

Answer 2.10.3. $-6 = (1110)$ and $3 = (0011)$.

Determine which operand has the larger absolute magnitude by comparing the base-2 representations. Do this by comparing the bits from most significant to least significant. If the most significant bits are equal continue checking the next most significant bit. If the two bits do not match then the operand with the bit set to 1 has the larger magnitude. This is due to $2^n > \sum_{i=0}^{n-1} 2^i$.

$$
\begin{array}{l|l}
1\ 1\ 0 & \text{Carry subtraction bit} \\
1\ 1\ 0 & \text{6 in base 2} \\
0\ 1\ 1 & \text{3 in base 2} \\
\hline
0\ 1\ 1 & \text{6 - 3 = 3}
\end{array} \quad -
$$

The result is negative as -6 has the larger magnitude, and therefore $-6 + 3 = -3 = (1011)$.

Answer 2.10.4. $3 = [0011]_{\overline{1}}$, $5 = [0101]_{\overline{1}}$, and $-5 = [1010]_{\overline{1}}$

$$
\begin{array}{l|l}
0\ 1\ 0\ 0 & \text{Carry bit} \\
0\ 0\ 1\ 1 & \text{3 in one's complement} \\
1\ 0\ 1\ 0 & \text{-5 in one's complement} \\
\hline
1\ 1\ 0\ 1 & \text{3 + (-5) = -8 + 1 + 5 = -2}
\end{array} \quad +
$$

D.3 Answers for Chapter 3

Answer 3.1.1. This circuit recalls whether the input *in* has ever been 0. If this has happened the output will be 0.

Answer 3.1.2.

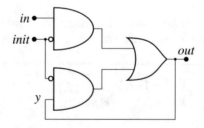

Answer 3.2.1. If both $\overline{reset}$ and $\overline{set}$ are equal to 1, the flip-flop keeps the value *out*. If $\overline{set}$ is equal to 0 and $\overline{reset}$ is equal to 1, then *out* becomes 1. This flip-flop is set when $\overline{set}$ is 0. Similarly, if $\overline{reset}$ is 0 and $\overline{set}$ is 1, the flip-flop will become 0. Metastability occurs when both inputs are 0.

Answer 3.2.2. The problem with the constructed circuit is that as soon as G is 1 the flip-flop will try to take over the new negated value and *out* will switch accordingly. But as soon *out* has switched it will try toggle its current value again. As long as G is enabled this will continue to happen. As there is only a very short delay between the toggles we need additional circuitry to guarantee that only a single toggle occurs when G is set to 1.

Answer 3.3.1.

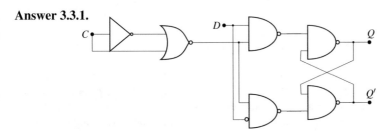

Answer 3.3.2. Gated D-latches can be used to replace the edge-triggered D-flip-flops in a master-slave D-flip-flop with almost the same behaviour. When the clock is high, the latch on the left passes D on to Q, while the right latch retains and forwards the old value of D. When the clock goes down, The input D is fixed in the left latch, and passed on in the second. When the clock goes up again, this value is stored in the second latch. The behaviour is the same as that of a master-slave D-flip-flop, except that the input is read at the down-going flank. To obtain exactly the same behaviour, the clock inputs need to be inverted.

Answer 3.3.3.

Answer 3.3.4.

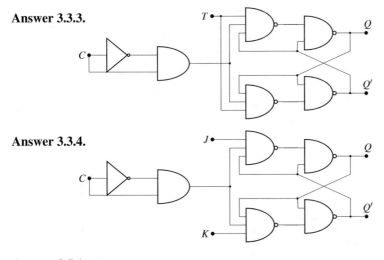

Answer 3.5.1.

state	s t	x
A	0 0	0
B	0 1	1
C	1 0	1
D	1 1	0

$x := s \oplus t$

state	s t (old)	p	state	s t (new)
A	0 0	0	A	0 0
A	0 0	1	B	0 1
B	0 1	0	C	1 0
B	0 1	1	B	0 1
C	1 0	0	C	1 0
C	1 0	1	D	1 1
D	1 1	0	A	0 0
D	1 1	1	D	1 1

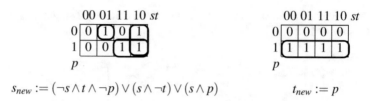

00 01 11 10 *st*

| 0 | 0 | 1 | 0 | 1 |

| 1 | 0 | 0 | 1 | 1 |

p

00 01 11 10 *st*

| 0 | 0 | 0 | 0 | 0 |

| 1 | 1 | 1 | 1 | 1 |

p

$$s_{new} := (\neg s \wedge t \wedge \neg p) \vee (s \wedge \neg t) \vee (s \wedge p)$$

$$t_{new} := p$$

For the unclocked circuit it would have to hold that p can be substituted for t in s because t is defined to be p by the Karnaugh diagram and $t := p$ incurs no extra propagation delay relative to p. This gives $s := (\neg s \wedge p \wedge \neg p) \vee (s \wedge \neg p) \vee (s \wedge p) = (s \wedge \neg p) \vee (s \wedge p) = s \wedge (p \vee \neg p) = s$. This leads to the conclusion that the input for the cells of the Karnaugh diagram of s where t and p have different boolean values cannot occur for this circuit. Notably the input of $s = 0 \wedge t = 1 \wedge p = 0$ cannot occur and therefore the s state variable can never become 1.

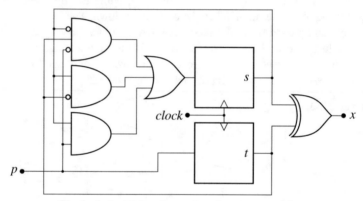

Clocked circuit implementing the state machine.

Answer 3.5.2.

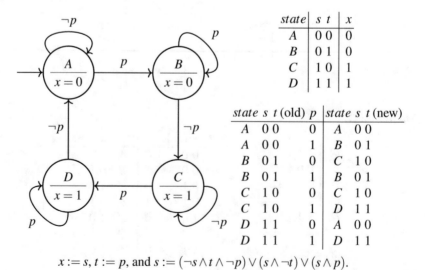

state	s t	x
A	0 0	0
B	0 1	0
C	1 0	1
D	1 1	1

state s t (old)		p	state s t (new)	
A	0 0	0	A	0 0
A	0 0	1	B	0 1
B	0 1	0	C	1 0
B	0 1	1	B	0 1
C	1 0	0	C	1 0
C	1 0	1	D	1 1
D	1 1	0	A	0 0
D	1 1	1	D	1 1

$x := s$, $t := p$, and $s := (\neg s \wedge t \wedge \neg p) \vee (s \wedge \neg t) \vee (s \wedge p)$.

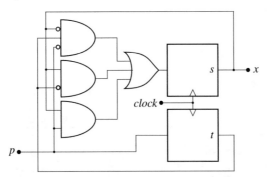

Clocked circuit implementing the state machine.

Answer 3.5.3.

state	s t	x
A	0 0	0
B	1 0	1
C	1 1	1
D	0 1	0

state s t (old)	r p	state s t (new)
A 0 0	0 0	A 0 0
A 0 0	0 1	B 1 0
A 0 0	1 X	A 0 0
B 1 0	0 0	C 1 1
B 1 0	0 1	B 1 0
B 1 0	1 X	A 0 0
C 1 1	0 0	C 1 1
C 1 1	0 1	D 0 1
C 1 1	1 X	A 0 0
D 0 1	0 0	A 0 0
D 0 1	0 1	D 0 1
D 0 1	1 X	A 0 0

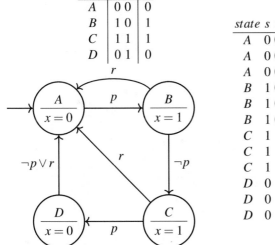

$x := s, t := (s \land \neg p \land \neg r) \lor (p \land t \land \neg r)$, and $s := (s \land \neg p \land \neg r) \lor (p \land \neg t \land \neg r)$.

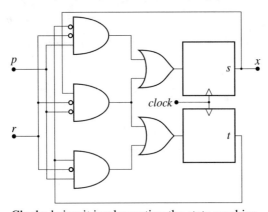

Clocked circuit implementing the state machine.

Answer 3.5.4.

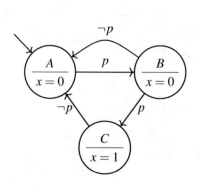

state	s t	x
A	0 0	0
B	0 1	0
C	1 0	1

$x := s$

state s t (old)	p	state s t (new)
A 0 0	0	A 0 0
A 0 0	1	B 0 1
B 0 1	0	A 0 0
B 0 1	1	C 1 0
C 1 0	0	A 0 0
C 1 0	1	C 1 0

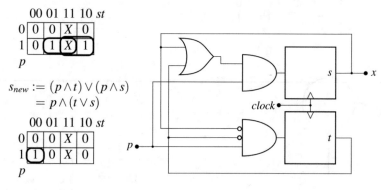

00 01 11 10 *st*

	0	0	X	0
0	0	0	X	0
1	0	1	X	1

p

$$s_{new} := (p \wedge t) \vee (p \wedge s)$$
$$= p \wedge (t \vee s)$$

00 01 11 10 *st*

	0	0	X	0
0	0	0	X	0
1	1	0	X	0

p

$$t_{new} := p \wedge \neg s \wedge \neg t$$

$p/x = 0$

$p/x = 1$

$\neg p/x = 0$

state s (old)	p	state s (new)	x
A 0	0	A 0	0
A 0	1	B 1	0
B 1	0	A 0	0
B 1	1	B 1	1

$s := p$ and $x := s \wedge p$

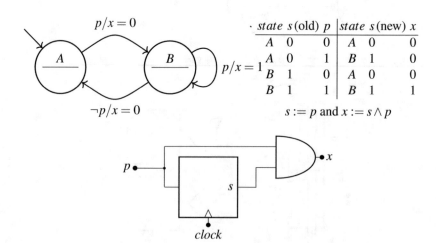

Answer 3.5.5.

state	s t	b l
A	0 0	0 0
B	0 1	1 1
C	1 0	0 1

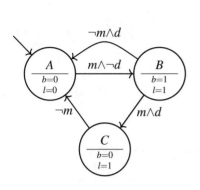

state	s t (old)	m d	state	s t (new)
A	0 0	0 X	A	0 0
A	0 0	1 0	B	0 1
A	0 0	1 1	A	0 0
B	0 1	0 0	B	0 1
B	0 1	0 1	A	0 0
B	0 1	1 0	B	0 1
B	0 1	1 1	C	1 0
C	1 0	0 X	A	0 0
C	1 0	1 X	C	1 0

$$b := t \qquad l := s \vee t$$
$$s := (t \wedge m \wedge d) \vee (m \wedge s) \qquad t := (\neg s \wedge m \wedge \neg d) \vee (t \wedge \neg d)$$

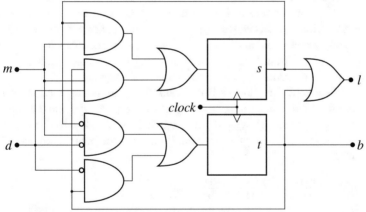

Answer 3.5.6.

state	s (old)	set	reset	state	s (new)
A	0	0	0	A	0
A	0	0	1	A	0
A	0	1	0	B	1
A	0	1	1	A	0
B	1	0	0	B	1
B	1	0	1	A	0
B	1	1	0	B	1
B	1	1	1	B	1

state	s	x
A	0	0
B	1	1

$$x := s \text{ and } s := (set \wedge \neg reset) \vee (set \wedge s) \vee (s \wedge \neg reset)$$

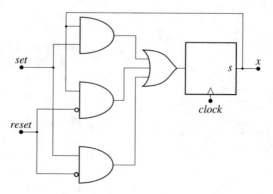

Clocked circuit implementing the state machine.

A set-reset flip-flop implemented via a (clocked) state machine has no metastability issues.

Answer 3.5.7. The circuit is drawn below with additional names of some signals. The initial stable situation is given in line 1. In line 2 p is set to 1. Signals that change are underlined. In line 3 the change of p leads to a_{12} to be set to 1. In line 4 o_{11} goes to 1. In line 5 both s and x are set to 1. In line 6 a_{21} responds to this change by going to 1. In line 7 this causes o_{21} to go to 1 and in line 8 t goes to 1. In line 9 a_{11} responds by going to 0 and in line 10 o_{11} does the same, causing s and x to go back to 0 in line 11. In line 12 a_{21} reacts by going to 0 again. In line 13 o_{21} reacts by going back to 0 and in line 14 t follows this by going to 0.

Line 15 is identical to line 4. This means that this sequence can repeat itself arbitrarily often. This causes the output x to change repeatedly from 0 to 1 and back again, as long as the signals $a_{22}, a_{31}, a_{32}, o_{12}$ and o_{22} are slow to change. In order for this circuit to work correctly, stringent timing requirements on the components are required.

	p	s	x	t	a_{11}	a_{12}	a_{21}	a_{22}	a_{31}	a_{32}	o_{11}	o_{12}	o_{21}	o_{22}
1	0	0	0	0	1	0	0	1	0	0	0	0	0	0
2	1	0	0	0	1	0	0	1	0	0	0	0	0	0
3	1	0	0	0	1	1	0	1	0	0	0	0	0	0
4	1	0	0	0	1	1	0	1	0	0	1	0	0	0
5	1	1	1	0	1	1	0	1	0	0	1	0	0	0
6	1	1	1	0	1	1	1	1	0	0	1	0	0	0
7	1	1	1	0	1	1	1	1	0	0	1	0	1	0
8	1	1	1	1	1	1	1	1	0	0	1	0	1	0
9	1	1	1	1	0	1	1	1	0	0	1	0	1	0
10	1	1	1	1	0	1	1	1	0	0	0	0	1	0
11	1	0	0	1	0	1	1	1	0	0	0	0	1	0
12	1	0	0	1	0	1	0	1	0	0	0	0	1	0
13	1	0	0	1	0	1	0	1	0	0	0	0	0	0
14	1	0	0	0	0	1	0	1	0	0	0	0	0	0
15	1	0	0	0	1	1	0	1	0	0	0	0	0	0

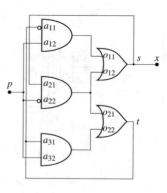

Answer 3.7.1.

state s t u(old)	read	write	state s t u(new)
$S_{0,0}$ 0 0 0	X	0	$S_{0,0}$ 0 0 0
$S_{0,0}$ 0 0 0	X	1	$S_{1,0}$ 0 0 1
$S_{1,0}$ 0 0 1	0	0	$S_{1,0}$ 0 0 1
$S_{1,0}$ 0 0 1	0	1	$S_{2,0}$ 0 1 0
$S_{1,0}$ 0 0 1	1	0	$S_{0,1}$ 0 1 1
$S_{1,0}$ 0 0 1	1	1	$S_{1,1}$ 1 0 0
$S_{2,0}$ 0 1 0	0	X	$S_{2,0}$ 0 1 0
$S_{2,0}$ 0 1 0	1	0	$S_{1,1}$ 1 0 0
$S_{2,0}$ 0 1 0	1	1	$S_{2,1}$ 1 0 1
$S_{0,1}$ 0 1 1	X	0	$S_{0,1}$ 0 1 1
$S_{0,1}$ 0 1 1	X	1	$S_{1,1}$ 1 0 0
$S_{1,1}$ 1 0 0	0	0	$S_{1,1}$ 1 0 0
$S_{1,1}$ 1 0 0	0	1	$S_{2,1}$ 1 0 1
$S_{1,1}$ 1 0 0	1	0	$S_{0,0}$ 0 0 0
$S_{1,1}$ 1 0 0	1	1	$S_{1,0}$ 0 0 1
$S_{2,1}$ 1 0 1	0	X	$S_{2,1}$ 1 0 1
$S_{2,1}$ 1 0 1	1	0	$S_{1,0}$ 0 0 1
$S_{2,1}$ 1 0 1	1	1	$S_{2,0}$ 0 1 0

state s t u	avail	full	input select	output select
$S_{0,0}$ 0 0 0	0	0	0	X
$S_{1,0}$ 0 0 1	1	0	1	0
$S_{2,0}$ 0 1 0	1	1	0	0
$S_{0,1}$ 0 1 1	0	0	1	X
$S_{1,1}$ 1 0 0	1	0	0	1
$S_{2,1}$ 1 0 1	1	1	1	1

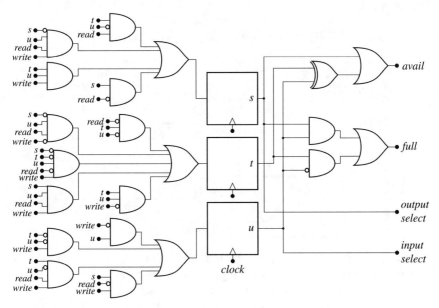

D.4 Answers for Chapter 4

Answer 4.1.1. Place the value of register R_0 on the Abus by setting *REGS.oea* to 1 and *IR.ra* to the correct bit sequence, which in the case of unsigned number encoding would be 00. Similarly R_0 is placed on the Bbus by setting *IR.rb* to 01 and *REGS.oeb* to 1. ALU.*op* is set to the bit sequence corresponding to $A+B$. To save the flags we set *CC.sel* to 1. *IR.ra* already specifies the correct register for the result; therefore, set *REGS.sel* to 1 to read the result from the Cbus into register R_0 at the end of the clock cycle.

Answer 4.1.2. First cycle: place the address via the Bbus into register ΣA by setting *IR.val* and $\Sigma A.sel$ to 1.

Second cycle: start retrieval from memory by setting $\Sigma A.oe$, $\Sigma R.sel$, and RAM.*oe* to 1. At the same time place the registers R_0 and R_1 onto the Abus and Bbus, respectively, by setting *IR.ra* to 00 and *IR.rb* to 01 together with setting both *REGS.oea* and *REGS.oeb* to 1. ALU.*op* is set to $A \lor B$. Collect the result into R_0 by setting *REGS.sel* to 1.

Third Cycle: Place R_0 and ΣR onto the Abus and the Bbus, respectively, by setting *IR.ra* to 00, *REGS.oea* to 1, and $\Sigma R.oe$ to 1. Set ALU.*op* to $A \lor B$ and save the flags by setting *CC.sel* to 1. Collect the result into R_0 by setting *REGS.sel* to 1.

Answer 4.1.3.

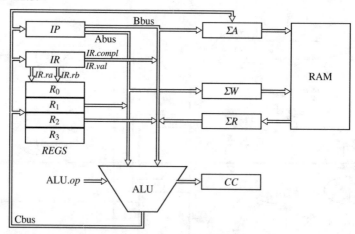

This instruction is not possible on the basic data path as the calculated address needs to be moved from the ALU output to register ΣA without going through a register. To solve this connect the Cbus to ΣA and add an extra select signal $\Sigma A.selc$.

The implementation on the modified basic data path depicted above is as follows: First cycle: place the value of R_0, via the Abus, into register ΣW by setting *IR.ra* to 00, and set *REGS.oea* and $\Sigma W.sel$ to 1. Second cycle: place the R_1 value on the Abus by setting *IR.ra* to 01 and *REGS.oea* to 1. Set *IR.compl* to 1, ALU.*op* to $A+B$ and $\Sigma A.selc$ to 1. Third Cycle: set $\Sigma W.oe$ and $\Sigma W.oe$ and RAM.*sel* to 1.

Answer 4.2.1. The data is stored and manipulated at addresses 0, 1 and 2. If the program is stored from address 0 onward, the addresses 0, 1 and 2 contain values corresponding to instructions that are meaningless as data. But a far more serious problem is that the content of register R_1 is written back to memory at the end of the program, replacing the instruction at address 1 with a value, which may or may not be a proper instruction but which is very likely different from LOAD R_1 [1]. This causes the program to have unpredictable behaviour when executed again. It is important to take care that data and programs in RAM are never mixed up.

Answer 4.2.2. In principle it is possible to store the return address in a register or at a fixed place in memory. There are, however, two problems. The first one is that this does not allow for nested function calls. If a function f calls another, say g, then the first address stored in the register is lost when the second return address is stored. This can be dealt with by storing the return address for each function separately. The second more severe problem is that it does not allow recursion where a function f calls itself. Storing the return address in a register has also the advantage that it is fast. The ARM processor facilitates this and leaves it to the program to store return addresses on the stack.

Answer 4.2.3. It is very well possible to have multiple stacks used by one program. Of course care must be taken that they used different parts of memory. It is, however, common to have only one stack in one program. This stack is used for other purposes as well, outside the control of the program, such as handling of interrupts.

Answer 4.3.1.
1. $\Sigma A \leftarrow RB(\text{Bbus})$.
2. $\Sigma R \leftarrow \text{RAM}[\Sigma A]$.
3. $RA, CC \leftarrow RA(\text{Abus}) + \Sigma R(\text{Bbus}), \text{ALU}.cc$.

Answer 4.3.2.
1. $\Sigma A, IP \leftarrow IP(\text{Bbus}), IP(\text{Abus}) + 1$.
2. $\Sigma R \leftarrow \text{RAM}[\Sigma A]$.
3. $IR \leftarrow \Sigma R(\text{Bbus})$.
4. $RA \leftarrow RA(\text{Abus}) \oplus RB(\text{Bbus})$.

Answer 4.3.3.
1. $\Sigma A, IP \leftarrow IP(\text{Bbus}), IP(\text{Abus}) + 1$.
2. $IR \leftarrow \text{RAM}[\Sigma A]$.

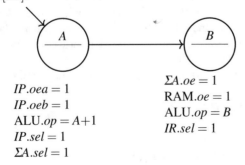

$IP.oea = 1$
$IP.oeb = 1$
$\text{ALU}.op = A + 1$
$IP.sel = 1$
$\Sigma A.sel = 1$

$\Sigma A.oe = 1$
$\text{RAM}.oe = 1$
$\text{ALU}.op = B$
$IR.sel = 1$

Answer 4.4.1. The arithmetic instructions use bit_9 to differentiate between an embedded value and a register. BRA and BRS are distinguished from each other by bit_9. The conditional branch instructions are discriminated by the bits 11 through 9.

bit_{15}	bit_{14}	bit_{13}	bit_{12}	Instructions
0	0	0	0	BRA, BRS
0	0	0	1	BCC, BCS, BPL, BMI, BVC, BVS, BNE, BEQ
0	0	1	0	RTS
0	0	1	1	STOR (direct/indirect)
0	1	0	0	LOAD (register/immediate)
0	1	0	1	LOAD (direct/indirect)
0	1	1	0	ADD (register/immediate)
0	1	1	1	ADD (direct/indirect)
1	0	0	0	SUB (register/immediate)
1	0	0	1	SUB (direct/indirect)
1	0	1	0	AND (register/immediate)
1	0	1	1	AND (direct/indirect)
1	1	0	0	OR (register/immediate)
1	1	0	1	OR (direct/indirect)
1	1	1	0	XOR (register/immediate)
1	1	1	1	XOR (direct/indirect)

The following table can be derived for available bit sequences:

$$
\begin{array}{cccccccccccccccc}
op & op & op & op & X & X & 1 & X & X & Y & Y & Y & Y & Y & Y & Y \\
0 & 0 & 1 & 0 & X & X & 1 & X & X & X & X & X & X & X & X & X \\
0 & 0 & 1 & 0 & X & X & 0 & Y & Y & Y & Y & Y & Y & Y & Y & Y \\
0 & 0 & 0 & 0 & Y & Y & 0 & X & X & X & X & X & X & X & X & X
\end{array}
$$

The symbols in the table have the following meaning:

- $op\ op\ op\ op \in \{\langle 0011 \rangle, \ldots, \langle 1111 \rangle\}$.
- any sequence of Y's cannot be all 0's.
- any X can either be a 1 or a 0.

Answer 4.4.2. On the simple processor the additive inverse can be calculated by either subtracting the value from 0, or inverting the bits and adding 1 (Theorem 2.2.5). The first method is not usable as an extra register is needed. The ALU only supports subtracting Bbus values from Abus values and the output from IR only connects to the Bbus. To invert the bits the value needs to be XORed with all 1's. This value can be obtained from $IR.compl$ which in sign extended form can be put on the Bbus.

Encoding for NEG R_i: $0\ 0\ 1\ 0\ r\ r\ 1\ 1\ 1\ 1\ 1\ 1\ 1\ 1\ 1\ 1$.

An implementation of the instruction that uses a minimal number of clock ticks is as follows:

1. $\Sigma A, IP \leftarrow IP(\text{Bbus}), IP(\text{Abus})+1$.
2. $\Sigma R \leftarrow RAM[\Sigma A]$.
3. $IR \leftarrow \Sigma R(\text{Bbus})$.
4. $RA \leftarrow RA(\text{Abus}) \oplus IR.compl(\text{Bbus})$; Uses that $IR = 111111111$.

5. $RA, CC \leftarrow RA(\text{Abus}) + 1$, ALU.*cc*.

Advantages:	Disadvantages:
• Only requires a single register.	• Uses up limited encoding space, making it impossible to add more instructions.
• Uses only 5 cycles versus a minimum of 8 if it would be implemented using multiple instructions.	• Adds states to the implementing state machine.
• Occupies less space in RAM.	• Makes the instruction set more complicated.

Answer 4.4.3. There are 13 store/load and arithmetic instructions, each occurring with *expr* as either a register or as a value. With eight registers the two register instructions require $13 * 2^3 * 2^3$ encodings, while instructions with values embedded need $13 * 2^3 * 2^9$ encodings. The subroutine instructions need $2^3 * 2^9 + 2^3$ encodings. The nine branch instructions are unchanged and require $9 * 2^9$ different encodings. In sum total, the $13 * 2^3 * (2^3 + 2^9) + 2^3 * 2^9 + 2^3 + 9 * 2^9 = 62792 \, (< 2^{16})$ encodings fit in 16 bits.

Answer 4.5.1. LOAD $R_i \, R_j$:
1. $\Sigma A, IP \leftarrow IP(\text{Bbus}), IP(\text{Abus}) + 1$.
2. $\Sigma R \leftarrow \text{RAM}[\Sigma A]$.
3. $IR \leftarrow \Sigma R(\text{Bbus})$.
4. $RA, CC \leftarrow RB(\text{Bbus})$, ALU.*cc*.
SUB $R_i \, [address]$:
1. $\Sigma A, IP \leftarrow IP(\text{Bbus}), IP(\text{Abus}) + 1$.
2. $\Sigma R \leftarrow \text{RAM}[\Sigma A]$.
3. $IR \leftarrow \Sigma R(\text{Bbus})$.
4. $\Sigma A \leftarrow IR.val(\text{Bbus})$.
5. $\Sigma R \leftarrow \text{RAM}[\Sigma A]$.
6. $RA, CC \leftarrow RA(\text{Abus}) - \Sigma R(\text{Bbus})$, ALU.*cc*.
BMI *disp* (flag N is 0, branch not taken):
1. $\Sigma A, IP \leftarrow IP(\text{Bbus}), IP(\text{Abus}) + 1$.
2. $\Sigma R \leftarrow \text{RAM}[\Sigma A]$.
3. $IR \leftarrow \Sigma R(\text{Bbus})$.
BMI *disp* (flag N is 1, branch is taken):
1. $\Sigma A, IP \leftarrow IP(\text{Bbus}), IP(\text{Abus}) + 1$.
2. $\Sigma R \leftarrow \text{RAM}[\Sigma A]$.
3. $IR \leftarrow \Sigma R(\text{Bbus})$.
4. $IP \leftarrow IP(\text{ABus}) + IR.compl(\text{Bbus})$.

Answer 4.5.2. ADD $R_i + [[R_j]]$:
4. $\Sigma A \leftarrow RB(\text{Bbus})$.
5. $\Sigma R \leftarrow \text{RAM}[\Sigma A]$.
6. $\Sigma A \leftarrow \Sigma R(\text{Bbus})$.
7. $\Sigma R \leftarrow \text{RAM}[\Sigma A]$.
8. $RA, CC \leftarrow RA(\text{Abus}) + \Sigma R(\text{Bbus})$, ALU.*cc*.

Answer 4.5.3.

1. $\Sigma A, IP \leftarrow IP(\text{Bbus}), IP(\text{Abus})+1.$
2. $\Sigma R \leftarrow \text{RAM}[\Sigma A].$
3. $IR \leftarrow \Sigma R(\text{Bbus}).$
4. $\Sigma A \leftarrow RB(\text{Bbus}).$
5. $\Sigma R \leftarrow \text{RAM}[\Sigma A].$
6. $RA, CC \leftarrow RA(\text{Abus}) \oplus \Sigma R(\text{Bbus}), \text{ALU}.cc.$

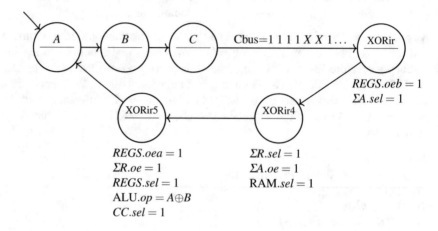

Answer 4.5.4.

BRS R_i *disp*:

1. $\Sigma A, IP \leftarrow IP(\text{Bbus}), IP(\text{Abus})+1.$
2. $\Sigma R \leftarrow \text{RAM}[\Sigma A].$
3. $IR \leftarrow \Sigma R(\text{Bbus}).$
4. $RA \leftarrow RA(\text{Abus})-1.$
5. $\Sigma A, \Sigma W \leftarrow RAB(\text{Bbus}), IP(\text{Abus}).$
6. $IP, \text{RAM}[\Sigma A] \leftarrow IP(\text{Abus})+IR.compl(\text{Bbus}), \Sigma W.$

RTS R_i:

1. $\Sigma A, IP \leftarrow IP(\text{Bbus}), IP(\text{Abus})+1.$
2. $\Sigma R \leftarrow \text{RAM}[\Sigma A].$
3. $IR \leftarrow \Sigma R(\text{Bbus}).$
4. $\Sigma A, RA \leftarrow RAB(\text{Bbus}), RA(\text{Abus})+1.$
5. $\Sigma R \leftarrow \text{RAM}[\Sigma A].$
6. $IP \leftarrow \Sigma R(\text{Bbus}).$

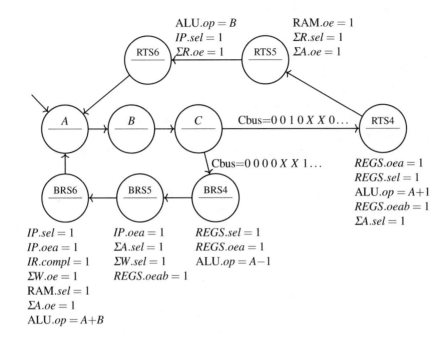

Answer 4.6.1. LOAD R_i *value*:
3. RA, IR, ΣA, IP, $CC \leftarrow IR.val$(Bbus), RAM[ΣA], IP, $IP+1$, ALU.cc.
STOR R_i [R_j]:
3. ΣA, ΣW, CC, $IPB \leftarrow RB$(Bbus), RA(Abus), ALU.cc, RAM[ΣA].
4. RAM[ΣA], IR, ΣA, $IP \leftarrow \Sigma W$, IPB, IP, $IP+1$.

Answer 4.6.2. BRS R_i *disp*:
3. $IP \leftarrow IP$(Abus)-1 (the instruction pointer points one instruction too far).
4. $RA \leftarrow RA$(Abus)-1.
5. ΣA, $\Sigma W \leftarrow RAB$(Bbus), IP(Abus).
6. IP, RAM[ΣA] $\leftarrow IP$(Abus)$+IR.compl$(Bbus), ΣW.
7. ΣA, $IP \leftarrow IP$(Abus), $IP+1$.
8. IR, ΣA, $IP \leftarrow$ RAM[ΣA] (Ibus), IP, $IP+1$.
   RTS R_i:
3. RA, $\Sigma A \leftarrow RA$(Abus) $+ 1$, RAB(Bbus).
4. $\Sigma R \leftarrow$ RAM[ΣA].
5. $IP \leftarrow \Sigma R$(Bbus).
6. ΣA, $IP \leftarrow IP$, $IP+1$.
7. IR, ΣA, $IP \leftarrow$ RAM[ΣA] (Ibus), IP, $IP+1$.

Answer 4.7.1. TESTSET [R_i] where RAM[R_i] $\neq 0$.:
4. $\Sigma A \leftarrow RAB$(Bbus).
5. $\Sigma R \leftarrow$ RAM[ΣA].

6. The value of RAM[ΣA] is put on the Bbus.

   _, $CC \leftarrow$ RAM[ΣA](Abus), ALU.cc (if Z is not set, jump to state A to fetch the next instruction).

TESTSET [R_i] where RAM[R_i] = 0.:

4. $\Sigma A \leftarrow RAB$(Bbus).
5. $\Sigma R \leftarrow$ RAM[ΣA].
6. _, $CC \leftarrow \Sigma R$(Bbus), ALU.cc (Z is set by sending ΣR through the ALU).
7. $\Sigma W \leftarrow IP.val$(Bbus) (set ΣW to 1; recall that ΣA is already set).
8. RAM[ΣA] $\leftarrow \Sigma W$.

Note that the register transfer during clock cycle 6 can be combined with earlier register transfers, saving one clock cycle.

Answer 4.8.1. The only requirement is to add an OUT instruction directly after the ADD instruction in the given polling program.

$$
\begin{aligned}
&\text{LOAD } R_1\ 0 \\
&\text{IN } R_0 \\
&\text{BVS } 4 \\
&\text{BCC } -3 \\
&\text{ADD } R_1\ 1 \\
&\text{OUT } R_1 \qquad \text{; Output the content of } R_1 \text{ to } OUT. \\
&\text{BRA } -7 \qquad \text{; Adapt the relative displacement.} \\
&\cdots
\end{aligned}
$$

Answer 4.8.2. IN R_i. We assume that *IN.cc* provides the correct settings for the CC flags.

1. $\Sigma A, IP \leftarrow IP$(Bbus), IP(Abus)+1.
2. $\Sigma R \leftarrow$ RAM[ΣA].
3. $IR \leftarrow \Sigma R$(Bbus).
4. $RA, CC \leftarrow IN$(Bbus), *IN.cc*.

OUT R_i:

1. $\Sigma A, IP \leftarrow IP$(Bbus), IP(Abus)+1.
2. $\Sigma R \leftarrow$ RAM[ΣA].
3. $IR \leftarrow \Sigma R$(Bbus).
4. $OUT \leftarrow RA$(Abus).

Answer 4.9.1. At any time an interrupt can come that will use and change addresses at and beyond the stack pointer. Therefore, all data outside the stack must be considered unstable and should never be used.

D.5 Answers for Chapter 5

Answer 5.1.1.

max_of_three:

	EQU $input_1$ 100	; Names for input and output addresses.
	EQU $input_2$ 101	;
	EQU $input_3$ 102	;
	EQU $output$ 103	;
	LOAD R_0 [$input_1$]	; Load the first input into register R_0.
	LOAD R_2 [$input_2$]	; Load the second input into register R_2.
	SUB R_0 R_2	; Subtract [$input_2$] from [$input_1$] and set the flags.
	BCS compare_third	; Branch if [$input_1$]<[$input_2$].
	LOAD R_2 [$input_1$]	; Load the larger of the two ($input_1$) into R_2.

compare_third:

	LOAD R_0 [$input_3$]	; $R_2 = \max([input_1],[input_2])$, load the third value.
	SUB R_0 R_2	; Perform subtraction to set flags.
	BCS third_smaller	; Branch if [$input_3$]< $\max([input_1],[input_2])$.
	LOAD R_0 [$input_3$]	; [$input_3$] is the largest, reload the value.
	STOR R_0 [$output$]	; Store the value at the output address.
	BRA end	; Branch to skip code as $input_3$ is not maximal.

third_smaller:

	STOR R_2 [$output$]	; R_2 holds maximum of [$input_1$] and [$input_2$].

end_max_of_tree:

	. . .	; Supervening code for this program.

Answer 5.1.2.

	EQU seq_start $\cdots$	; Names for given variables.
	EQU seq_length $\cdots$	;
	EQU $cumul\_sum$ $\cdots$	;
	LOAD R_2 0	; Initialise R_2. Used to keep track of the sum.
	LOAD R_0 seq_start	; Load the address of the first element.
	LOAD R_1 R_0	; Make a copy.
	ADD R_1 seq_length	; Calculate the stopping address, i.e., the first
		; address not in the sequence and store it in R_1.

sum_loop:

	SUB R_1 R_0	; Subtract to set esp. the Z flag.
	BEQ save_sum	; If equal then the entire sequence is traversed.
	ADD R_1 R_0	; Restore the stopping address in R_1.
	ADD R_2 [R_0]	; Add the next value to current sum.
	ADD R_0 1	; Increment the address to prepare to add the
		; next element.
	BRA sum_loop	; Branch back to check if the next address is
		; valid.

save_sum:

	STOR R_2 [$cumul\_sum$]	; R_2 holds the correct sum for the entire
		; sequence. Save it to the specified address.

Answer 5.1.3. Labels not used in jumps refer to the position of the instruction in the code as if the code is loaded at address 0. The value loaded in register R_0 is the value at RAM[constant_store] whereas the value 10 is stored at RAM[*offset* + constant_store] where *offset* is the address from which the program is loaded in memory. Only if *offset* = 0 do these addresses coincide.

Answer 5.2.1.

```
convert: LOAD R₁ R₀          ; Set the N flag.
         BMI conversion_error ; R₀ contained a negative number.
                             ; Conversion is not possible.
         ...                 ; R₁ contains the required positive number.
```

Answer 5.2.2.

```
add_tc:                      ; R₀ and R₁ both contain two's complement numbers.
       ADD R₀ R₁     ; Add the registers and set the overflow flag.
       BVS overflow ; If V is set an overflow occurred,
                    ; jump to the error handler.
       ...          ; Normal continuation of the program.
overflow: ...        ; Error handler for an overflow.
```

Answer 5.2.3. We copy the content of *input* to *output* bit for bit shifting it one position to the right. Register R_1 contains a mask in which only one bit at position i is set and in register R_2 a single bit is set at position $i-1$. Initially, $i=1$, register R_1 contains 2 and R_1 contains 1. Repeatedly, a bit in *input* at the position where R_1 contains a 1 is copied to *output* at the position indicated by the 1 in R_2.

```
divide_by_2:
        EQU input  ...        ; The location of the input in memory.
        EQU output ...        ; The location of the output in memory.
        LOAD R₀ 0             ; Clear R₀.
        STORE R₀ [output]     ; Clear the output.
        LOAD R₁ 2             ; Bit i = 1 of the input is the first to be copied.
        LOAD R₂ 1             ; And it is copied to bit 0.
divide_loop:
        LOAD R₀ R₁            ; Register R₀ is used for temporary calculations.
        AND R₀ [input]        ; Check whether bit i is set in the input.
        BEQ prepare_next_loop ; If the bit is not set, prepare for the next iteration.
        LOAD R₀ R₂            ; Perform the calculation in R₀.
        OR R₀ [output]        ; Set the required bit in the output.
        STOR R₀ [output]      ; Store the intermediate result in memory.
prepare_next_loop:
        ADD R₁ R₁            ; Shift the bit in R₂ to the left.
        BEQ end_divide_loop ; If R₁ becomes 0 all bits have been copied.
        ADD R₂ R₂           ; Shift R₁ to the left.
        BRA divide_loop     ; Loop back. At this point i := i+1.
end_divide_loop:
        ...                 ; Normal continuation of the program.
overflow_handler:
        ...                 ; Error handler for an overflow.
```

Answer 5.3.1.

countdown:

        EQU timer 1234   ; Use an arbitrary address for the timer value.

        EQU counter 121 ; EQUs do not run during code execution.

        LOAD R_0 counter ; LOAD requires 4 clock cycles (basic fetch).

burn_cycles:

        SUB R_0 1   ; Takes 4 cycles. Decrements counter for inner loop.

        BNE burn_cycles ; 4 cycles when taken, else 3 cycles.

                                  ; Loop runs $(121-1)*(4+4)+1*(4+3)=967$ cycles.

        LOAD R_0 [timer] ; 6 cycles.

        SUB R_0 1   ; 4 cycles.

        LOAD R_0 R_0 ; 4 cycles. Just for timing.

        STOR R_0 [timer] ; 5 cycles.

        BEQ timer_end   ; 4 when taken, else 3. Branches when timer reaches

        BEQ timer_end   ; 0. Due to the instruction above this will execute

                                  ; in 3 cycles.

        BNE countdown   ; Due to the branch above this executes as a 4

                                  ; cycle branch.

                                  ; Branches take $3+3+4=10$ cycles when timer $\neq 0$,

                                  ; else only the first branch executes in 4 cycles.

timer_end:

        LOAD R_0 [timer] ; 6 cycles. Used to precisely reach multiple of 1000.

        . . .

$$\text{countdown}(timer) =$$
$$\begin{cases} 4+(121-1)*8+1*(4+3)+6+4+5+3+3+4 = 1000 & \text{if } timer > 1, \\ 4+(121-1)*8+1*(4+3)+6+4+5+4 = 994 & \text{if } timer = 1. \end{cases}$$

Answer 5.4.1. The program assumes register R_3 is available, if this is not the case a local variable can be used.

        LOAD R_0 source_start   ; Load initial positions in arrays.

        LOAD R_0 dest_start   ;

        LOAD R_2 source_length ; Load length of first array.

        LOAD R_3 dest_length   ; Load length of second array.

        SUB R_2 R_3 ; Perform subtraction to compare the two.

        BCS source_shorter   ; Jump if source array is shorter.

        LOAD R_3 R_3 ; Reload the shorter length to set flags.

        BRA copying_loop   ; Keep length used for looping in R_3.

source_shorter:

        LOAD R_3 source_length ; Source array was shorter, reload length.

copying_loop:

        BEQ done_copying   ; Length has reached zero, copying is done.

        LOAD R_2 [R_0]   ; Load word at position in source array.

        STOR R_2 [R_0]   ; Store word at same position in dest array.

        ADD R_0 1   ; Increment the array pointers at the same time.

        ADD R_0 1   ;

        SUB R_3 1   ; Length is decremented for each iteration.
        BRA copying_loop   ; Jump back to condition check
                                              ; (flags set for length).
    done_copying:
        ...   ; Done.

Answer 5.4.2.

        LOAD R_0 e_1 ; Load the first value encountered in the parse tree.
        ADD R_3 1   ; Prepare stack for this value.
        STOR R_0 [R_3-1]   ; Place value on top of stack.
        LOAD R_0 e_2 ; Visit the next leaf node and load its value.
        ADD R_3 1   ;
        STOR R_0 [R_3-1]   ; Place on top of stack.
        LOAD R_0 e_3 ; Visit the third leaf node and load its value.
        ADD R_3 1   ;
        STOR R_0 [R_3-1]   ; Place on top of stack.
        LOAD R_0 [R_3-2]   ; Load the left hand side of minus expression.
        SUB R_0 [R_3-1]   ; Subtract right hand side minus expression.
        SUB R_3 1   ; The two values on top are replaced by one value.
        STOR R_0 [R_3-1]   ; Store the result of the minus operation on the stack.
        LOAD R_0 [R_3-2]   ; Load left hand side of first multiplication.
        MUL R_0 [R_3-1]   ; Perform multiplication.
        SUB R_3 1   ; The two values on top are replaced by one value.
        STOR R_0 [R_3-1]   ; Store the result of the mult operation on the stack.
        LOAD R_0 e_4 ; Traverse through the root to arrive at leaf e_4.
        ADD R_3 1   ;
        STOR R_0 [R_3-1]   ; Place the value on top of the stack.
        LOAD R_0 e_5 ; Plus node needs last leaf to be loaded first.
        ADD R_3 1   ;
        STOR R_0 [R_3-1]   ; Place the last value on top of stack.
        LOAD R_0 [R_3-2]   ; Strict translation means loading left hand side plus
                                              ; operation.
        ADD R_0 [R_3-1]   ; Calculate plus expression.
        SUB R_3 1   ; The two values on top are replaced by one value.
        STOR R_0 [R_3-1]   ; Store the result of the plus operation on the stack.
        LOAD R_0 [R_3-2]   ; Load the value generated in left hand side of root.
        MUL R_0 [R_3-1]   ; Multiply this value with value from right sub-tree.
        SUB R_3 1   ; The two values on top are replaced by one value.
        STOR R_0 [R_3-1]   ; Store the result of the plus operation on the stack.

Answer 5.4.3.

```
        LOAD R₁ [R₀]   ; Register R₁ contains the address of the next
                       ; element of e₁, could be the null pointer.
        BEQ end_delete ; There is no next element, no removal necessary.
        LOAD R₁ [R₁]   ; Register R₁ contains the address of the next next
                       ; element of e₁.
        STOR R₁ [R₀]   ; Set the next next element of e₁ to become
                       ; the next element.
  end_delete:
```

The LOAD R_1 $[R_0]$ instruction: Register R_1 contains the address of the next element of e_1, could be the null pointer. BEQ end_delete: There is no next element, no removal necessary. LOAD R_1 $[R_1]$: Register R_1 contains the address of the next next element of e_1. STOR R_1 $[R_0]$: Set the next next element of e_1 to become the next element.

Answer 5.5.1.

```
        EQU var_one 0           ; Names and offsets of the global variables.
        EQU var_two 1           ;
        EQU var_three 2         ;
  main: LOAD R₀ initial_one     ; Load initial value for first global.
        STOR R₀ [R₂+var_one]    ; Store value in variable located in global
                                ; data segment.
        LOAD R₀ initial_two     ; Repeat steps for other two globals.
        STOR R₀ [R₂+var_two]    ; Note that indexed addressing is used
        LOAD R₀ initial_three   ; for convenience, adding and subtracting
                                ; the offsets works equivalently.
        STOR R₀ [R₂+var_three]  ;
  loop: LOAD R₀ [R₂+var_one]    ; Load the first global in main loop.
        ADD R₀ 1                ; Increment the value.
        STOR R₀ [R₂+var_one]    ; Store the incremented value.
        LOAD R₀ [R₂+var_two]    ; Exactly the same as above.
        ADD R₀ 1                ;
        STOR R₀ [R₂+var_two]    ;
        LOAD R₀ [R₂+var_three]  ;
        ADD R₀ 1                ;
        STOR R₀ [R₂+var_three]  ;
        BRA loop                ; Continue looping ad infinitum.
```

Answer 5.5.2. The RTS instruction pulls the top-most word from the stack and unconditionally jumps to this address. Therefore, it is possible to branch to a fixed address by placing this address on top of the stack and executing the RTS instruction.

Answer 5.6.1. If the called code allocates the space on the stack, on executing the RTS instruction the address of the return value would be beyond the stack pointer. This means that it will be overwritten when an interrupt occurs directly before or after the RTS instruction.

Answer 5.6.2.

```
        EQU result 3              ; Relative stack position for the return value.
        EQU arg1 2                ; Relative stack position for the first argument.
        EQU arg2 1                ; Relative stack position for the second arg.
        EQU arg3 0                ; Relative stack position for the third argument.
sum_three:
    SUB SP 1                      ; Make space for saving the value of R0.
    STOR R0 [SP]                  ; Save the value of R0.
    LOAD R0 [SP+arg1+2]           ; Load the first argument to register R0.
    ADD R0 [SP + arg2 + 2]        ; Add the second argument.
    ADD R0 [SP + arg3 + 2]        ; Add the third argument.
    STOR R0 [SP+result+2]         ; Save the resulting sum to the stack.
    LOAD R0 [SP]                  ; Restore the value of R0.
    ADD SP 1                      ; Deallocate stack space.
    RTS SP                        ; Return from the subroutine.
call_sum_three:
    . . .
    SUB SP 4                      ; Add space for the arguments and the return
                                  ; value.
    LOAD R0 1                     ; An arbitrary first argument.
    STOR R0 [SP + arg1]           ; Store the first argument on the stack.
    LOAD R1 2                     ; An arbitrary second argument.
    STOR R1 [SP + arg2]           ; Store the second argument on the stack.
    LOAD R2 3                     ; An arbitrary third argument
    STOR R2 [SP + arg3]           ; Store the third argument on the stack.
    BRS SP sum_three              ; Call the subroutine.
    LOAD R0 [SP + result]         ; Load the result in register R0 for further
                                  ; processing.
    ADD SP 4                      ; Deallocate stack space for arguments.
    . . .
```

Answer 5.6.3.

```
            EQU quadratic_term 1            ;
            EQU linear_term 2              ;
            EQU argument_a 4               ;
            EQU argument_b 5               ;
            EQU argument_c 6               ;
quadratic: SUB SP 3                        ; Make space for saving R0 and two
                                           ; local variables.
    STOR R0 [SP]                           ; Save R0's value.
    MUL R0 [SP + argument_b]               ; Calculate x * b.
    STOR R0 [SP + linear_term]             ; Store result in local.
    LOAD R0 [SP]                           ; Load x's value.
    MUL R0 R0                              ; Take the square of x.
    MUL R0 [SP + argument_a]               ; Multiply the square with a.
```

         STOR R_0 [SP + quadratic_term] ; Store the quadratic component.
         LOAD R_0 [SP + argument_c]   ;
         ADD R_0 [SP + linear_term]   ;
         ADD R_0 [SP + quadratic_term] ;
         LOAD R_0 [SP]   ; R_0 contains result.
         ADD SP 3   ; Restore stack pointer.
         RTS SP ;

Answer 5.6.4.

         EQU quadratic_term 0   ;
         EQU linear_term 1   ;
         EQU constant 3   ;
         EQU sum_result 4   ;
         EQU argument_a 5   ;
         EQU argument_b 6   ;
         EQU argument_c 7   ;
quadratic: SUB SP 4   ; Make space for 3 local variables and
                                          ; the result.
         STOR R_0 [SP + linear_term]   ; Temporally save the value of x.
         MUL R_0 R_0 ; Take the square of x.
         MUL R_0 [SP + argument_a]   ; Multiply the square with a.
         STOR R_0 [SP+quadratic_term] ; Store the quadratic component.
         LOAD R_0 [SP+linear_term]   ; Load the value of x.
         MUL R_0 [SP+argument_b]   ; Calculate $x * b$.
         STOR R_0 [SP+linear_term]   ; Store result locally.
         LOAD R_0 [SP+argument_c]   ;
         STOR R_0 [SP+constant]   ; Move c to the stack position for
         BRS SP sum_three   ; sum_three. Call summing function
                                          ; with the stack prepared.
         LOAD R_0 [SP+sum_result]   ; Move the result to R_0 for returning.
         ADD SP 4   ; Restore the stack pointer.
         RTS SP ;

Answer 5.6.5. It is possible to optimise the use of the stack by using an argument position for the return value, provided that this is clearly agreed in the calling convention, and the calling program does not need to use the value of the argument after the subroutine returns.

Answer 5.7.1. If all registers are saved, this requires substantial space on the stack and it may also require unnecessary time. It is a wise strategy for a hardware designer to provide the programmer with maximum control over how he or she uses memory and instruction space.

Answer 5.7.2. If interrupts are disabled during an interrupt handler, an interrupt that comes during the execution of the interrupt handler may be missed. This may mean that the processor does not respond appropriately to external stimuli, for instance by missing a key-stroke. If interrupts are enabled during the execution of the

interrupt handler, the interrupt handler is interrupted during its execution, putting a
new return address and flags on the stack. If this happens repeatedly, the stack will
grow unlimitedly, for instance overwriting the heap of the program. This will be
evident because the program will quickly crash.

Answer 5.7.3.

```
                EQU clock_var 100        ; Variable to store the time.
        clock_handler:
                SUB SP 1                 ; Create space to save the register R_0.
                STOR R_0 [SP]            ; Save R_0.
                LOAD R_0 [clock_var]     ; Load the value of the clock variable.
                ADD R_0 1                ; Increment the clock variable.
                STOR R_0 [clock_variable] ; Write the incremented value back.
        flag_exit: LOAD R_0 [SP]         ; Restore register R_0 from the stack.
                ADD SP 1                 ; Deallocate space from the stack.
                RTI
```

Answer 5.7.4.

```
                EQU display_char 23     ; The address used to write a character.
                EQU display_pos 24      ; The address used to indicate a character
        fatal_handler:                  ; position.
                LOAD R_0 0              ; The initial character index.
                LOAD R_1 69            ; Load the ASCII value for 'E'.
                STOR R_0 [display_pos]  ; Set the character position to the first
                                        ; position on the left.
                STOR R_1 [display_char] ; Write 'E' to the display.
                ADD R_0 1              ; Increment the character index.
                LOAD R_1 82           ; Load the ASCII value for 'R'.
                STOR R_0 [display_pos]  ;
                STOR R_1 [display_char] ; Write 'R' to the display.
                ADD R_0 1              ; Increment the character index.
                STOR R_0 [display_pos]  ;
                STOR R_1 [display_char] ; Write 'R' to the display.
                ADD R_0 1              ; Increment the character index.
                LOAD R_2 79           ; Load the ASCII value for 'O'.
                STOR R_0 [display_pos]  ;
                STOR R_2 [display_char] ; Write 'O' to the display.
                ADD R_0 1              ; Increment the character index.
                STOR R_0 [display_pos]  ;
                STOR R_1 [display_char] ; Write 'R' to the display.
                LOAD R_1 32           ; Load the ASCII space character to clear the
        spaces_loop:                    ; line.
                ADD R_0 1              ; Increment the character position.
                STOR R_0 [display_pos]  ; Write the character position to the display.
                STOR R_1 [display_char] ; Write the space character to the display.
```

```
            LOAD R2 15              ; Final position to write to.
            SUB R2 R0               ; Perform comparison.
            BNE spaces_loop         ;
infinite_loop:
            BRA infinite_loop       ; Never return.
            ...
    main: LOAD R0 fatal_handler     ; Load the relative address of the interrupt
                                    ; routine.
            ADD R0 R2               ; Calculate the actual address of the routine
                                    ; assuming the processor provides the code
                                    ; segment address in R2.
            STOR R0 [36]            ; Directly use the given installation address.
            ...
```

Answer 5.8.1.

```
    EQU intr_table_addr 57      ; Arbitrary external interrupt installation address.
    EQU wait_queue 1000         ; Address pointing to the first waiting process.
    EQU last_wait_proc 1001     ; Address pointing to the last waiting process.
    EQU running_proc 1002       ; Address of the pointer to the running process.
    EQU main_fr 1003            ; Address of the PCB for the main process.
    EQU second_fr 1006          ; Address of the PCB for the second process.
    EQU stack_proc2 12345       ; Arbitrary address to start the stack.
    LOAD R0 waiting_status      ; Initialise the second PCB to the waiting state.
    STOR R0 [second_fr+status]  ;
    LOAD R0 subroutine          ; Calculate the entry point for the second process.
    ADD R0 R2                   ; Assume R2 points to start of the code segment.
    LOAD R0 stack_proc2+1       ; Load the address RTI is going to return from.
    STOR R0 [R0]                ; Store the entry point address at this address.
    ADD R0 5                    ; Add 4 to SP for register values and
                                ; 1 to point to an empty spot on stack.
    STOR R0 [second_fr
                +stackpointer]  ; Store the calculated stack pointer.
    LOAD R0 0                   ; End of list indicator.
    STOR R0 [second_fr+next]    ; The second PCB is the last PCB in the list.
    LOAD R0 second_fr           ; Store the address of the second PCB as both
    STOR R0 [wait_queue]        ; the first one in the list
    STOR R0 [last_wait_proc]    ; and the last one in the list.
    LOAD R0 main_fr             ; Set the main process as the currently executing
    STOR R0 [running_proc]      ; process. The handler will handle the
                                ; initialisation of the PCB.
    LOAD R0 context_sw_hndlr    ; Load the relative address of the interrupt routine.
    ADD R0 R2                   ; Calculate the actual address of this routine.
    STOR R0 [intr_table_addr]   ; Install the handler address in the handler table.
    LOAD R0 0                   ; Write zero to the timer, which
    STOR R0 [timer_address]     ; immediately triggers the context switch handler.
    ...                         ; Rest of the main process, e.g., an infinite loop.
```

D.6 Answers for Chapter 6

Answer 6.1.1. The function *min* calculates the minimum of two values and the function min_3 of three. The function max_3 calculates the maximum of three values. Note that this program only works properly if the numbers are small, and no overflow occurs.

> **function int** *min*(**int** x, **int** y)
>   **if** $(x < y)$ **then return** x **else return** y **fi**
> **end**;
> **function int** min_3(**int** x_1, **int** x_2, **int** x_3)
>   **return** $min(x_1, min(x_2, x_3))$
> **end**;
> **function int** max_3(**int** x_1, **int** x_2, **int** x_3)
>   **return** $- min(-x_1, min(-x_2, -x_3))$
> **end**;
> **function int** *middle*(**int** x_1, **int** x_2, **int** x_3)
>   **return** $x_1 + x_2 + x_3 - min_3(x_1, x_2, x_3) - max_3(x_1, x_2, x_3)$
> **end**;
> **nat** *result*;
> *result* := $middle(1, 3, -4)$;

Answer 6.2.1. The strings $1 - 2$, $1 + 2 + 3$, **and not** *correct* are not syntactically correct expressions. In the string *true* **and** *false* the substrings *true* and *false* are variables.

Answer 6.2.2. The parse tree is given in Figure D.1.

Answer 6.2.3. There are many conceivable forms that a print statement and a for loop can have. The solution below is just one way to do it.

> *Statement* ::= ... |
>   **print** *Expression* |
>   **for** *Type Variable* ':=' *Expression* **to** *Expression* **do** *Statement* **od**
> *Expression* ::= ...
>   *Expression* '/' *Expression* |

Answer 6.3.1. The argument of a print statement can be of any type. In a for loop, the variable and all expressions must be of type **nat** or **int**, in accordance with the explicitly indicated type. The arguments of '/' must be of type **int** or **nat**, and the result is only of type **nat** if both arguments are of type **nat**. It is not possible to require that the second argument cannot be 0, as there is no algorithm that can, for all programs, decide whether an expression can be 0 or not.

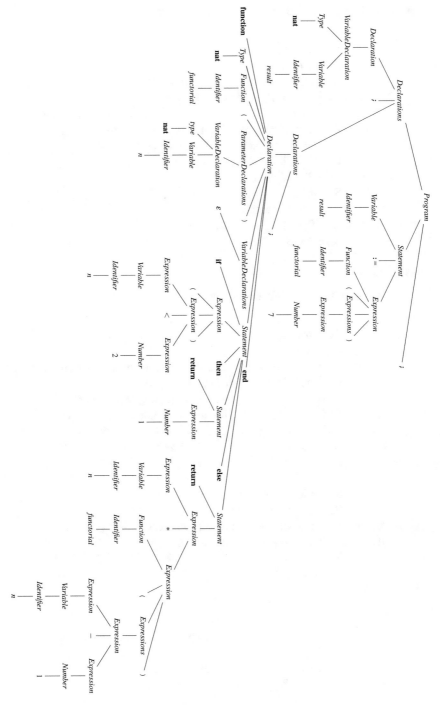

Fig. D.1 Parse tree for Exercise 6.2.2

Answer 6.4.1. The translation for unsigned numbers.

```
                EQU a 2            ;
                EQU b 1            ;
                EQU c 0            ;
                LOAD R₀ [SP + a]   ; Translation of the unsigned interpretation
                LOAD R₁ [SP₃ + b] ; of the if statement.
                SUB R₀ R₁          ; Perform the subtraction, set the flags.
                BEQ unsigned_then  ; Then part should be executed iff the zero
                BCS unsigned_then  ; or the carry flag is set.
                LOAD R₀ [SP + b]   ; c := b − a.
                SUB R₀ [SP + a]    ;
                STOR R₀ [SP + c]   ;
                BRA unsigned_end   ;
unsigned_then: LOAD R₀ [SP + a]   ; c := a − b.
                SUB R₀ [SP + b]    ;
                STOR R₀ [SP + c]   ;
unsigned_end:  ...                ;
```

The translation for two's complement numbers.

```
                EQU a 2            ;
                EQU b 1            ;
                EQU c 0            ;
                LOAD R₀ [SP + a]   ; Translation of the unsigned interpretation
                LOAD R₁ [SP₃ + b] ; of the if statement.
                SUB R₀ R₁          ; Perform the subtraction, set the flags.
                BEQ integer_then   ; If a and b are equal the zero flag is set.
                BMI minus_flag_set ; If N = 1 branch to check that V = 0.
                BVS integer_then   ; N = 0, branch to "then" part if V = 1.
integer_else:   LOAD R₀ [SP + b]   ; c := b − a.
                SUB R₀ [SP + a]    ;
                STOR R₀ [SP + c]   ;
                BRA integer_end    ;
minus_flag_set: BVS integer_else   ; N = 1, branch to "else" part if V = 1.
integer_then:   LOAD R₀ [SP + a]   ; c := a − b.
                SUB R₀ [SP + b]    ;
                STOR R₀ [SP + c]   ;
integer_end:    ...                ;
```

Answer 6.4.2.

```
code_for_f: EQU x₁ 2              ; There are no local variables;
            EQU x₂ 1              ;
            LOAD R₀ [SP + x₁]     ; Calculate x₁ + x₂;
            ADD R₀ [SP + x₂]      ;
            STORE R₀ [SP + x₁] ;
            RTS SP               ; End of function f.
```

```
EQU x 2            ; Relative addresses on the stack for the
EQU y 1            ; variables.
EQU z 0            ;
SUB SP 3           ; Make space for variables.
LOAD R₀ 0          ; x := 0. Note that putting 0 on the stack is
STOR R₀ [SP + x]   ; optimised away.
LOAD R₀ [SP + x]   ; y := x + 1.
ADD R₀ 1           ; Optimise putting 1 on the stack.
STOR R₀ [SP + y]   ;
LOAD R₀ [SP + x]   ; z := f(x + y, y + y).
ADD R₀ [SP + y]    ; Avoid storing both x and y on the stack.
SUB SP 1           ; Put the first argument for f on the stack.
STOR R₀ [SP]       ;
LOAD R₀ [SP + y + 1] ; Load y. Note there is one extra element
                   ; on the stack.
ADD R₀ [SP + y + 1] ; Calculate y + y. Do not put y on the stack.
SUB SP 1           ; Make room for the second argument of f.
STOR R₀ [SP]       ; Store the second argument on the stack.
BRS SP code_for_f  ; Calculate the value of the function
                   ; application expression.
ADD SP 1           ; Remove superfluous args from the stack.
LOAD R₀ [SP]       ; Retrieve the result of f.
ADD SP 1           ; Remove the result from the stack.
STOR R₀ [SP + z]   ; Assign the result to z.
```

Answer 6.5.1. There are several levels of optimisation. Assume the compiler can inline and evaluate constant expressions.

```
start_: LOAD R₀ 9   ; Load the answer 9.
        STOR R₀ [SP] ; Store the result in variable x.
```

If the compiler cannot or is not allowed to inline, an optimised version could look like

```
code_for_square: SUB SP 2          ; function nat square(nat
                                   ; y)  y := y*y ; return y.
                 STOR R₀ [SP]      ; Put y twice on the stack.
                 STOR R₀ [SP + 1]  ;
                 BRS multiplication ; Multiply the top values on the stack.
                 LOAD R₀ [SP + 1]  ; Put the result in y, which is R₀.
                 ADD SP 2          ; Remove the arguments from the stack.
                 RTS SP            ; End of the function square.
start_:          LOAD R₀ 3         ; Main program: x := square(3).
                 BRS code_for_square ; Pass the argument and the result in R₀.
                 STOR R₀ [SP]      ; Store the result in variable x.
```

Answer 6.5.2. The argument n is passed in register R_0 and the result is passed in register R_1.

```
code_for_sum: LOAD R₁ R₀    ; result := n.
loop_sum:     BEQ end_sum   ; Jump to the end if n = 0.
              ADD R₁ R₀;    ; result := result + n.
              SUB R₀ 1      ; n := n − 1.
              BRA loop_sum  ; Remove the arguments from the stack.
end_sum:      RTS SP        ; End of the function sum.
```

Answer 6.5.3.

```
code_for_f: ADD R₀ R₁       ; Pass arguments in registers R₀ and R₁.
            RTS SP          ; Return the result in R₀.
                            ; End of function f.
            EQU x 2         ; Relative addresses on the stack for the
                            ; variables.
            EQU y 1         ;
            EQU z 0         ;
            ADD SP 3        ; Make space for variables.
            LOAD R₁ 0       ; x := 0.
            STOR R₁ [SP+x]  ;
            LOAD R₀ 1       ; y := x + 1.
            STOR R₀ [SP+y]  ;
                            ; Register R₀ contains the first argument of f.
            LOAD R₁ 2       ; Set the second argument.
            BRS SP code_for_f ; Calculate the function.
            STOR R₀ [SP+z]  ; z := f(x+y, y+y).
```

Answer 6.6.1.

print e $[\![e]\!]_{pos}$	**readnat** BRS SP $readnat$
LOAD R_0 [SP]	SUB SP 1
ADD SP 1	STOR R_0 [SP]
BRS SP $printnat$	

D.7 Answers for Chapter 7

Answer 7.1.1. The operating system would require much more memory than the BIOS. Hence, it may have to be put in a different address space than where the BIOS now resides, although this depends on the properties of the processor. Technically, it is possible though. The system would be very inflexible in the sense that there is only one operating system that cannot be updated. As most computers with a full-fledged operating system also have mass storage devices, the operating system can easily be stored there.

Answer 7.2.1. No. If a program can write its MMU tables, it can change which parts of the memory it has access to. This would render the notion of memory protection unusable.

Answer 7.2.2. The first reason is that when common tasks that are done often, such as drawing a figure on a screen, are offered by an operating system or other library, such routines do not have to be provided in each application program. Another reason is that it is much faster to write a complete figure in one call than to incur the overhead of an operating system call for each pixel in this figure.

Answer 7.3.1. Multiple programs can share code and data by letting the translation table map the virtual addresses of these programs to the same physical addresses.

Answer 7.3.2. The translation table has $6TB/4096 = 1.6\ 10^6$ entries.

Answer 7.4.1. Assume both programs use the better part of the cache. When one program is swapped out, the other program starts to replace all the data in the cache, which is time consuming. With the next context switch the first program needs its own data from memory and starts filling the cache with its own data. The overhead of refilling the cache in this case is much larger than switching the stack pointer and adapting the administration of the program threads.

Answer 7.4.2. With the random strategy, there is a probability of $\frac{1}{2}$ that cache line l is used and a probability of $\frac{1}{2}$ that the data at address a_i is put in cache line l_{a_i}. When the same data is visited again 50% of the data elements are already in l_{a_i} and the remainder are put with a probability of $\frac{1}{2}$ in l_{a_i}. When the data is visited for the third time, only 25% of the data elements must be loaded. Summing this up, this means that if there are n addresses that are read, a cache line must only be loaded $2n$ times. With the LRU strategy, all but the first data elements will be loaded in l_{a_i}. This means that only n cache lines need to be filled, which is in this case optimal.

Answer 7.5.1. The most important reason is the difficulty to write correct and efficient programs for many-core systems. It is very costly to transfer existing software from single or multicore systems to many-core processors in such a way that the performance potential of many-core systems bears fruit. Besides that, multi-core systems are more than adequate for most purposes for which computers are used.

Answer 7.5.2. If the first program is executed first, and then the second, but the assignment $x = 1$ is written to memory with a delay, this is possible.

D.8 Answers for Chapter 8

Answer 8.4.1. As there are only 12 bits to represent a number only 2^{12} numbers can be generated. But some numbers can be made in different ways. For instance, 1 equals $0000\,0001$ rotated 0 positions, but also $0000\,0100$ rotated $2 * 1$ positions to the right. This reduces the number of different values that can be represented.

Answer 8.4.2. In the case of a left shift the output of flip-flop$_n$ must be connected to the input of flip-flop$_{n+1}$. In the case of a right shift this requires the output of flip-flop$_n$ to be connected to the input of flip-flop$_{n-1}$. Therefore, to create a single-direction shift, no logic gates are required. Implementing a bi-directional shift requires a single 2-bit multiplexer, composed of three gates, for each flip-flop in the register.

Answer 8.4.3. MVN R_i, #0.

Answer 8.4.4. Suppose value v is stored in the program n bytes before the place where the current instruction is located. The instruction LDR R_i, [PC, $-\#(n+12)$] loads the value v in R_i.

Answer 8.4.5. If the PC were the base register in an STM or LDM instruction, the registers would be stored in the code that is currently being executed or fetched. Generally, this is very undesirable, especially when the PC is being changed during this process, in which case the results of the program may be unpredictable. Using the PC in the set of registers is very useful, as it can be used to pull all registers at the end of a subroutine, including the return address in just one instruction.

Answer 8.5.1. It is almost correct. It should be LDR PC, [SP, #4] as the stack grows downward. Actually, as this instruction is more efficient than an LDM with one register, the assembler often replaces such an LDM with an LDR.

Answer 8.5.2. Yes, this is indeed possible, and it does not only reduce the program size, but it is also faster.

Answer 8.6.1. The value can be obtained as the program counter points to the instruction after SWI n.

```
interrupt_handler:
        STMFD SP!, {LR,R4,R5}  ; Push LR, R4 and R5 on the stack.
        MOV R4, [LR, -#4]      ; Load the instruction SWI n in register R4.
        LDR R5, =0x0FFF FFFF   ; Meta instruction to load a mask in R5.
        AND R4, R4, R5         ; Set the first byte of the instruction to 0.
        ...
```

References

1. P1076 VHDL Analysis and Standardization Group. 1076-2019 - IEEE standard for VHDL language reference manual. Technical report, IEEE, 2019.
2. ARM. Introducing the Arm architecture. Technical Report ARM062-948681440-3277, Arm limited, 2019.
3. Arm Ltd. Arm instruction set. version 1.0. reference guide, 2018. Available at https://developer.arm.com/.
4. Arm Ltd. Procedure call standard for the ARM© architecture, 2019. Available at https://developer.arm.com/.
5. John W. Backus. The syntax and semantics of the proposed international algebraic language of the Zurich ACM-GAMM conference. In *Information Processing, Proceedings of the 1st International Conference on Information Processing, UNESCO, Paris 15-20 June 1959*, pages 125–131. UNESCO (Paris), 1959.
6. Armin Biere, Marijn Heule, Hans van Maaren, and Toby Walsh, editors. *Handbook of Satisfiability*, volume 185 of *Frontiers in Artificial Intelligence and Applications*. IOS Press, 2009.
7. Emily R. Blem, Jaikrishnan Menon, and Karthikeyan Sankaralingam. Power struggles: Revisiting the RISC vs. CISC debate on contemporary ARM and x86 architectures. In *19th IEEE International Symposium on High Performance Computer Architecture, HPCA 2013, Shenzhen, China, February 23-27, 2013*, pages 1–12. IEEE Computer Society, 2013.
8. Bram A.G. Bosch. A formal processor model in mCRL2. Master's thesis, Eindhoven University of Technology, Eindhoven, The Netherlands, 2017.
9. Randal E. Bryant. Graph-based algorithms for boolean function manipulation. *IEEE Trans. Computers*, 35(8):677–691, 1986.
10. The Unicode Consortium. The unicode standard version 13.0 - core specification. Technical report, Unicode Consortium, 2020.
11. Stephen A. Cook. The complexity of theorem-proving procedures. In Michael A. Harrison, Ranan B. Banerji, and Jeffrey D. Ullman, editors, *Proceedings of the 3rd Annual ACM Symposium on Theory of Computing, May 3-5, 1971, Shaker Heights, Ohio, USA*, pages 151–158. ACM, 1971.
12. Edsger W. Dijkstra. Letters to the editor: go to statement considered harmful. *Commun. ACM*, 11(3):147–148, 1968.
13. Guy Even and Moti Medina. *Digital Logic Design - A Rigorous Approach*. Cambridge University Press, 2012.
14. James R. Groff, Paul N. Weinberg, and Andrew J. Oppel. *SQL: The complete reference, third edition*. McGraw-Hill, 2009.
15. F.-R. Güntsch. *Logischer Entwurf eines digitalen Rechengeräts mit mehreren asynchron laufenden Trommeln und automatischem Schnellspeicherbetrieb*. PhD thesis, Technische Universität Berlin, Berlin, Germany, 1957.

© The Editor(s) (if applicable) and The Author(s), under exclusive license to Springer Nature Switzerland AG 2021
J. F. Groote et al., *Logic Gates, Circuits, Processors, Compilers and Computers*,
https://doi.org/10.1007/978-3-030-68553-9

16. Microchip Technology Inc. AVR instruction set manual. Technical report, Microchip Technology Inc. The Embedded Control Solutions Company, Chandler, USA, 2016.

17. Intel. Intel 64 and IA-32 architectures. volume 1: Basic architecture. Technical Report 253665-072US, Intel, Santa Clara, USA, 2020.

18. Kathleen Jensen and Niklaus Wirth. *Pascal user manual and report - ISO Pascal standard, 4th Edition*. Springer, 1991.

19. Raspberry Pi (Trading) Ltd. Raspberry Pi compute module 3+, 2019. Available at https://www.raspberrypi.org.

20. Gordon E. Moore. Cramming more components onto integrated circuits. *Electronics*, pages 114–117, 1965. Reprinted in the Proceedings of the IEEE 86(1):82-85, 1998.

21. Noam Nisan and Shimon Schocken. *The Elements of Computing Systems - Building a Modern Computer from First Principles*. MIT Press, 2008.

22. Linda M. Null and Julia Lobur. *The essentials of computer organization and architecture (2. ed.)*. Jones and Bartlett Publishers, 2006.

23. Staff of the Computation Laboratory. *A Manual for the Operation for the Automatic Sequence Controlled Calculator*. Harvard University Press, 1946.

24. David A. Patterson and John L. Hennessy. *Computer Organization and Design. ARM edition. The Hardware/Software Interface, 1st edition*. Morgan Kaufmann, 2016.

25. David A. Patterson and John L. Hennessy. *Computer Organization and Design. MIPS edition. The Hardware/Software Interface, 6th edition*. Morgan Kaufmann, 2020.

26. Thomas A. Powell. *HTML & CSS: The complete reference, fifth edition*. McGraw-Hill, 2010.

27. Siobhan Roberts. The curious creativity of John Horton Conway. In *Bridges 2015: Mathematics, Music, Art, Architecture, Culture*, pages 317–322, 2015.

28. Claude Shannon. A symbolic analysis of relay and switching circuits. Master's thesis, Massachusetts Institute of Technology, 1937.

29. Bruce Smith. *Raspberry Pi. Assembly Language. Raspbian*. BSB, 2016.

30. Jon Stokes. *Inside the machine: an illustrated introduction to microprocessors and computer architecture*. No Starch Press, 2006.

31. 1800_WG SystemVerilog Language Working Group. 1800-2017 - IEEE standard for SystemVerilog–unified hardware design, specification, and verification language. Technical report, IEEE, 2017.

32. Andrew S. Tanenbaum. *Structured computer organization, 5th Edition*. Pearson Education, 2006.

33. Wil M. P. van der Aalst. Business process execution language. In Ling Liu and M. Tamer Özsu, editors, *Encyclopedia of Database Systems, Second Edition*. Springer, 2018.

34. John von Neumann. First draft of a report on the EDVAC. *IEEE Annals of the History of Computing*, 15(4):27–75, 1993.

35. Li Wenhao. A technical report on TEE and ARM TrustZone, 2014. Available at https://community.arm.com.

Index

Index 251

Printed in the United States
by Baker & Taylor Publisher Services